CLASSIC WALKS IN

EUROPE

Edited by Walt Unsworth

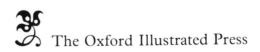

The Oxford Illustrated Press

The Oxford Illustrated Press

© 1987
Brian Evans, Walks 1, 6
Andrew Harper, Walks 2, 17
Walt Unsworth, Walks 3, 12, The Introduction and Appendices
Fleur & Colin Speakman, Walk 4
Martin Collins, Walks 5, 9, 10
Kev Reynolds, Walks 7, 8
Hamish Brown, Walk 11
Stephen Lee, Walk 13
Roger Smith, Walk 14
Cecil Davies, Walk 15
Ingrid High, Walk 16

Printed in England by J. H. Haynes and Co Limited, Sparkford, Nr Yeovil, Somerset

ISBN 0 946609 31 4

Published by:
The Oxford Illustrated Press, Sparkford, Nr. Yeovil, Somerset

Haynes Publications Inc, 861 Lawrence Drive, Newbury Park, California 91320 USA

British Library Cataloguing in Publication Data:

Classic walks in Europe —(Classic walks series).
  1. Voyages and travels—1951– —Guide-books
  I. Unsworth, Walt
  910'.202   G153.4

ISBN 0-946609-31-4

Library of Congress Catalog Card Number 87-81701

Contents

CLASSIC WALKS OF EUROPE

INTRODUCTION

Over the years it has been my good fortune to visit a great many countries of the world and to travel through them by all sorts of transport, from helicopters to elephants and everything in between. It didn't take me long to discover that the more one observes, the less one sees and that travel is not so much a matter of distance as time. A tourist rushing through a country on a bus sees less than a young man or woman cycling along the same road, and the cyclist in turn sees less than the walker. This is one of the reasons for a walking trip.

> What is this life if, full of care,
> We have no time to stand and stare?

So wrote W.H. Davies, the self styled super-tramp, in his poem *Leisure* and he was right. Walking gives you time to stand and stare, but the pace of walking in itself gives you time to see what is going on around you and even perhaps, to stop and take part. There is a one-ness between a walker and the countryside which does not exist with other forms of transport.

The one-ness is enhanced by the fact that all the senses come into play when you are walking. The scent of new mown hay is difficult to detect from the back of a motor car and you'll never hear the distant rumble of an avalanche from that position. Yet these are commonplace on many of the walks described in this book, as is the feel of rough rock grasped between the fingers or the taste of water from a mountain stream. Walking totally immerses you in the environment and so you experience it to the full.

I had a very vivid illustration of this recently. I was fortunate enough to accompany a ranger on foot through the Kruger National Park in South Africa. Most visitors, of course, are not allowed to get out of their cars in the park because of the obvious danger from wild animals. As I walked through the bush, my shirt being plucked by the thorns of the wait-a-bit tree, I was very keenly aware of the environment—some of which was stalking us! The difference in perception between walking through the park and driving through the park was immense.

Of course, the Kruger Park is an extreme case in a somewhat extreme environment, but it is really only a matter of degree.

The second great advantage of a walking trip is that it allows you to reach places that you cannot reach by any other means. Only the walker can see the myriad gentians spread like a blue carpet on the Col de la Vanoise or watch the chamois on the Pas de Chevre. Mind you, I write this with an anxious glance over my shoulder at that horrid modern invention, the trail bike, whose rasping noise threatens to ruin the peace of the hills and whose tyres threaten to erode our paths quicker than any number of walkers. Unless trail bikes are rigorously controlled I see little hope for either the gentians or the chamois.

So there are two good reasons for a walking tour. There is another, less easily explained—walking is enjoyable in itself. It is an activity which can be indulged in at many levels. Like the layers of an onion skin: peel off one and there's an equally valid one underneath. Some walkers are fitness freaks whose aim is to walk as far and as fast as possible, like the members of the Bob Graham Club whose qualification for admission is to gallop round a 72-mile course in the Lake District, taking in 42 summits and 27,000 ft of ascent—all within 24 hours. This is really fell-running, of course, but there are lots of so called 'Challenge Walks' of up to a hundred miles or so, where the aim is to travel fast and furious in order to clock up a good time and win a badge or certificate. Meanwhile, at the other extreme there are walkers who park in a lay-by and stroll to the nearest viewpoint, before strolling back again to the car. The average walker is somewhere in between. I like to visualise the average walker as someone who can knock off a dozen miles in the mountains of Wales or the Lakes without feeling the strain and maybe twice that distance for a big effort. Such a performance does not require super fitness; it is well within the capabilities of the average man or woman. Age hardly comes into it either; quite young children can manage these distances and I know several 70 year-olds who could manage it too. Perhaps this is why a recent survey showed that walking was the most popular outdoor pursuit in Britain!

The Fitness Factor

Although this book is concerned with long walks lasting a week or more, the fitness factor is no more critical than it is for a day out in the hills. After all, what is a long walk but a series of day walks strung together? There might even be benefit in so far as each day gets easier as the walk progresses and you get into your swing! This does not hold indefinitely, however—there seems to be a point in ultra-long walks where physical and mental stress begins to take its toll. Needless to say, none of the walks in this book are of that length.

Even so, it would be foolish to imagine that you can lead a completely sedentary lifestyle for fifty weeks of the year then go straight out and tackle the Coast to Coast Walk or Tour of Mont Blanc. The first few days would not be pleasant because you would be extremely tired and it would require great determination to continue with the trip. This crisis can be avoided by simple exercise, and the best exercise for walkers is walking. A day out on the local moors once a month is all that is needed to keep in shape. If you are not accustomed to walking far then build up your performance over the months. Start with five miles of gentle stroll, then add some ups and downs and build up to fifteen miles. You should be able to accomplish this standard within four or five walks of commencement. If you do this regularly—not necessarily very frequently—then you should be able to manage anything in this book.

Of equal importance to physical fitness is mental fitness. It is very important to be mentally tuned to the trip you are embarking upon and to have the mental reserves necessary to carry it through.

Proper planning sees to the first requirement. The initial enthusiasm may be roused by a book such as this one with its detailed text and attractive pictures, but a winter spent poring over maps and guidebooks is calculated to give the enthusiasm a sounder base. Any real adventurer loves maps and an ability to map-read is as great a social asset as learning to type, or play the piano. To anyone who can read one the map tells all—well, nearly all.

The planning stage should cover details of travel and gear, accommodation and food. All these matters need sorting out in advance and the knowledge that they *have* been sorted out is excellent preparation.

Once on the walk all sorts of things can crop up which require a fine mixture of decision and determination. In the face of continual bad weather, for instance, it is easy to give up. Sometimes this is the right decision. On one occasion a friend and I were at the Prinz Luitpold Haus in the Bavarian Alps (see Walk 12) when it rained so hard that we never moved out of the hut all day. On the *next* day we woke to find it snowing! A foot of snow lay round the hut and as we were expecting to tackle the tricky Heilbronner Weg, an airy route with fixed cables to hang on to, we aborted the walk.

That was a right decision because it would have been dangerous to go on, but I can think of other walks where a bit of snow wouldn't make much difference except psychologically—sometimes just *seeing* snow in the middle of July can be off-putting and a strong mental attitude is needed to overcome the tendency to give up. It is something we are all prone to, especially if we are out of sorts with our companion, ourselves, or the world in general. A combination of bad weather and bad humour is often fatal to the success of a walk.

Companions

Walk alone, or walk with friends? The professionals—Hamish Brown, John Merrill, Chris Conroy—when they are doing one of their ultra long-distance walks invariably tackle it alone. A friend may join in for a mile or two now and then, but basically the thing is a contest between the walker and his willpower, in which outsiders should not intrude. Even in less exalted circles some people prefer to walk alone for they are then beholden to nobody as regards pace or even direction. It is the ultimate freedom—if that is what you are looking for.

There are problems for the lone walker in mountains and wilderness areas should anything go wrong. The International Alpine Distress Signal is six blasts on a whistle (or at night six flashes from a torch) in a minute, with a minute's pause between signals. In popular areas this should bring someone to your aid pretty quickly, but in more remote parts you might be blowing your whistle for a long time!

With a group, this problem hardly exists. It should be possible to send someone for help. If the victim has to be left alone, then warm clothes and emergency rations should be left too, and the location of the accident carefully noted.

A large group—and by this I mean half-a-dozen or so—can be good fun. There's lots of chat and banter, plenty of hands to help in any chore and a good time is had by all. But a large group travels very slowly and is just as open to dissention as to camaraderie. It's harder to keep together, too, because the chances are that different members will be at different levels of fitness or ability.

This should never happen if the group is professionally led by an experienced tour leader from one of the well established trekking companies. Such a group might be the answer for anyone who doesn't wish to walk alone but who has no like-minded companions. Many companies have regular clients who go on a walking tour every year, preferring to pay a bit extra in order to be relieved of the hassle of organising the trip themselves.

I've walked alone and I've walked in groups and enjoyed both. Perhaps my greatest pleasure has come from walking with a single like-minded companion of similar interests and ability.

Equipment

In these inflationary times equipment tends to be expensive and it is well worthwhile considering what is absolutely necessary and what is not. There is no sense in kitting yourself out with gear fit for Everest if all you intend to walk is the Pembroke Coast Path. Yet many walkers do; impressed perhaps by the macho image of the hard men.

There is a balance to be struck, and I will be the first to admit that it is not easy getting just the right balance. All the walks in this book, for example, can be done in simple walking gear such as you might use for a day out on the fells in summer but sometimes—just sometimes—you might wish you'd brought along an ice-axe, perhaps, or worn gaiters. No book can make allowance for that; the subtleties are things you have to discover for yourself through experience. Sometimes painful experience.

So what gear is essential? Boots and a rucksack. Both should be comfortable to wear, and you should get the best you can afford.

There are some very good lightweight boots around nowadays—no need for the heavy mountain boots which walkers were once condemned to wear. Go to a specialist shop (good advice for all your gear) and get them to explain the advantages and disadvantages of the various types. Remember—they don't need a stiffened sole and they don't even need to be 100% waterproof, but they do need to be *light*.

A fashion has developed recently for walking in training shoes, but though they are light and comfortable they have no protection for the ankle and they are miserable in muddy conditions or the odd patch of snow. Thin soled trainers can be painful on a stony track. My personal preference is to wear lightweight boots and carry trainers for emergency wear.

Rucksacks have developed astonishingly during the last few years and are now so sophisticated you need a specialist retailer to fit you out with one, individually tailored to your size and shape! The capacity depends on what you intend to do. If you intend to camp then you'll need a bigger capacity sack than if you don't have to carry camping gear. Again, the retailer will advise you.

Avoid like the plague all those cheapie rucksacks you see in some general stores. They are not up to the job, and if your rucksack strap breaks in the middle of a long tour, you're in trouble. I once had a chat with a man who manufactured cheap rucksacks. "Don't you get complaints?" I asked.

"All the time," he said, with a pained expression. "A guy wrote last week to say he'd taken his rucksack to Snowdon and it had fallen to bits. I wrote back and said what did he expect if he took it up Snowdon? I mean, you gotta be reasonable."

Waterproofs

For some years I used to keep out the rain with an old army gas cape. As a youngster it was all I could afford, and I seem to remember it worked quite well. I wonder if they still make them? Not that it would do today when we need to protect the image as much as anything else!

I suppose a cycle cape would be the modern equivalent of my gas cape but the problem here is that the wind can get under the cape and this can be dangerous. Winds strong enough to lift you off your feet are not uncommon in the mountains. I remember on one occasion being with some friends on the Pennine moors near Saddleworth when the wind was so strong we had to lie down and hang onto something—the moment we raised our bodies the wind flipped us over like pancakes! If we'd been wearing capes we'd have been sent hang-gliding into Yorkshire!

Over the last twenty years or so the style of outdoor weather gear has gone from anoraks to cagoules to the present all purpose 'alpine' jacket. This will be waterproof and windproof to a greater or lesser degree depending on the materials used and the quality of manufacture. The cheap jackets found in general stores are not good enough for our purpose, but even among the better quality jackets there is a wide range.

A good jacket should have a generous hood, good pockets, including an inside map pocket, windproof cuffs and sufficient length of skirt—almost knee length, for preference. The seams should be taped and doped because this is where leakage is likely. Nowadays, the materials used to make these jackets are very varied and quite complex. The following is just a simple outline:

Polyurethane coatings: Prices range from the cheapest to quite expensive. Every manufacturer seems to have his own secret coating formula these days, some of which are said to be 'breathable'. In general they are totally windproof and waterproof, but suffer from condensation.

Breathable fabrics: Expensive to very expensive. The first modern breathable fabric was Gore-Tex by W.L. Gore & Associates, but there are now several types on the market. The idea is that the fabric has numerous tiny holes large enough to let water vapour from the body out, but too small to let water molecules (rain) in. It seems to work better for some people than others.

Various cottons etc: Oiled cottons, tarps and so forth are not so common these days although the old wartime material called Ventile is making a comeback. A bit on the heavy side and very expensive, it does breathe and is excellent, especially in cold conditions.

As well as a jacket a pair of waterproof overtrousers is useful. These should have long zips on the legs so that they can be pulled on over boots quite easily. On a day of intermittent heavy showers you may have to put your overtrousers on and off several times, so make it easy for yourself!

I suppose you could count gaiters as waterproofs. Originally they were developed to keep snow out of boot tops, then they were lengthened to keep snow off stockings and now some walkers like to wear them all the time. They help to keep stockings dry and they keep stones out of boots. They are rather warm though and I prefer to keep them for their original function—combating snow.

Other Gear

There is really no need to buy any other special gear for a summer walking holiday in Britain or Europe. Ordinary casual clothes will suffice, though you will need thicker socks than usual and walking breeches, which are knee length and are more comfortable than ordinary slacks. Avoid cotton jeans which are poor protection in inclement weather and tend to be tight fitting anyway, which is not what you want for walking. Some walkers prefer shorts, which is alright until the weather turns nasty, as it has a habit of doing in the hills, when you need something warmer. A pair of slacks should be carried just in case. Old time mountaineers used to dismiss the idea of shorts: 'You never see a shepherd in shorts,' they'd say, knowingly.

Many walkers like to wear two pairs of socks and, of course, you have to take this into account when buying new boots. Personally, I've never seen the need for this. If just means you have to carry twice the quantity of socks!

First Aid

In *Classic Walks of the World* I went into considerable detail regarding tummy bugs and altitude sickness, but no such dramatic illnesses are likely to occur in Europe where the standard of hygiene is much higher than in some of the more remote parts of the world. Even our food tends to be much the same nowadays—you can get lasagne in Nottingham just as easily as in Naples. Nevertheless, making the effort to keep everything clean is worthwhile especially when you are camping and the weather is bad and you don't feel like washing up properly . . .

No walks in this book have the slightest chance of giving you serious altitude sickness, but some things are universal and one of them is midges. Biting bugs of various kinds seem to sharpen their fangs specially for walkers. It is worth using insect repellent even for the temporary relief it offers, but the bites themselves are often untreatable and have to be put up with. Some, like those of the horse-fly or cleg, can become infected and they can be treated with an antiseptic cream. If the bite becomes septic then medical help should be sought.

Sunburn is another common ailment which can totally spoil a holiday. It is the result of ignorance or carelessness. Bare flesh should not be exposed to the sun for long periods without an effective barrier cream, especially in the mountains where the ultra-violet rays are strong. On snow or ice it can be particularly dangerous and the sunshine does not need to be bright. A few years ago I was with a man who spent a couple of hours on a glacier in Switzerland without bothering to put on suncream. It was thick mist at the time and the sun was quite invisible—nevertheless, his arms and face were raw by the evening.

My advice is to seek out a high-altitude barrier cream from the chemist and a good lip-salve too. Sun glasses help to reduce glare—especially from snowy mountains—and prevent headaches.

What about when the weather is the very opposite of hot? Summer walkers along the routes in this book are not likely to suffer from frostbite, but they could suffer from hypothermia if conditions were really bad. Wet through, chilled, miserable—a loss of body heat can become serious and in extremity, lead to death from exposure. The symptoms are unreasonable behaviour, slurred speech, violent shivering, excessive tiredness, collapsing and failure of vision. Warmth, protection from the elements and a stop to all physical activity are essential for the victim.

The first aid kit for a long walk can be

Facing page: **Backpackers of necessity use lightweight gear—the tents and rucksacks seen here are of very high quality as is the man's Alpine jacket.**
(Photo: Camper Magazine/Mel Dew.)

considered in two parts. First, the universal items that each member of the party should carry for him or herself: creams, aspirin, plasters, indigestion tablets, toilet paper, a whistle and a torch, and secondly the things which can be shared to save weight such as larger bandages and scissors. The kit should be carried in an easily accessible pocket of the rucksack.

Insurance

Though some other countries in Europe have a health service similar to that in Britain it does not always work in the same way. In France, for example, you pay for your visit to the doctor and claim the money back afterwards. To do this you need to *have with you* the DHSS form E111, obtained from your local office before departure.

This cover is minimal and most people prefer to back it up with extra insurance which includes not only health but travel and equipment as well. If you are in a private patient plan in the UK you may well find that you are covered for abroad too as far as hospitalisation goes (but not transport to the hospital!). Similarly, the use of certain charge cards when booking flights can give some insurance against cancellation and so on.

None of the usual insurances cover *rescue*, however, which though free at home is very expensive abroad. Guides have to be paid for, and so does the helicopter—the latter costs about £50 per minute. Let me give a recent example. A friend of mine slipped whilst scrambling down a gorge in some Alpine foothills. He dislocated his arm and lost his glasses, which meant he could not see, as well as suffering from bodily bruising. He could not move in such dangerous circumstances and his companion left him to go and fetch the rescue helicopter, which duly arrived and lifted him to hospital, down the valley. The helicopter cost £1,700 and an overnight stay in hospital, with treatment, another £200. In other words, £2,000 for a simple mishap. No guides were involved, nor extensive searches and the time taken from calling out the rescue to arrival at hospital was rather less than five hours. Imagine what the cost could be for a complicated rescue!

To cope with this there are three firms offering special insurances. Basically they cover liability, rescue, medical and travel expenses, though they can be extended to cover gear as well. The policy can be adapted for the UK, Europe or Worldwide. Members of clubs affiliated to the British Mountaineering Council (or individual members of the BMC) can avail themselves of the BMC insurance, which is very comprehensive. The addresses are:

Insurance Dept., BMC Services Ltd, Crawford House, Booth St East, Manchester M13 9RZ (061 273 5163).

West Mercia Insurance Services, High St, Womborne, Nr Wolverhampton WV5 9DN (0902 892661).

Endsleigh Insurance Services Ltd, Endsleigh House, Cheltenham Spa, Gloucestershire GL50 3NR (0242 36151).

Travel and Accommodation

Do not expect to get much help from national tourist offices if you are going walking! Even the countries with a strong outdoors tradition, like Switzerland and Austria, know very little about walking tours, paths or available services. You must learn to rely on the map and—if there is one—the guidebook. In the Alpine villages the Guides' Bureau is often helpful with the weather forecast and they will tell you whether any of the passes are under snow.

Getting to any area in Europe from Britain is not difficult these days whether by public transport or car. I have taken a car to the Alps on numerous occasions when I've been on a climbing holiday, based at one or two centres and if there's enough people to share the petrol it is probably the cheapest way. However, it isn't suitable for the sort of walking holiday described in this book because the car has to be abandoned for a week or a fortnight—expensive or risky, depending on how you leave it.

Public transport is more satisfactory. The de-luxe way is to fly to the nearest airport and take a bus or train to the start of the walk, but the ferries from these shores are frequent and varied (if you haven't looked at ferry services lately, you'll be amazed where they go to and from) and train or even bus travel is possible from Britain. A good travel agent will advise on costs and timetables.

Once on the walk the choice lies between camping and some sort of permanent shelter—it could be a mixture of the two. Lightweight camping, moving on from place to place, is called backpacking—an American word precisely descriptive of what is involved. You carry everything with you; a considerable load, but one which gives you absolute freedom over route and distance. But if you don't want to backpack consider the wide variety of alternative accommodation available, though not all of it on any one walk. There are hotels and guest houses, youth hostels, *gîtes d'étape,* alpine huts and various bothies and howffs. Readers will be familiar with most of these though a word or two on *gîtes d'étape* and alpine huts might not come amiss.

A *gîte d'étape* is essentially a bunkhouse offering simple overnight accommodation. There is cooking provision and sometimes simple meals are provided. They are to be found along all the major footpaths of France (the *Grandes Randonées*) and at various other places throughout Europe in a variety of disguises. In Switzerland and Austria they are called *dortoirs* or *matratzenlager* and can vary from comfortably adapted chalets to the loft over an ancient inn. In Scotland and Wales they are called bunkhouses, whilst in the Peak District and Yorkshire the national park authorities have adapted some old barns to the same purpose. A bothy or a howff is a spartan version of the same thing, peculiar to Scotland!

In some ways mountain huts are similar, but they have a tradition all their own. Some are private but most of them belong to a national mountaineering club—the Swiss Alpine Club, for example. They are looked after by a guardian, though some small huts are unsupervised bivouac shelters with very minimal facilities (usually in fairly inaccessible positions and not likely to be met with by anyone but experienced climbers). On the other hand some huts are big—the Berliner Hut in the Zillertal, for example, or the Felix Faure Hut in the Vanoise—and they have a busy staff running what is essentially a mountain hotel.

You do not need to be a club member to use a mountain hut, though members are supposed to have preference if there's a shortage of accommodation. Accommodation (but not meals) is cheaper for members—about half in most huts, though it can vary—so it could be worth joining a club if you intended to use the huts a lot. It doesn't really matter which one because all the alpine clubs have what are called reciprocal rights—that is, a mutual use of huts at reduced rates. The Austrian Alpine Club is the most popular with British walkers—no doubt because it is less expensive than the others!

There are certain elementary rules to be observed in huts unless you wish to incur the wrath of the guardian.
1. Do not enter the hut in mountain boots. Remove them in the porch and wear hut shoes or stocking feet.
2. Do not try to book a bed during a busy meal period. Book immediately upon arrival, which should be mid-afternoon.
3. Do not pitch your tent next to a hut expecting to cook your own food, but using the hut's facilities.

Most huts provide food these days but it varies from the simplest to quite extensive menus (one of the best I've ever come across is the Landsberger Hut. See Walk 12). It saves quite a bit of money to provide your own breakfast of simple crispbread and jam, and to have your own coffee making ingredients, just buying the hot water.

Photography

I wrote extensively about this in the companion volume *Classic Walks of the World*, because some of the trips described there were literally once in a lifetime treks and it seemed a pity not to record them properly. The same could be said of the European walks, of course, though not with the same urgency. Decisions have to be made, in this as most other things, and the following notes might help.
1. The standard format for film is 35mm. Professionals may use bigger sizes from time to time but most of us would find it too expensive. Smaller sizes are not, in my opinion, suitable for anything serious, though they are admirable for snapping Dad and the kids at the seaside.
2. Transparencies (slides) are the most flexible form of photograph since prints can be made from them if necessary. Colour pictures in books and magazines usually require trannies, so if you have publication in mind or a slide show, this is the medium to go for. On the other hand colour print film is much cheaper if you just want something for the album.
3. A good quality automatic compact will give excellent results and is light in weight and simple to use. A UV filter will be useful in the mountains and should be kept on at all times because it protects the lens—you can replace the filter for a fiver, but it will cost you fifty to replace the lens.

The Walks

In *Classic Walks of the World* I graded the routes in a comprehensive list which went from the easiest to the hardest. It was meant as a rough guide at best, but I thought it valid because the walks were so different from one another, influenced by climate and altitude. In this book there are no extremes of either and though some of the walks are tougher than others, the spectrum is not too wide.

The walks are of two types. In the first kind, like the Scottish walk described by Roger Smith, the author has picked a route of his own making through some outstanding countryside. There may or may not be paths, and obviously the route is open to variation. This is not always possible with the second kind of walk, which is a designated 'Way'—a marked trail, usually easy to follow, and often provided

In spring the high hills might be out of bounds through snow, but the valleys will be full of flowers. The hamlet of Osa, Norddal, Norway. (Photo: Walt Unsworth.)

throughout its length with huts or *gîtes d'étapes*. The French call them *Grandes Randonées*, like the GR 54, Tour d'Oisans, described by Andrew Harper; the Germans call them *Wegs* as in the Jubiläums Weg (see Walk 12) and the Italian word is *Via*—as in the famous Dolomite walk described by Martin Collins, the Alta Via 1.

The advantages of an organised path are:
1. They are often specially marked on maps and there is always a guidebook; sometimes several.
2. The route is 'way-marked' ie. a distinctive symbol or sign appears on rocks, signposts etc., throughout its length. On the Continent the usual way-mark is a splash of paint. In theory all you need do is stagger from one way-mark to the next, though it is seldom so simple in practice.
3. They are usually well provided with accommodation along the route.

The disadvantages are:
1. The route might be crowded.
2. The path may be well worn by human erosion.

3. Some walkers feel the loss of freedom inherent in an organised route. They also feel there is a threat in that people might be legislated along prescribed routes and denied access elsewhere.

In Britain fierce argument rages over the desirability of 'ways'. The Ramblers' Association strongly supports them but the British Mountaineering Council is strongly opposed to them in the mountains.

There is no doubt that such paths lessen initiative and detract from route-finding skills, but on the other hand they do provide access routes through rural and urban areas where no access was previously possible. In the mountains this doesn't apply. A freedom to roam policy must be guarded.

But whether we follow the beaten way or wander at will in the lonely hills we should share a curiosity about the world around us. Each journey should be the 'Golden Road to Samarkand'.

We are the Pilgrims, master; we shall go
Always a little further; it may be
Beyond that last blue mountain barred with snow
(J.E. Flecker: Hassan)

Walk 1 FRANCE: The Traverse of the Vercors by the Balcon Est by R. Brian Evans

An Adventurous Route through a Limestone Wonderland

The limestone Prealpes of France are humble mountains. They pay homage to the queen, Mont Blanc, visible from most of the higher summits; and bow to the nearer nobles of the Oisans with their silver coats and sparkling crowns. The walking is modest too, and as a change from the constant steep up or steep down of Alpine areas, there are level stretches where you can stride out. Many visitors eager to reach well known alpine regions, rush through the Prealpes, conscious perhaps that the road twists through rocky gorges with forested slopes topped by fretted cliffs. Then

they are through to the industry of the Isère, Arc or Arve and the teeming hordes of holidaymakers around the popular centres. For many years I broke the journey to the Alps with a day in the Prealpes, or retreated there in bad weather, until I realised that the Prealpes were just as attractive in their own way and deserved more detailed exploration.

They are walkers' mountains. Paths traverse their length at different levels, amongst forest or higher on more open crests. White ribbons of limestone crags dance along for miles. It is still possible to find solitude and the best areas are not ruined by commercialism. Skiing has only blighted a few limited slopes and equally important, the character of the mountains is

Mont Aiguille from the plateau. This startling peak saw the birth of mountaineering in 1492. (Photo: R.B. Evans.)

13

not ruined by huge hotel-like huts. In the Prealpes, the huts are just that—simple spartan shelters.

Like ramparts which defend the Alps, the northern Prealpes stretch in a long curve from north east to south west, from the Jura, through the Bornes, the Bauges, the Aravis, the Chartreuse, to culminate in the Vercors. Rivers separate the massifs where they cut through the limestone to form a gap or *cluse*. The most southerly massif, the Vercors, spreads into a rough triangular shape with its northern apex overlooking Grenoble and the *cluse* of the Isère. Much of the Vercors is a Parc Régional of great beauty and interest, whilst the Haut Plateau is a special nature reserve, totally uninhabited. On all sides the Vercors is defended by steep crags like a fortress—which it effectively was for the Resistance during World War II. There is a central north-south high-level valley, that of the Vernaison and Romayère, split east-west by the deep gorges of the Borne. The rest of the massif is a series of complex plateaux, less forested as height is gained. Along the eastern edge of the plateau the peaks sweep into a wave-like crest which drops dramatically in almost unbroken cliffs for 80km (50 miles) from the outskirts of Grenoble to the Col de Menée. Passes bite deeply into the cliffs here and there, and dominating the views for many a mile is the isolated peak of Mont Aiguille.

The first ascent of Mont Aiguille in 1492 is considered by many to be the birth of mountaineering, if not rock climbing, for the climb is well documented. The exact line of ascent remains a mystery and despite the use of ladders and other devices it was a formidable feat. On the orders of the king, Charles VIII, who saw the impressive peak whilst travelling past, it was climbed by Antoine de Ville and seven companions. The second ascent was made three and a half centuries later, in 1834.

There are many traverses of the Vercors, each worthwhile and often of very contrasting character. The GTA (Grande Traversée des Alpes) passes through the massif on its western side, as does the GR9, traversing forested plateau and deep gorges. Most challenging is the GR91, which explores the interesting wild country of the Haut Plateau, but this is best done in winter on cross country skis—surely the finest traverse of its kind in the Alps? Even more challenging is the traverse by the *Balcon Est*, the footpath which runs below the eastern escarpment. This route, with its extensions, is described here.

The Balcon Est

The path starts near St Nizier, a little village perched high above Grenoble and famous for its Olympic ski jump below the floodlit towers of Les Trois Pucelles (the Three Maidens). It then runs almost horizontally for 50km (30 miles) to the head of the Gresse valley below the huge cliffs of the Grand Veymont, at 2,341 m (7,700ft) the highest peak in the Vercors. To continue the traverse, the route crosses a steep col to another valley below Mont Aiguille. Here one can cross the Col de l'Aupet, between Mont Aiguille and the main plateau, to finish at Chichilianne; or mount the Pas des Bachassons onto the edge of the plateau. The wild southern reaches of the high plateau make a memorable finish to the trip.

French guide books give two days for a shorter version of the Balcon Est from Plateau de St Ange to Gresse, but this entails hard walking with no account taken of possible route finding errors in the forest, stops for photographs or admiration of scenery, flowers etc—or sheer fatigue if carrying a backpacking load. The complete walk as described is most easily accomplished by backpacking and will take most people a week. Parts of the walk are very popular, other parts rarely traversed: to complete the whole route is a very satisfying experience.

Unlike the GR91 which traverses the plateau, the Balcon Est is a sporting challenge with several sections of gripping exposure. Early in the season there are many awkward ravines which may be snow filled and require an ice axe to negotiate. After the snow has gone, the same ravines carry little trace of a path until passing walkers have beaten the clay into shape.

There is another major problem—water. The Vercors is a limestone area riddled with caves and shafts so all precipitation sinks to re-appear at odd places as sources, marked on the maps with a tear drop symbol. Some are excellent and flow strongly all summer. Others are feeble and diminish to extinction if the summer is dry. June and July are the best months. September after a long dry summer could be awkward on the first three days. Forewarned about the water, it is prudent to fill up at every source and be prepared to descend to camp near a certain water supply.

There are two tiny foresters' huts which form logical stages, but they are merely shelters, with walls, a roof and a wooden-floored sleeping area. A tent is less gloomy and should be carried anyway to give freedom of choice. Alternative accommodation is available just below the path at several villages, whilst there is a *gîte d'étape* almost on the path above the Col d'Arzelier. There are comfortable *Refuges* near Gresse, Prelenfrey and at

Chichilianne, whilst the more spartan Abri des Chaumailloux on the plateau is the only one remaining of six purpose-built huts—the others have all been burned down, more the result of a design fault than misuse.

Gresse is the only village en route where provisions can be bought because Prelenfrey and other villages close to the path do not have a shop. Travelling shops call on certain days but cannot be relied upon. There is a shop at Chichilianne at the end of the walk.

Don't be put off by the foregoing comments, the rewards more than amply justify the effort. A glorious array of flowers are constant companions along the path. You are continually surrounded by a delicate blend of hues and scents and distant panoramas which mingle to form an exquisite experience.

The walk is based on Grenoble, easily reached by train in a day from many parts of England, including a memorable superfast whisk from Paris on the TGV. On completion of the walk a return to Grenoble is made from Clelles on the Veynes-Grenoble line, a well-used little railway of great character.

If travelling by car, it is advisable to leave the vehicle at the southern end of the walk, perhaps at Chichilianne, preferably where it can be looked after. Return to Grenoble by train to start the walk. St Nizier, the start of the footpath, overlooks Grenoble but is 900m (3,000ft) above the city. You will be lucky to find that your journey coincides with the bus to Villard de Lans which travels the road, and the best solution, particularly with a small group, is to take a taxi. If it is late at night and you intend to camp discreetly at the start of the path, remember to take water with you. There is a *gite* in St Nizier.

Distance: 68km (42 miles).
Time Required: 6 days.
Type of Walk: The traversing nature of much of this walk makes it less strenuous than most mountain tours, but parts are very exposed and demand a steady head. An ice axe is essential in June.
Base: Grenoble.
Start: St Nizier.
Best Time of Year: June – October; snow may pose problems in June, lack of water in late summer.
Maps: IGN *Massif du Vercors* 1:25,000 (Three sheets, *Vercors Nord, Hauts Plateaux Nord, Hauts Plateau Sud)*, or D&R *Massif du Vercors* 1:50,000.
Guidebooks: No English guide available, although a guide to the Prealpes is in preparation (Cicerone Press).

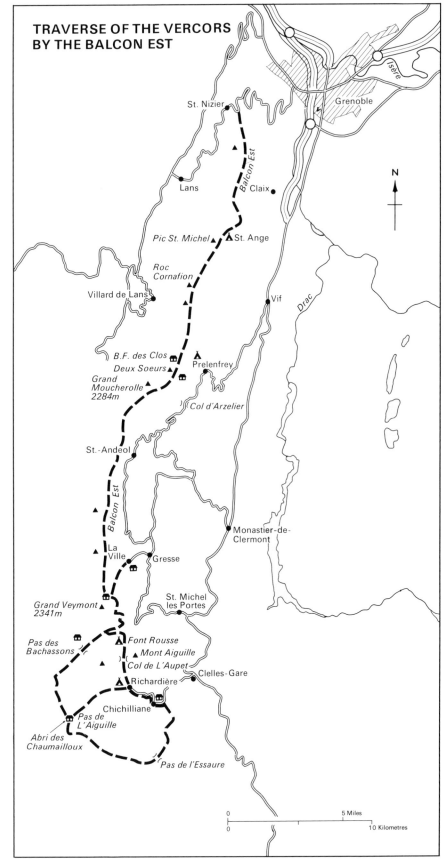

TRAVERSE OF THE VERCORS BY THE BALCON EST

Day 1: St Nizier to St Ange

This is a short day, to recover from the journey and to break yourself in gently whilst carrying a full pack. Much of the walking is in forest, where breaks reveal Grenoble spread like a street plan and glimpses of the snow-flecked Belledonne and Grandes Rousses beyond.

The path, awkward to find at first, is marked with blue/yellow flecks, and runs below Les Trois Pucelles, three limestone towers which hint at things to come. It is easy to miss another branch in the path and find you are heading up towards the Grand Moucherolle. You should be traversing its shoulder to cross a major ravine which carries water well into summer. Round the next spur descend to the Plateau du Peuil where a gently rising path re-enters the forest. Several small ravines are passed, but a more prominent one, la Pissarde, should contain water in early summer. Fill up your water containers here and mount a very steep spur for about 200m (650ft) to its level top where it is possible to pitch a tent. There are fine views towards Mont Aiguille, even now a landmark to the south. Immediately above towers the fine rocky Pic St Michel. The nearest alternative water sources are on either side of the Col de l'Arc, but the steepness of the ground there is not conducive to camping.

Day 2: St Ange to Baraque des Clos or Col d'Arzelier

Another short day, but with enough time to ascend the Roc Cornafion, and enjoy the intricacies of its exposed rocky path. This is a key passage in an early season walk—I have been defeated in early June when new snow transformed the path into a serious winter mountaineering expedition. A year later only a few patches of old snow posed little difficulty. If there is any doubt as to the feasibility of this section, cross the Col de l'Arc to take the easier GR91 path on the western side of the mountain, to regain the eastern flank over the Col Vert. When all the snow has gone there is no difficulty for experienced walkers who enjoy tremendous exposure and easy rock scrambling.

The forest is soon left behind as the open ground below the Col de l'Arc is reached. A path rising left goes to a source, the only water of the day, then still rising leftwards mounts a rocky barrier to join a better path which comes from the col. The next section of path is one of the most exhilarating on the route as it traverses a very rocky mountainside above a cirque of crags, with the green meadows of St Paul 1,400m (4,600ft) below. The path is well marked but sometimes one wonders where it

can possibly go next. Twice it squeezes through natural arches in rock buttresses, sometimes it follows an airy balcony, always in spectacular surroundings. The intricate route winds high up the mountainside and it is well worth the extra effort to scramble up the twin summit of the Roc Cornafion (2,049m, 6,720ft). Needless to say, the views are impressive, for this peak is on a knife edge arête which stretches both north and south.

Regain the Balcon path which descends then crosses another craggy area before easy slopes are reached below the Col Vert. Join a popular path, on which rapid progress is made. Looking back, it seems impossible that a walkers' path traverses the rock peak of the Cornafion.

(At the edge of the forest a path descends left to Prélenfrey: good camping at the picnic site just above the village, water in the village, but no shop, other accommodation is available at the recently built Maison de l'Escalade.)

The Balcon Est continues almost horizontally below the extensive cliffs of the Gerbier, one of the prime climbing crags of the Vercors. At the end of the huge rock wall are two aiguilles which guard the entrance to a stony combe, where perched below a protective avalanche boulder is a little stone hut, the Baraque Forestiére des Clos. A tent could be pitched nearby with some ingenuity, and water is available early in the season, though by August it may have dried up. The alternative is to continue to the *gîte* at the top of the ski lift above the Col de l'Arzelier—or to camp where the angle eases just past the Fontaine des Sarrasins.

A night at the Baraque des Clos is a memorable experience, particularly if mist swirls around the pinnacles and crags which enclose the head of the cirque. Cloud is a feature of the area and you should encounter some memorable effects. Often there is a thick sea of cloud like cotton wool in the valley, or you may see a line of cloud pouring like a waterfall over the escarpment. Overhead soar the twin buttresses of the Deux Soeurs, Agathe and Sophie, with their classic rock climbs. An improbable path wends easily up the narrow gully between the two, an interesting diversion if you have energy and time to spare.

Day 3: Baraque des Clos to La Ville

A long and arduous day as the path traverses below the continuous escarpment and crosses several difficult ravines. There is no guarantee of water between the Fontaine des Sarrasins and the Source of the Grand Veymont. If you are walking the route early in

Facing page: **Pic St Michel from the path below the Col d'Arc.** (Photo: R.B. Evans.)

Below: **On the southern part of the plateau. In the background is the Grand Veymont.**

the season much snow will be encountered in the ravines and an ice axe is essential to aid a safe passage. In these conditions it is unlikely that you will complete this stretch in a day and it is recommended you drop down to camp at the Grand Clos, a prominent clearing,

although the nearest water is still well below. Once embarked on the ravines, there is only one escape path and that is steep!

Forewarned about the difficulties, make an early start and you will be rewarded by seeing the array of crags glowing pink in the early morning sun. The path traverses steep slopes below the Deux Soeurs, to cross the head of a ski lift (with the *gîte* just below) and continue to the important water source round the corner. It is named after the Saracens who are reputed to have retreated there after being repulsed from the nearby Pas de Balme in the 9th century. The pass has an enormous man-made defensive wall above the path.

The escarpment stretches into the distance with the Grand Veymont assuming its rightful place as the most dominant peak. Below the array of colourful crags and screes, long spurs poke like fingers into the forest. Across the valley is another parallel, but lower crest, with the prow of the Devoluy visible behind.

Join the path from the Pas de Balme and descend several hairpins before branching along the horizontal again, below the Rochers de Balme. As the path traverses a huge cirque there are good retrospective views to the rocky dome of the Grand Moucherolle, at 2,284m (7,490ft) one of the highest summits of the Vercors. The corner of the cirque is marked by the Rochers du Playnet, an imposing tower. (A path descends to St Andeol where there is water but no shop.) Continue below the seven towers which here give the area its closest resemblance to the Dolomites.

The path keeps more or less horizontal, just skirting the upper limit of the forest. The IGN map marks a long section here with dots, which denote a difficult passage, and just when you think it's not so bad after all, you are faced with an awesome ravine of crumbling rock bands above a big drop. Now you know why the path has dwindled in size, for this section is not traversed by the average walker out for a gentle stroll! Ravine follows ravine, and great care is necessary. You may find that some carry protection wires, although these may be demolished by winter snows and rockfall.

At last you escape the clutches of the ravines to gain gentler slopes. A notch in the skyline ahead is the Pas de Berrièves, an important easy col. Join the path below the col and descend to the top of a spur below the Rocher de Séguret. Now for the sting in the tail—yet another broad ravine and its crumbly ledges. You can opt out here and descend the spur directly to les Petits Deux and so to La Ville, but the Balcon Est continues on its airy course.

The Ravine de Farnaud safely crossed, there are no further hazards as the path crosses the

head of ski slopes above La Ville. Ahead towers the rock face of the Grand Veymont, at 2,341m (7,680ft) the highest peak of the Vercors. Cross the path which goes to the Pas de la Ville, another major pass across the range, and continue below the cliffs of the Grand Veymont, where a strong stream issues from a source at the foot of the crags. Descend gradually to the head of a delightful valley, where the little Baraque Forestière du Veymont is situated amongst the trees. This could still be used overnight in 1986, although it was showing signs of decay. There are good camping pitches in the valley nearby.

If you prefer comfort to the spartan accommodation of a bothy, then follow the forest road down the valley to La Ville, a recently developed ski village. Here there is a modern Refuge du Parc, with central heating, cooking facilities and genuine bunks—at a very reasonable overnight fee (about £1.50). Gresse, an attractive old village, lies 2km further, with a small general store. Its proprietor has no idea of the importance it has assumed in the eyes of hungry British backpackers. Fresh bread, incomparable French sausages and wine seem all the better after a hard trek.

Day 4: La Ville to Font Rousse

A semi-rest day after the rigours of the Balcon Est, for this marks the end of that path, and you will certainly want to wander down to Gresse to re-stock with food. Don't be completely fooled however, the crossing of the crest to the next cirque was strenuous enough to draw the comment from one member of my party: 'If that's your idea of a semi-rest day, I wouldn't like to sample a full one!' It is very tempting to linger at the valley head, a more alpine situation than many in the Vercors.

If you have spent the night at La Ville return to the Baraque Forestiére du Veymont—the footpath on the right of the stream, starting at a small dam, is a pleasant alternative to the forest road. The Balcon Est completed, the walk now changes character—it goes steeply uphill to mount the north-west flank of the Côte de Quinquanbaye. Once on the crest the views are breathtaking—the route of the Balcon Est can be seen from the bastion of the Deux Soeurs to its finale as a thin ribbon below the buttresses of the Grand Veymont. Turn

Top: **The Rochers du Parquet from the Col de l'Aupet.**
Middle: **Crossing an exposed ravine; in early season an ice axe is essential.**
Bottom: **The lone tree on the Plain de la Querie is marked on the map!** (All photos: R.B. Evans)

around and there is incredible Mont Aiguille like a sheer walled fortress on top of a conical base. Below, deceivingly near, is the forested cirque where you may choose to spend the night.

To avoid the vertiginous gullies below, the path strikes along the crest until it can safely zig-zag to easier ground amongst forest, where it assumes its more familiar horizontal role. Deep ravines again cut into the mountain and the path traverses first one side then the other. The Ravine des Challanches may prove awkward, for every winter parts of the path are eaten away and a new passage has to be devised to cross the stream bed. Cross a shaly shoulder to reach the Ravines des Chauvines which carries a strong stream—there are no further problems with water supplies on the walk. Once again, the old path has crumbled away and the ascent of the ravine side to its forested spur is devious.

You could continue up the valley to reach the plateau, but the cirque below Mont Aiguille is so idyllic that I strongly recommend a stay. So descend the spur into its more gentle base where woodland and clearing frame the surrounding peaks. There is a stream with attractive camping pitches on the edge of the woods. You may see the charred remains of the burnt Font Rousse *refuge,* once a popular base for climbers heading for Mont Aiguille. Now they use a barn just down a rough road on the east side of the stream.

It is of course possible to extend the day's walk over the steep Col de l'Aupet below Mont Aiguille to reach Chichilianne, but this would terminate the trip too early and there is much of interest still to see. If you have energy to spare after pitching camp, take a walk up the track to the Col de l'Aupet, a fine belvedere, to study the crags of Mont Aiguille, whose western face is now revealed as a complicated mass of towers and gullies. The *Voie Normale* ascends this face and whilst it has protection wires in place, similar to a Dolomite *Via Ferrata,* it does involve easy rock climbing and is very exposed. The cliffs of the Rochers du Parquet which dominate the western side of the col, are almost equally impressive. A strenuous return to the camp can be made by a path which heads along the crest towards the Rochers du Parquet then turns along the edge of the cirque to gain another path through the forest which regains the ascent path at the foot of the Cascade de la Pisse.

Day 5: Font Rousse to Abri des Chaumailloux

Another change of character, for this days' walk explores the plateau. Views are tre-mendous. In 1987, the timber-built Refuge des Chaumailloux was still there—but don't count on it!

Start by retracing the previous day's route up the forested spur by the side of the Ravine des Chauvines, then continue up the narrowing valley, quite steep in parts, to the Pas des Bachassons (1,913m, 6,280ft) on the edge of the plateau. Surprisingly, there is a source here, which runs strongly all summer. Just over the hill towards the Grand Veymont is another tiny *refuge,* the Cabane des Aiguillettes, which is yet another alternative. A night here in good weather instead of at Font Rousse, would allow time for an ascent of the Grand Veymont by its easy south ridge.

Gain the flat-topped spur on the right of the Pas des Bachassons and follow it south west to a large upland hollow, the Plaine de la Querie. The distinctive lone tree is even marked on the map, whilst just beyond on the right are ancient Roman quarries. The stone, some of which was used in Die, must have been very special to warrant such a trek.

Just past the lone tree bear left across a slight col between low hills, where the plateau becomes much stonier as the path circles a little hollow with a *bergerie,* the Jasse de Peyre Rouge. In summer the *bergeries* are often occupied as huge flocks of sheep are brought to the Vercors from the more arid Midi. Give the flocks a wide berth to avoid disturbance.

Ahead, the plateau is a tortured landscape of rocky hillocks and hollows. There is a path going the way we want—if you can find it. A prominent rounded hill, the Tourte-Barreaux is kept on the right as progress is made, then surmount a region of little conical mounds. The route finding is interesting even in perfect visibility. In mist it is totally confusing unless you know the area well. If you have success-fully solved the intricacies you will emerge on the edge of a grassy hollow at the top of a deep-cut valley—the Pas de l'Aiguille, well named for Mont Aiguille provides a perfect backcloth. The Abri de Chaumailloux is a welcome sight, a tiny timber hut which nestles below a little knoll. The hut has a central wood burning stove (which must not be used in summer), a two-tier wooden sleeping platform, a table and benches. The overnight fee, payable to the Parc authorities is about 50p. There are several water sources close by.

On a winter ski trip, this is a delectable spot, difficult to reach and committing in bad weather. In summer it is just as attractive in a different way. Stroll down the head of the Pas, where there is a stirring monument to the Resistance. A path leads to two small caves on the left, where a handful of local men held the pass against overwhelming odds for over 24 hours. Several died but most escaped to continue harrying the enemy.

Day 6: Chaumailloux to Chichilianne

Once again there are options—you can simply descend the steep path down the Pas de l'Aiguille to Richardière and then along quiet lanes to Chichilianne, or continue the traverse of the southern plateau. The former is shorter and the scenery at the head of the Pas is wild, for there are impressive waterfalls which form major winter ice climbs in the style now so popular in Britain.

The way along the plateau is also interesting for those who like the feel of space and wilderness. Follow the tiny stream by the side of the hut, up a narrow cut, then branch left to zig-zag up the side of the steep Tête des Baumiers. A rising terrace makes a pleasant path around the northern slopes of the hill to level out and cross a low col. Ahead is a shallow valley, which you follow past the Bergerie de Chamousset to mount the slopes beyond to a col. Views are extensive. The plateau stretches away to the west, with hints of the cliff edges which guard its rim.

The path continues dropping gradually to an obvious nick, the head of the Vallée de Combau. Descend a more abrupt slope to a plateau on the left of the stream. There is another stone *refuge,* the Abri de l'Essaure, on this shelf, but branch left well before it to a col on the edge of the escarpment. There is another lone tree landmark hereabouts.

The gap is the Pas de l'Essaure, and the path dips steeply into the forest and zig-zags down a seemingly endless spur to reach the pleasant village of Chichilianne, journeys end.

Chichilianne is a pleasant village with a shop, cafes and an unusual but very comfortable Refuge du Parc situated on the ground floor of the Mairie. Three kilometres down the valley is Clelles Gare, where you can catch the train back to Grenoble.

Walk 2 FRANCE: The Tour of the Oisans by Andrew Harper

The Balcony path after Col de Souchet. (Photo: Andrew Harper.)

An Exhilarating Walk amidst Glorious Mountain Scenery

Walkers should be grateful that in addition to the good paths in Britain, they need venture no further than our nearest neighbour to unlock the treasure chest that awaits them there. There are the obvious routes like the Tour of Mont Blanc and the long-distance GR5 which are relatively well known, but surely there is nobody who can be conversant with the whole extent of footpaths throughout France? They abound in the lowlands as well as mountainous areas, even following the shore along stretches of coastline. Nice though seascapes and quaint little villages may be, the grandeur of the mountain backdrop is surely unchallengeable for visual impact and reward.

Such, then, is the setting for the walk described here. The area encompassed by the route is to a large extent designated as one of France's National Parks where there is a positive approach to protecting the floral growth and the animal life within its confines as well as a policy to guard against exploitation. The starting point of this circuit is a large village called Bourg d'Oisans, some 50km (30 miles) east of Grenoble; a regular bus service links the two. Grenoble is served on one of the routes from Paris run by the TGV express rail network and there is at least one coach operator that features it throughout the summer from London.

At Bourg d'Oisans (717m, 2,352ft) there are numerous hotels, some with dormitory-style accommodation (called a *dortoir*), and camping sites where one can rely on spending the first night. From then on the route is punctuated with *refuges* and villages where overnight opportunities are adequate. There are some campsites as well and in consequence wayside pitching is discouraged: bivouacing 'above the tree-line' is evident, but even this is forbidden within the confines of the National Park boundaries (with certain exceptions).

The First Pace

The path starts adjacent to the Sarenne Campsite which is about a mile from the centre of Bourg d'Oisans on the road leading towards the winter ski-ing resort of l'Alpe d'Huez and immediately before the roadway commences its zig-zagging to gain height. It is not unknown for walkers to take the bus that continues up this road, alighting at the mountainside village of d'Huez, reckoning that the bulk of the day's ascent is best avoided in this manner: this is nonsense as the path it by-passes is one of the nicest and shouldn't be snubbed. Gaining height in the shade, it opens out eventually to give the first unhampered and glorious view of the day where a hospitable hotel with restaurant facilities is conveniently sited—but all of this prior to the point at which the path would be joined by the 'bus people'.

Walk down awhile to cross a narrow river by means of an age-old stone bridge, followed by a steady climb that takes the path above the tree-line to approach the first col—Sarenne (2,009m, 6,591ft). Rather bleak just there but a few paces beyond will show the wee village of Clavans (1,407m, 4,616ft) right down at the base of the cleft. The legs start to complain as they 'change gear' to descend the steep slopes towards the place. Clavans is made up of two separate clusters with few facilities, but a bar and simple sleeping facilities can be found. A lot of walkers aim for the next village, Besse-en-Oisans (1,550m, 5,085ft), but this involves climbing for an hour at the end of the first day and so it is not to everyone's liking. Maybe it might be best to make a halt at Clavans and get up to Besse in good time for breakfast.

After this bigger village the path sweeps upwards until drawing level with Col Bichet (2,245m, 7,365ft) producing one of the most sensational and far-reaching views. For the first time you can see some of the large peaks comprising the range, crowned here by la Meije (3,982m, 13,064ft). Even if you are tired beyond belief, it is doubtful if you would notice the effort needed to walk the three hours or so to pass Col Souchet (2,362m, 7,749ft) and reach the village at le Chazelet (1,786m, 5,860ft) because the sights to the right are so absorbing!

La Grave

The village of la Grave (1,474m, 4,836ft) lies at the base of a narrow valley and is very picturesque in its setting. It has plenty of accommodation and eating establishments as well as essential stores. The path leaves the village and dips to cross the river Romanche, climbing to surmount an intervening ridge before dipping again to rejoin the river adjacent to a charming little village called Villar d'Arène. From here it hugs the watercourse for a couple of miles to reach a large campsite and roadhead, eventually narrowing to climb alongside an enormous waterfall to get to the general upper level surrounding the Refuge de l'Alpe du Villar d'Arène. This *refuge* is situated amongst some wild and fascinating scenery: typical of the glories gradually opening up as the Tour gets underway.

A short distance further on takes you to the Col d'Arsine (2,348m, 7,7703ft) with its attendant glacier, and then the lengthy descent to le Casset begins. Negotiating a steep hairpin it drops to skirt lake Douche before entering thin woodland and joining the roadway. Le Casset has limited facilities, and it is usually better to make for the lower and much larger village of Monêtier-les-Bains (1,495m, 4,905ft), so as to be favourably positioned for the next day.

To Vallouise

It is always nice to have a *refuge* or a hut not too far from the highest point of the day's walk, attracting a nucleus of people where ideas can be exchanged and the sound of laughter heard. Not only can the tasteless soup become the most welcome thing on earth but the knowledge of shelter 'being there' can be comforting. There's nothing like this, though, on the next stretch until you have gone a long way down the other side of Col de l'Eychauda (2,425m, 7,956ft). The final approach to this col is bleak indeed, undoubtedly horrid on a wet day and probably cauldron-like when the weather goes to the opposite extreme. It must also be said that the surroundings are not representative of the best that the area can offer although the path itself is substantial. It takes some four hours to drop down to the roadway at St. Antoine and at least another hour to reach the resort of Vallouise (1,166m, 3,825ft). There are numerous places to lodge along the roadside, but Vallouise will be found

Top: **The Oratoire du Chazelet with la Meije in the distance.**

Above: **The waymark post for the GR54.**
(Photos: Andrew Harper.)

23

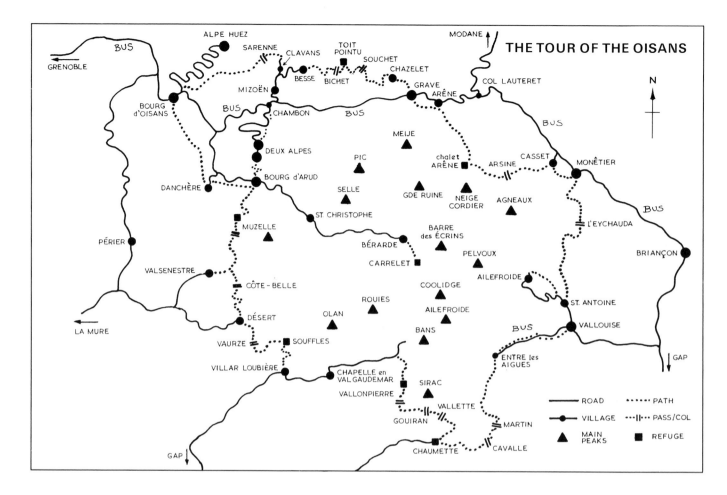

THE TOUR OF THE OISANS

N

Legend:
— ROAD
●— VILLAGE
—‖— PASS/COL
▲ MAIN PEAKS
■ REFUGE
····· PATH

Distance: 180km (115 miles).
Ascent/Descent: 12,000m (40,000ft). These figures presume the adoption of all the recommendations.
Time Required: 10 to 14 days.
Type of Walk: Previous experience of dedicated alpine walking preferable if not essential. Several long stretches without shelter.
Two of the cols demand particular care and good judgement.
Paths well defined and waymarking reasonably good.
Base: Grenoble.
Start: Bourg d'Oisans.
Best Time: Mid-July to mid-September.
Map: *Massifs Ecrins Haut Dauphiné* 1:50,000 Didier & Richard.
Guidebook: *Tour of the Oisans:* GR54 by Andrew Harper (Cicerone Press).
Additional Information: French Government Tourist Office, 178 Piccadily, London W1. Tourist Office, Bourg d'Oisans, France.

to be well-equipped to cater for all categories of visitor.

Ailefroide

This charming mountaineering centre is off the direct course of the Tour d'Oisans and is at the head of the road which goes through St. Antoine. It can also be reached by path, which takes slightly over the hour to climb to the village at a height of 1,506m (4,941ft). Vallouise represents almost the halfway point on the circuit and so it should be possible to assess progress and judge if it is feasible to make such a diversion. Maybe it will depend just as much on how the eye judges the weather prospects? Ailefroide is a place 'truly of the mountains' and you are encouraged to go there.

Col de l'Aup Martin and the Chaumette Refuge

Those who took the bus on the first day will be pleased to learn that there is a minibus service operating out of Vallouise which cuts out the two-hour-plus slog up the narrow road to reach Entre-les-Aigues. Even for experi-

enced mountain walkers it will be quite a long day, so the knowledge of this form of assistance might be welcomed! The road is not at all unpleasant and if handled with the dawn it should be nice enough. From the roadhead the path goes up the left-hand valley of the two that join there, immediately engaging rough country where it accompanies a tumbling stream for most of the remaining ascent.

After surmounting a couple of gigantic shoulders and hairpinning past a waterchute, it gets quite slippery underfoot where the terrain seems to be composed of damp black shale. The extremely narrow ledges that form the path in this sweeping slope appear quite inadequate for the task but with a little caution it will lead you up to the highest part on the circuit: Col de l'Aup Martin (2,761m, 9,058ft). This can be regarded as a real achievement and the prize for this will be a superb vista of new things beyond. You will be at the top end of a large valley coming up from the left and you can see the next pass on the other edge of the valleyhead. This will be the Pas de la Cavale (2,735m, 8,973ft) and it does not take long to get to it by the almost-contouring linking path. It is a safe descent, although a trifle steep initially and care will have to be exercised if there is any snow covering the track. As the slope lessens, the new enchanting scenery ahead will begin to occupy the mind: this point in the walk represents the southernmost extreme of the circuit. At the very bottom a stream has to be crossed and it will then only be a few paces up the opposing slope to the Refuge de Pré de la Chaumette (1,790m, 5,873ft), which usually offers a substantial evening meal and can accommodate a large number of people in its many dormitories. This can be a haven in inclement weather as there is absolutely nowhere else to shelter.

Three Cols

In very bad weather a *refuge* attracts everyone, including those of the backpacking brigade who find it all too much to take. So, after a rainy night, it can be a noisy affair getting breakfast in such a place. The path goes past the *refuge* and gradually gains height up a rock-strewn, stubby valley behind it. It surmounts various plateaux before slanting up the side of a hanging valley where, in places, it is cut into the rock. At a point where there is a miniscular pond it is possible to overlook the ridge and see into the tumbling mountain backdrop beyond.

The Col de la Vallette (2,668m, 8,753ft) is the first of three cols and the second can be seen over on the other side of the glen into which the path dips when crossing to it. Forty minutes later you reach the Col Gouiran (2,597m, 8,520ft) from where the path ahead can be seen under the shaly watershed of the right-hand slopes. Finally it jerks upwards to reach the grass-covered final approach to the third pass encountered on this section. Arrival at the Col de Vallonpierre (2,607m, 8,553ft) will allow a splendid view right into the heartland of the Ecrins National Park. The major mountain of the area is the mighty Sirac and it is shown in fine perspective from the neighbourhood of the col.

The start of the descent is somewhat tricky and the head of the path will be found some few paces along the crest to the left: don't go straight down the other side. It will be uncomfortably steep initially, but from the point where the Vallonpierre *refuge* can be seen (on the far shore of a small lake), the going gets easier. At 2,280m (7,480ft), this *refuge* is situated at an idyllic corner of the world. Some people like it so much that they plan to spend the night there even though they could otherwise make more progress and reach the next *refuge* long before nightfall. The path linking the two, drops through bush-clad hillsides and has the company of turbulent streams and rivers along its course.

It takes some two hours to get to the Refuge Xavier Blanc (1,397m, 4,583ft) and this is about as far as most people want to go in a day, although strong walkers might prefer to continue to reach la Chapelle-en-Valgaudemar (1,100m, 3,608ft) where they will have the opportunity of staying in a hotel instead. On a good evening it is no bad thing to amble down the road leading to this attractive village: the scenery is magnificent and the small hamlet of le Casset which is passed on the way is very photogenic.

Le Désert and Valsenestre

Passing through Valgaudemar it is necessary to continue on the road for another hour (hardly a problem: not many cars) until coming to a delightful but slightly smaller village called Villar-Loubière (1,033m, 3,389ft). Be well advised to take fresh supplies on board because of the limited availability of provisions during the ensuing three days.

The path cants up from the village and is gently graded throughout its whole length up to the next pass. It will take just short of five hours to get there but the nicely positioned Refuge des Souffles (1,975m, 6,480ft) provides a welcome break almost at the half-way point. The path scours wide arcs over the upper grassy slopes before drawing level with Col de la Vaurze (2,498m, 8,196ft) and once there you will not only be able to see the crest of the next col but beyond that to the next one as well.

The eye will eventually lower to discover the small cluster of houses and buildings that represent Le Désert and the steepness of the path leading down to the village seems to have been designed specifically to torment the leg muscles. But isn't the scenery magnificent? The drop to the village will seem never ending but the thought of getting a cool lager on arrival is inducement enough to keep up the good work! Le Désert (1,255m, 4,117ft) is probably the smallest place encountered on the route with facilities: *dortoir,* modest restaurant, a bar and a very simple provisions store. French mountain rural life personified.

Leave the village at its 'high' end by way of a jeep track that curves up to the left. Approaching a defile it narrows significantly, immediately becoming a good quality path which only steepens to surmount a promontory. It then continues in wide sweeps to gain the height necessary to reach the Col de Côte Belle, (2,290m, 7,513ft) which will be found to be grassy, gently curved and with plenty of space to stretch out. This is the shortest day in terms of the walking hours, so not only would a late start have been feasible but there is absolutely

A picturesque waterfall passed en route. (Photo: Andrew Harper.)

no restraint upon taking a lengthy lounge at the crest. The views fore and aft are very good and so, too, is the path leading down to the next valley, being extremely rich with bushy vegetation for most of its drop.

At its base you will come to a junction of paths and the way to the col de la Muzelle goes off to the right. The strenuous going to Bourg d'Arud by way of this particular pass absorbs a day in its own right and only a fell-runner or the foolhardy would tack it onto the crossing of the Côte Belle. This dictates a turn to the left at the junction for a 40-minute woodland descent into the small village of Valsenestre (1,295m, 4,249ft). There will be found a well-run campsite as well as a *dortoir* where it is possible to acquire an evening meal. (An alternative route over to Bourg d'Arud commences its climb directly from this village, though this is not without its share of difficulties).

Bourg d'Arud by way of Col de la Muzelle

Retrace your steps to the path junction where you must veer left to start the section leading to the col. Initially it is almost identical to the climb of the preceding day but the major difference will not become noticeable until the latter stages. Where the grass ends it becomes necessary to traverse an easy scree slope which is immediately followed by some devilish compacted shale which steepens to such an extent that it is sometimes difficult to maintain a reasonable stance whilst planning the next foot position. The final assault is handled with a prayer rather than elegance and once at the Col de la Muzelle (2,625m, 8,612ft) it will be found to be a place that holds no comforts and will not encourage anyone to linger.

My philosophy is this: show me a *path* and I reckon to walk along it. Whilst admitting that the Muzelle is a *route* it is certainly not a path. I get no additional satisfaction out of a day by encountering and overcoming 'difficulties' of this kind, but what would life be like if everything was easy? Apart from being an essential element in progressing the circuit, is there anything about the col that pleases? Certainly—the view in both directions from it. The backwards view will hold no surprises but that ahead is unexpected. The Refuge de la Muzelle comes to view alongside the striking blue lake and a long way beyond the ridge at its rear will be seen the saddle straddling the main range which houses the large winter resort villages of les Deux Alpes.

Going down the other side is awkward, although its lesser ferocity makes for welcome change. Surprisingly, it will take over an hour

to reach the *refuge* which can be relied on to provide the customary things. The col looks insignificant when compared to the enormous glacier that can now be seen to its left. The path goes over the crest behind the *refuge* and after striking some marshy ground drops down with determination to a spot where two waterchutes join and then with the amalgamated water for company the path takes an eternity in continuing down to l'Alleau. The mountainsides are richly clad with pine trees and the sight of numerous waterfalls will make even the most determined walker stop to admire them.

It takes only a few paces to pass the small number of houses at l'Alleau where it will be necessary to cross a girder-constructed road bridge if you want to go into the larger Bourg d'Arud (942m, 3,091ft) with its two hotels, campsite and shop.

Final Paces

After a good sleep, the body will be anxious for the 'off' again, having by this time attuned itself to any demand made upon it: the nightmare that was Muzelle has become a thing of the past, creating a sense of relief with the knowledge that only lesser problems can lay ahead. As it happens, the contrast could not be greater because the remaining section is the least demanding of all. Going back over the bridge to l'Alleau there is a signposted path off to the right which immediately leads into woods that line the left-hand side of the valley floor. This is a pleasant stroll, taking over an hour to emerge at la Danchère which is a smashing little community. From there the path continues much as before, eventually crossing open countryside, taking a total of about four hours to get to Borg d'Oisans from Bourg d'Arud.

Two Suggestions

1. Certain stages of the Tour d'Oisans have alternative paths with merits of their own but the route described is *traditional*. There are also a few offshoots that can be explored (the diversion to Ailefroide having already been mentioned) and right at the end of the holiday another splendid opportunity presents itself. Regarded by many as being the Mecca of the Alps, the village of la Bérarde (1,711m, 5,614ft) can be visited in just one day by using the bus that passes through Bourg d'Arud around 10am to return about 6pm (check). Once there the most popular path takes an hour to reach the Chalet Hotel du Carrelet, although the tag 'hotel' is surely somewhat pretentious: the surroundings, however, are simply stupendous!

2. If it is of no great consequence that the circuit be completed by returning to Bourg d'Oisans entirely on foot, there is a much more rewarding way of terminating the vacation although this will absorb a whole day. When ready to leave Bourg d'Arud, instead of going to Bourg d'Oisans through the woods, go up the short path to Venosc, which is a pretty little place. Continue to the upper extent of this village where the narrow streets converge to develop into a path which takes 2hrs 40 mins to climb to Alpe-de-Venosc (the first of 'les Deaux Alpes' that could be seen from the Col de la Muzelle). Here there is a wealth of restaurants and other facilities, just as there are at the next place called Alpe de Mont-de-Lans (the second one). The route, having gone along the main street which links the two resorts, becomes a path once more and starts to descend, shortly going through the lovely village of Mont-de-Lans. After this landmark it should be possible to look across the rich blue water of the dam at lac Chambon and when eventually you get to the cluster of premises adjacent to the dam wall it will be possible to board a bus to complete the return to Bourg d'Oisans. A much nicer way of spending a day.

'GR54' with its variants offers some of the grandest scenery that France can put on show. If you were to go there and walk its length it would be more than likely that you would want to return over and over again.

Top: **The Refuge de l'Alpe du Villar d'Arêne.**

Middle: **Logs are piled high at Bourg d'Arud.**

Bottom: **The Refuge Xavier Blanc.**
(Photos: Andrew Harper.)

The Dents du Midi. (Photo: John Cleare.)

Walk 3 FRANCE, SWITZERLAND: Through the Chablais Alps by Walt Unsworth

Through the gentle Chablais Hills from Lac Leman to Mont Blanc

There could hardly be a better introduction to hill-walking in the Alps than the first few days of the GR5 from the Lake of Geneva to Chamonix. Except in one or two places the path is well marked, quite without difficulty, and there is plenty of accommodation on the way. The stages can be almost as long or short as you wish and there is nothing committing about the walk either, because road or rail can be reached quite easily throughout its length.

Day 1

Geneva is probably the best base from which to start this walk, though Montreux would do just as well. Both places are connected by public transport with the start and finish of the route.

It begins in the little lakeside town of St Gingolph which is reached romantically by lake steamer from Montreux or more prosaically by train from Geneva, right round the lake's edge in a journey which more than anything demonstrates the efficiency of the Swiss railways. The town itself sits astride the Franco-Swiss border which is actually at the bridge in the middle of the high street.

The walk stays on the French side, following the border stream of the Morge, to the hamlet of Novel. It follows a delightful, though at times steep, path through the woods until after about one and a half hours of toil the hamlet appears, clustered prettily hugger-mugger in a manner suited to its seven hundred years. You would scarcely suspect that the whole place was burnt to the ground in 1924!

Once beyond the hamlet the trees are soon left behind. Ahead the valley terminates in a ring of limestone peaks. Pleasant pastures lead towards these and it is worthwhile to pause here and look back down the Morge valley towards the lake, now a thousand metres below. On either hand the peaks rear up, especially on the Swiss side where the sharp grey spires of the Grammont look savagely attractive.

Turning again to the task in hand it seems as though the path follows a natural valley away to the left, climbing gently to a col, but this is just deception. Before long the path starts to climb steeply up a spur, broken by outcrops of limestone. Away to the right the splendidly craggy Dent d'Oche rears up to 2222m (7,283ft) and the view back towards the lake becomes increasingly panoramic. Eventually the path zig-zags up to a gap in a ridge beyond which lies a curious upland valley, reminiscent of a Derbyshire moor.

The path goes along here past a ruined chalet called de Neuteu, which offers splendid refuge in a storm as I can testify only too well! I sat out a thunderstorm here a few years ago when the rain came down like glass stair-rods; unfortunately, I foolishly left the friendly shelter of the chalet too soon, mistaking a break in the storm as the all-clear signal. I had scarcely got more than a few hundred yards from the hut when the rain came down with all its previous intensity. Of course I had waterproofs—but in my experience nothing yet invented is proof against a downpour on the outside and sweat on the inside; you get wet one way or the other.

It is important at this point to identify the place at which the path turns sharp left towards the Col de Bise (1916m, 6,285ft) or you are likely to go wandering off along the track to Thonon-les-Bains. In clear weather the wooden cross which guards the col acts as a marker, but in bad weather it isn't always easy to spot. Fortunately, there isn't much of a climb and the col is soon reached.

From the col the way ahead extends down a valley reminiscent of a Highland glen. A spur cuts off any sign of habitation and at the end of the glen there is a splendid limestone peak, the Cornettes de Bise, all bulky and craggy.

The descent is pleasant and quite short. In well under the hour the Chalets de Bise appear; a group of farm buildings in a lonely setting,

famous for their herds of cows and goats. At milking time the concentrated clanging of the cowbells is an unforgettable noise. At such times it is best to seek the quiet of the hut belonging to the Club Alpin Français, where one can stay the night.

Day 2

The next day is short and sharp. From the door of the club hut a track leads below the Cornettes de Bise to climb in steep zig-zags to the pas de la Bosse (1815m, 5955ft). It is difficult to understand why some alpine ridge crossings are called *cols* (saddles) and others given the more important title of *pas* (pass), when often there isn't a scrap of difference between them. This particular *pas* gives glorious views down to the valley of the Dranse. From the top of the pass a lovely wooded vale, fringed with white limestone crags, funnels narrowly down to the main valley. This is followed to the chalets of Chevanne where the track becomes a road leading down to the little village of La Chapelle d'Abondance.

It takes about three hours to reach Chapelle from the Bise hut, so the day has hardly started and yet it may be worth staying here for the night, preparing for the rigours of the next day rather than pushing on. There isn't much in Chapelle d'Abondance to while away the time, but down the valley lies the larger parent village of Abondance itself where there is a 14th-century abbey. The walk takes about one and a half hours, or you may be lucky enough to catch the bus which serves the Dranse valley—traffic is heavy here because it is a popular way to Morgins and Champéry; the only vehicular access across the mountains to Switzerland between the Lake of Geneva and the Chamonix valley.

Day 3

Even the guidebook warns you about the start to this part of the walk. No doubt the authorities will sort it out one day but at present the climb out of the Dranse valley is very confusing. A friend and I struggled for hours in thick forest trying to find the path, led astray by forestry signs which are identical with those used to mark the GR5. So beware! (Note: since writing this the tourist office in Chapelle assure me the route has been made clearer.)

It starts innocently enough with a steep but charming ascent by the side of a tumbling cascade, up through the woods to the old chalet of Sur Bayard. From this point a close scrutiny of the guidebook text is needed, along with an even closer scrutiny of the map. If you do get lost then make for the valley again

The Abondance Valley. In the background, left, is the Cornettes de Bise and the Pas de la Bosse. (Photo: Walt Unsworth.)

where, in the village of Châtel, you can get a taxi to hoist you effortlessly (and quite cheaply) to the Col de Bassachaux. (Note: in 1986 the road was closed by landslide.)

But assuming that all goes well, you emerge from the trees onto a ridge with splendid views of the distant snowy alps from the Col des Mattes (1,910m, 6,267ft). From there the path contours round the spur called Crête de Coicon to the farm at Lenlevay where cheese is still made in the old way, in a big vat over an open wood fire. Whether this cheese still requires the sort of attention described by Edward Whymper in his famous book *Scrambles Amongst The Alps* is doubtful! Whymper described how a 'foul native' blew into the bubbling cheese, in between taking a few whiffs from his pipe. 'It accounts, perhaps, for the flavour possessed by certain Swiss cheeses.' Whymper remarks laconically. Oh well, we are still in France, not Switzerland—though we are heading towards that country quite rapidly.

The Col de Bassachaux (1,783m, 5,850ft) comes next, and I have already described how it was once possible to cheat your way to this spot by taxi, but no longer. There's a well patronised restaurant at the col and a broad track leads from it towards a valley head and the Col de Chésery (2,025m, 6,644ft). The climb here resembles that up Sty Head from Borrowdale, in the English Lake District: a meandering path, never too steep, which idles its way to a broad hummocky col, littered with a few old custom buildings. This is the Swiss border, though you'd hardly know it—there

isn't even a sign saying 'Switzerland'.

It isn't the best introduction to the land of the cuckoo clock. The mountains are small, shaly and drab and the chief object of attention is a miserable looking lake, the Lac Vert, on the far side of which can be seen the path leading to the next col, Porte du Lac Vert (2,157m, 7,077ft). (*Porte* is another, and much rarer, variation on *col* or *pas* and is equally indistinguishable.) The trudge up to the col is brutally steep but mercifully short. And at the top . . .

Well, at the top there is one of the greatest *coups d'oeil* in the Alps. Below your feet the land falls away into a wide valley, at the far side of which rises the majestic Dents du Midi, a towering white wall of peaks. The foreground is bright green alpage, dotted with chocolate box chalets; the background blues, purples and white of the high mountains.

From the col it is only twenty minutes down the path to the simple hotel at Planachaux.

Day 4

There is a broad track leading from Planachaux below the frontier ridge until it climbs steeply, through clumps of alpenrose, to the Col de Coux (1,925m, 6,315ft). The walk is pretty enough, especially with the Dents du Midi as a background, but one is conscious all the time of the plethora of wires zooming everywhere, like the work of some mad telegraphist. It isn't telegraphy of course, but the insidious téléférique—the cable cars, ski tows and chair lifts that litter our mountains in the name of the Great Ski God. Skiing rules the Alps these days; all other time-honoured activities like mountain walking or climbing— even farming—must bend the knee to the God.

At the Col de Coux the path passes back into France after its brief visit to Switzerland. As you breast the top the prospect is that of a wide valley head—almost like a bowl in the hills—well wooded and extremely pretty. On the left there is an immense range of crags, aptly named Les Terres Maudites, with spectacularly folded strata. The path descends swiftly, plunging into the woods where, unfortunately, it has been bulldozed and is difficult to follow. However, it isn't long before things improve and a lovely little path runs out round the valley head, below the contorted cliffs, to climb to the Col de la Golèse (1,659m, 5,443ft).

This gap in the hills is an important migratory passage for birds and insects. Researchers have discovered that some birds, like coal-tits, only pass through every other year on their way south to sunnier climes, whereas others, like blue-tits, use the col every year. One blue-tit was caught seven years in a row! Researchers are also studying migratory insects like bluebottles and mosquitoes.

It is a pity that, unlike the birds and insects, we can't fly, because the descent from the Col de la Golèse to the town of Samoëns is long and laborious. It just seems to go on and on, first as a steep track, then as a metalled road—a good three hours of steady tramping. The only consolation is the thought that at least you are not doing it in the opposite direction! In the lower stages there is a footpath which avoids the road, but by then most people are too tired to care about such niceties and anyway the road gives access now and then to a delightful river with clear pools. There is even a *bise* of crystal clear water—a mill race which presumably once fed the mills at the hamlet of Moulins, on the edge of Samoëns.

Until Chamonix is reached at the end of the walk, Samoëns is by far the largest habitation. It is a pleasant town and I have happy memories of a *jour de fête* once spent here, when the brass band played in the square and the hoop-la stalls did a roaring trade. At one time it was connected to Annemasse, on the outskirts of Geneva, by a steam tram which took three hours for the 50-km (31-mile) journey and traces of this transport system can still be detected by the observant. Nowadays the journey is made more prosaically by bus, in about half the time.

Day 5

Although, strictly speaking, it is not on the route of the GR5, it would be a shame to travel this way and not visit the Fer-à-Cheval in the valley of Sixt. The rock architecture is amongst the most dramatic in the Alps. Indeed, the whole of day 5 can be an object lesson in landforms.

From Samoëns the road to Sixt is followed for some three quarters of an hour to the bridge at Perret. This point can also be reached by a path through the meadows, or even by bus if you are feeling lazy. Cross the stream of the Giffre and follow a good path to where the river cuts through a gorge of surprising depth. The water roars through the narrows, emphasising that the Giffre is second only to the Arve in Savoyard rivers when it comes to rate of flow. And over the years it has changed course because within a few minutes the path climbs up to the Old Gorge des Tines which used to be the bed of the Giffre. The place has an air of excitement about it: limestone cliffs, soaring up and three rock passages to climb with the aid of fixed ladders.

The path rejoins the valley road at le Fay and from there into Sixt is a walk of about twenty minutes. The village itself is rather a disappointment, though it was a great favourite with the Victorian mountaineers and Genevese society of that period. Alfred Wills, whose ascent of the Wetterhorn in 1854 is sometimes regarded as the birth of alpinism as a sport, built himself a chalet here called 'The

The view from Brévent looking towards the Aiguilles Verte and Drus. (Photo: Walt Unsworth.)

Eagle's Nest' and on the wall of the local school there is a plaque to Jacques Balmat, the first man to climb Mont Blanc in 1786. He disappeared in the mountains above Sixt in 1834—some say as the result of foul play.

The walk up the valley towards the Fer-à-Cheval takes over an hour and is along a narrow motor road, quite busy. It is possible to avoid this by taking a bus to the terminus at Plan du Lac where there is a restaurant set in an area of scrubland by the banks of the Giffre. From here a broad path leads further up the valley to a bridge over the river and a little cafe. There is no point in going further for everything worth seeing can be seen between the Plan du Lac and here.

The head of the valley is hemmed in by wild looking limestone mountains: Mont Ruan, Pic de Tenneverge and Dents Blanches, but the real spectacle is the great cirque of the Fer-à-Cheval which frowns down on the Plan du Lac. Cliffs and pinnacles soar up in wild profusion and waterfalls leap out of holes in the rock. In spring, when the winter snows are melting, there can be as many as thirty waterfalls. In bad weather the cirque has all the appearance of a set from Götterdämmerung as clouds shred themselves amongst the wild pinnacles.

The return along the valley to Sixt can be speeded by bus and the path picked up again at Maison Neuve, though at this point it is actually a road which continues up the valley as far as the Chalets du Lignon. On the way you pass the impressive Cascade de Rouget where the water pours over two rock steps for more than sixty metres (200ft). Once the road ends the path climbs steeply through woods and rough hillside to some more waterfalls, the Cascades de Pleureuse and La Sauffla, where it divides, one branch climbing up the Sales glen to the Pas de Sales and the other climbing steep slopes below the Pt de Sales to the Collet d'Anterne (1,800m, 5,905ft). Our route takes the latter and leaves us wondering at yet another word describing a saddle—collet—which I suppose is meant to indicate a little col, though once again you'd be hard put to tell the difference. There are wonderful views back towards Samoëns and the Col de la Golèse and with luck you might even catch your first glimpse of Mont Blanc.

From the col it is only half an hour through a wild upland valley, dotted with rock outcrops, to the night's shelter at the Refuge Chalet d'Anterne. It has been a long day—nine hours, probably—and the hardest part is at the end, so a bed is welcome. It can be eased considerably by using the bus to visit the Fer-à-Cheval.

Day 6

Next day the way lies across the rolling moorland of the Plateau d'Anterne to the dark, mysterious Lac d'Anterne, lying in its lonely hollow. Sometimes the surface is frozen, even in summer, and there may well be patches of snow lying late in these wild uplands. The lake has no outlet; the water escapes through fissures in the limestone.

The route we have followed up from Sixt is a very old one, but at the turn of the last century it had been virtually abandoned in favour of a new mule track which climbed up the Fonts valley through Les Frassettes and the Chalets des Fonts, where it passed Wills' Eagle's Nest. It reached the Lac d'Anterne by the Bas de Col d'Anterne—an abrupt edge to the moorland of the plateau. This route offers superb views of Le Buet—a mountain which played an important part in the early history of mountain exploration, and is probably still viable. The old route, now restored in popularity, has turned the tables on this upstart.

A gradual ascent leads in a half hour or so to the wooden cross at the Col d'Anterne (2,265m, 7,431ft), where for the first time the full glory of the Mont Blanc range bursts into view. The contrast between the limestone desolation of the foreground and the white beauty of the great peaks is most striking.

Very steeply the path zig-zags down from the col to cross the wild glen at the head of the Diosaz stream, passing the *refuge* in the old Chalets de Moëde. This is indeed a wilderness area, with gaunt limestone cliffs all round and the deepening valley which lower down becomes the splendid Gorges of Diosaz (these are worth a visit from Servoz on a half day). Height is gained gradually to just beyond some ruined chalets when the track forks and the left-hand branch—the one you want—zig-zags steeply up the mountainside into the cleft of the Col de Brévent (2,368m, 7,769ft). The way is rocky but the path is good. There may well be snow patches.

From the col it is a simple matter to follow the ridge to the summit of the Brévent (2,526m, 8,288ft), the highest point and climax of the whole walk. And what can one say about the view across the Chamonix valley towards Mont Blanc and the Aiguilles? It is one of the most famous panoramas in the world and yet it never palls, no matter how many times you see it. Suddenly, the whole plan of this fascinating walk becomes clear, perhaps for the first time: how from the Lake of Geneva the cols have got progressively higher, step by step, revealing first tentative glimpses of the high Alps from the Col des Mattes, the Porte du Lac Vert, the Col d'Anterne, each adding to the previous one and building towards this remarkable climax on the Brévent.

Chamonix lies below; the end of the walk. A cable-car connects the summit of the mountain with the village, but the walk demands a better ending than that. Perhaps the well known path to les Houches used by the Tour du Mont Blanc, which also passes this way, or a descent by way of the Col du Brévent and Planpraz (la Cheminée is a more exciting variant on this which demands a simple pitch of easy rock climbing down a prominent fissure in the ridge). But in fact there are many ways down to the valley and you can choose whichever suits your mood. Nor does it matter much where you come down, for there is an excellent bus service along the valley which will carry you swiftly to Chamonix.

Distance: 60Km (37 miles).
Time Required: 6 days.
Type of Walk: Across the grain of the country over a series of high cols.
Base: Geneva or Montreux.
Start: St. Gingolph on Lake Geneva.
Best Time of Year: July – September.
Maps: IGN 1:50,000 *Thonon-Chatel, Samoëns-Pas de Morgins; Cluses; Chamonix*
Guidebook: *Walking the French Alps:* GR5 by Martin Collins (Cicerone Press).

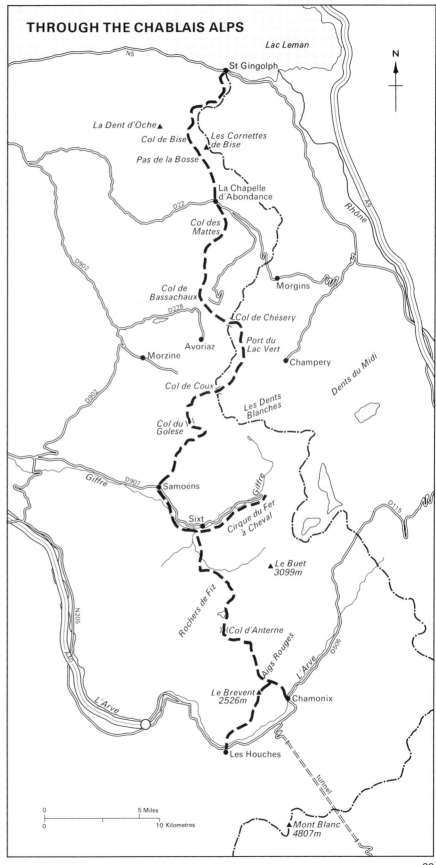

THROUGH THE CHABLAIS ALPS

A bridge over the Ammer Gorge, one of the most exciting parts of the walk. (Photo: Colin Speakman.)

Walk 4 GERMANY: The King Ludwig Way by Fleur and Colin Speakman

Following the path of Wagner's Dream King

A simple wooden cross standing in a lake, close to the lake shore, is a curious place to begin a long distance footpath. But then the King Ludwig Way isn't your ordinary kind of walking route taking its name from a geographic or historic feature, but one which is associated with one of the most colourful and paradoxical of European Kings—Ludwig II of Bavaria, the 'Dream King'.

This 120-km (75-mile) route through southern Bavaria takes in some fine scenery of the Voralpenland, which loosely translated means the Foothills of the Alps. The walk takes you from Lake Starnberg, on the outskirts of Munich, to Ludwig's fairy tale castle and the town of Füssen, on the Austrian border, and the first of the mighty Alpine ranges which rear up dramatically from the soft Bavarian countryside.

It's easy, fairly relaxed kind of walking, with few dizzy heights, no scrambles, mostly along forest tracks and farm roads, yet with some real moments of drama. But what it does offer is an astonishingly rich cultural experience, both through the associations with King Ludwig himself, and equally significantly, through a series of stunningly beautiful Baroque churches to be found on the route.

The route was created in 1977, and has rapidly developed to become one of the most popular long-distance paths in Germany; something which obviously appeals to the sense of culture and history in most Germans. It is excellent for the middle-distance walker: someone for whom 18 to 26 kilometres (12—17 miles) a day on well-waymarked paths is a most attractive option.

Its promotion is undertaken by the Arbeitsgemeinschaft Fernwanderwege im Voralpenland—the Voralpen Long Distance Footpath Union—which is not, as its name might seem to imply, a users' group, but a loose federation of the local tourist offices along the route. They market the walk very effectively indeed, mainly in Germany, and organise an excellent package holiday based on pre-booked bed and breakfast in small hotels and guest houses. Clients' luggage is carried between overnight accommodation, thus saving the need to carry 30lb or so on one's back—the curse of most long-distance walking.

Where does King Ludwig II come into the story? Ludwig, of course, is a kind of folk-hero in Bavaria, their last truly independent monarch. His life ended mysteriously on June 13th, 1886 when his body, and that of his doctor, were found floating in Lake Starnberg. To this day no one knows if it was a case of murder or suicide, and it ended the controversial reign of a king who had ascended the throne in 1864 at the age of 18 as one of the most gifted young monarchs in history, and who died a deeply unhappy, isolated man, accused of insanity and wild extravagances. If he was an incompetent leader, he nevertheless left his mark upon his kingdom, with an astonishing legacy of romantic castles which are now of extraordinary value and benefit to the Bavarian economy as tourists, in their millions, flock to see them.

It isn't entirely inappropriate that a long distance footpath should be named after him, for Ludwig was a complex, contradictory personality who was himself a passionate walker who loved the Bavarian countryside, particularly its forests. He was a king isolated at court yet able to communicate easily with ordinary country people.

His downfall was linked to many complex factors of politics and personality. After a promising, even a brilliant start, it rapidly became clear to him that the realities of European power-politics, dominated by the ruthless 'Iron Chancellor' Bismarck of Prussia, determined to create a united Germany, left little room for an independent Bavaria. It was soon evident to Ludwig that he was powerless to influence events and increasingly he began to retreat away from affairs of state into an inner world dominated by art—in particular the music of Richard Wagner, whom he had championed, rescuing the composer from disgrace and oblivion—and sponsoring performances of such great works as *Tristan and Isolde* and even the completion of *The Ring, The Mastersingers* and *Parsifal*.

Ludwig's generosity to Wagner created scandal and dissent in Munich, but it didn't prevent Ludwig from creating, at Neuschwanstein, an extraordinary embodiment of the Wagnerian chivalric-heroic-romantic ideal in a building which has been described as one of the world's greatest playthings. This can be seen at the end of the walk. As he grew older, Ludwig's eccentricities, including dressing up in 18th-century costume, taking long night rides by sleigh, and putting on private theatrical performances, persuaded many people that he was mentally unstable and unfit to rule. A medical report was prepared to prove his 'madness' and a Commission left for Neuschwanstein to arrest him. Though this first attempt failed—the Commission itself was arrested—Ludwig's own lack of direction and drive resulted in the desertion of his loyal followers, and led to the success of a second Commission and Ludwig's forced abdication in favour of his uncle Luitpold who was to act as Regent.

Ludwig was taken a virtual prisoner, from Neuschwanstein to Castle Berg, his own palace on the Starnberg See where he was to be kept under close confinement but where, soon after his arrival, he was found dead in the lake under circumstances which to this day have never been satisfactorily explained.

So the cross in the Starnberg Lake, at Berg, just five kilometres from the town of Starnberg, is a highly emotional shrine for most Bavarians, and the following route to Neuschwanstein—in the reverse direction of Ludwig's own sad, last journey—ends at what is perhaps his greatest glory, that piece of pure theatre in stone which now attracts millions of visitors to Bavaria.

But what lies between? This is a countryside of forest and farms, of lovely rolling hills, forested gorges and fast moving rivers, an area which is at once very distinctive yet very typical of South Germany.

Forests dominate. It is difficult for Anglo-Saxons to fully appreciate the significance, for Germans, of their forest or *Wald*. About a third of Germany is forest, and forest is something which runs deep in German culture and folk-lore—something mysterious, wild, and very precious. The recent damage done by acid rainfall, caused by power station emissions and vehicle exhaust fumes, is a major

The cross in the Starnberg Lake at Berg is a memorial to King Ludwig who was drowned in mysterious circumstances. (Photo: Colin Speakman.)

political issue, a threat not only to the environment but to the German's sense of national identity. Fortunately, the forests of upper Bavaria are relatively little affected as yet, and you walk through woodlands of indescribable richness and beauty on the King Ludwig Way.

It has been said of Bavaria, with some justification, that it is a land of 'Farmers, Artists and Monks'. The farming will be self evident, mainly dairy farming in large, scattered farms between the forest. The monks and artists arise from the fact that the monasteries were not 'secularised' in Bavaria until 1803, which meant that in the 17th and 18th centuries they were extraordinarily rich and powerful, their abbots and bishops great patrons of the arts. This shows itself along the King Ludwig Way in the magnificent Baroque and Rococo monastic churches, richly decorated by some of the greatest artists of their period, many of them local, such as the great Zimmermann brothers of Wessobrunn. Churches at Andechs, Diessen, Rottenbuch, Steingaden, Wessobrunn itself, and above all Wies are stunning masterpieces of 18th-century Baroque art, places of worthy pilgrimage for walkers on the King Ludwig Way which has been devised to take full advantage of them.

But to the route itself. Pathfinding is no problem. The route is well waymarked with the little blue crowned 'K' waymark, and with rare exception is visible at all points of indecision. It is also clearly shown on most walking maps, including the popular Kompass Wanderkarte which are readily available in Munich or larger towns. An interesting aspect of the Kompass maps is that they also include details of cafes and restaurants, as well as the usual walking and tourist information—useful if your plans for a civilised day's walking include a lunch stop, perhaps with half or even a full litre of the world famous Bavarian beer.

A number of variants exist on the King Ludwig route, in particular an entirely land-based route which avoids the Ammersee ferry. It is easier, however, to concentrate on the most popular 'main' route which takes in all the characteristic features of interest.

The official start of the King Ludwig Way is at Starnberg, a pleasant lakeside resort easily reached by S-Bahn (suburban electric train) which operates from Munich Station as an underground line and then becomes a surface railway, line S6, to Starnberg. Starnberg has a good choice of hotels and guest houses, and the usual facilities of a small resort.

But it is assumed that most King Ludwig Way walkers will want to make the journey out to Berg to visit the Memorial Chapel to Ludwig in the Castle Grounds before starting the first day's walk. The best way of doing this in the summer months is by steamer, one of the lake boats which every hour operate from Starnberg landing stage (near the station) around the lake, first stop Berg. A short walk from the landing stage at Berg leads to the woodland path to the Votivkapelle and the Memorial Cross. You can then follow the lakeside track and path back along the lake shore into Starnberg—all this forms part of the 'official' King Ludwig Way, and it's worth planning your arrival at Starnberg to include it.

Day 1

The first full day on the Way, 21km (13 miles) is from Starnberg to Herrsching on Lake Ammersee, and includes taking the ferry across the lake.

From Starnberg's scattered suburbs the route heads southwestwards into the Maisinger Schlucht, a forested gorge whose mature beech trees offer a foretaste of things to come. Beyond Maisinger the Way winds through a nature reserve, by Lake Maisinger and an area of low lying marshes, all reeds and willows and wildflowers (one of the glories of the King Ludwig Way, particularly in early summer, is the incredible richness of the flora, particularly in the sub-Alpine meadows, relatively unharmed by herbicides). After the hamlet of Aschering the route climbs into pine woods, by the Eßsee, then cuts across meadowland to reach a little peace chapel and a path bordered by shrines symbolising the Stations of the Cross leading down to the village of Andechs. On a hillock—the Holy Hill—immediately above the village is the Monastery of Andechs crowned by its noble Pilgrimage Church, founded in the Middle Ages to house relics brought back by Crusaders from the Holy Land. The Church, magnificently decorated, houses an astonishing collection of richly-decorated Votive candles, many of them dating from the 17th and 18th centuries.

The monastery has another claim to fame in the shape of a world-famous brewery noted for excellent beers which are happily on sale in the adjacent Beer Garden and Beer Room!

From the church the King Ludwig Way plunges into another thickly wooded gorge this time forming the steep Kiental valley, from where a track leads to the resort of Herrsching on Lake Ammersee, and a regular ferry service across the lake to Dießen. There is a good choice of accommodation in both Herrsching and Dießen to make either town an excellent

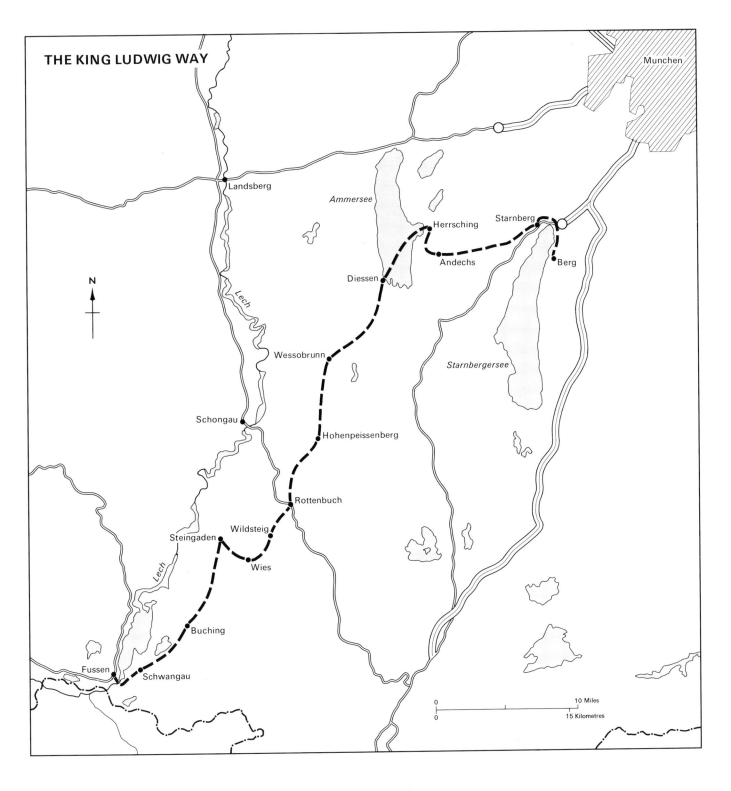

THE KING LUDWIG WAY

concluding point for a first day's ramble on the King Ludwig Way.

Day 2

Day Two begins with another architectural treasure, this time Diessen Monastery Church, its strikingly beautiful entrance facade now much improved by the restoration, in 1986, of

DISTANCE: 120km (75 miles).
MAPS: Kompass Wanderkarte 1:50,000 Sheets 180 (Starnberger—Ammersee); 179 (Pfaffenwinkel-Schongauer Land); 4 (Fussen-Ausserfern).
Start: Starnberg, reached from Munich by S-Bahn.
Time Required: 5 days.
Best Time: May–October. For details of accommodation along the route and the

special 'without luggage' package weeks on the route in May, June, September and October write to Arbeitsgemeinchaft in Fernwanderwege im Voralpenland, Von-Kühlmann-Strasse 15., 8910 Landsberg a. Lech, West Germany.
Guidebook: *King Ludwig Way* by Fleur and Colin Speakman (Cicerone Press).

the original handsome copper cupola on its tower. Originally a Collegiate Church of the Augustinian Canons, it was rebuilt a number of times, lastly under the direction of the great Baroque architect Johann Michael Fisher in the 1730s. It is notable for some magnificent frescoes and highly decorative stucco work: a riot of white and gold, and richly blending colours.

Path-finding from this attractive little town requires care, with quite a few awkward turns before, beyond the suburbs of St. Georgen, the Way turns south into another lovely stretch of forestry nature reserve, by the Mechtilds Spring. It then winds along farm and forestry tracks into the dense pine and fir woodland of the Bayerdiessen State Forest, (where foresters still employ horses to drag timber from the narrow forest glades), before reaching a farm road into Wessobrunn.

The monastery at Wessobrunn has a long and distinguished history. It was founded in the 8th century when one Count Tassilo dreamt of a ladder stretched over three springs of running water. Next day his huntsman discovered the three springs and taking the occurence to be a sign from God, Tassilo established a Benedictine monastery there whose name Wezzo's Brunnen or Wezzo's Springs still survives.

The monastery developed as a great centre of learning, and it was here that the Wessobrunn Prayer was written, inserted into a Latin text, by a 9th-century monk. It is the oldest surviving example of the written German language. A copy of the inscription was made in 1875 and carved on the stone by the tree in the little green opposite the Hotel zum Post.

At certain times (check beforehand) it is possible to visit the abbey, now a convalescent home. It is notable for its fine interior decoration, especially the beautiful Fürstengang—the Gallery of Princes—in a richly decorated rococo style. The Abbey Church was built and decorated in 1758 by the local craftsmen from Wessobrunn who were famous throughout Bavaria.

You leave Wessobrunn along Zimmermann Strasse where the famous painter Johann Baptist Zimmermann (1680-1758) and his brother Dominkus (1685-1766), the great architect, lived. The Way cuts across another small gorge, and now picks up paths and tracks to St Leonhard in the Forest, due south, before going along an extended forest track to Hohenpeißenberg, a remarkable outlier of the Alps, 988m (3,241 ft) high and a notable viewpoint. The path climbs the back of the little peak, the first real climb on the King Ludwig Way to reward the walker with a

superb Alpine panorama, and the great peaks, now intriguingly close, form a splendid backcloth across the horizon. The summit is shared with yet another fine Baroque church and a Meteorological Observatory dating from 1780. It was founded by the Augustinian Canons of Rottenbuch and is the oldest weather station in Bavaria. Continuous weather records have been kept here since 1781.

Hohenpeißenberg village, lying immediately below the hilltop whose name it has taken, is a quiet country town and resort. Astonishingly it was once a coal mining town, but industry has long vanished, and it makes an excellent place for rest, food and accommodation, the natural termination of the second day's 26-km (16-mile) stage.

Day 3

The third day (23km, 14 miles) contains one of the walk's highlights, the dramatic Ammerschlucht. It also contains one of the most beautiful stretches of forest on the whole route, soon reached after a three kilometre walk along quiet farm roads. The Way plunges into deep forest, a route which wanders through mature beech and pine trees, the ancient German forest of legend, with dark brown squirrels that leap between branches. In a little clearing at Schnaltz there is a hunting lodge and drinking fountain and a welcoming bench, before the way turns westwards to join a track leading to the Ammer Gorge.

The River Ammer here is a true Alpine river, its swift movement and greenish tinge familiar to anyone who knows the Alps. As it forces its way through the accumulated rocks and debris that form the gorge, it is gradually eroding a deep ravine.

You pass the picturesque wooden-roofed lime-works bridge—avoid the temptation to cross—before ascending the steep steps that form the start of the most tricky section of the King Ludwig Way. This is a magnificent stretch of path, much of it artificially created, along the side of the Ammerschlucht. There are places where care will be needed, particularly in wet weather, when some of the timber bridges and walkways can be a little slippy. There are no handrails, and the less agile in particular may need a helping hand. In extreme conditions the lower section can flood, and if that happens then it may be necessary to retreat, along the path signed to the Schnaidalm, to the main road above.

But by any standards this is a beautiful stretch of path, as it contours around the gorge, the rushing river below, through beech, ash and alder woods, rich in wildflowers at almost any season, offering the occasional glimpse, if you're lucky, of wild deer.

The path emerges from the Gorge to join a farm track ascending to give some fine views before the Way turns off back along the side of the gorge to Rottenbuch.

Rottenbuch—its name meaning 'clearance in the beeches'—has had a monastery here since the 10th century, and later an establishment of Black Monks or Augustinian Canons. The Collegiate Church is yet another showpiece of 18th-century architecture with breathtakingly rich and elaborate rococo decor, including work by another of the great Wessobrunn masters, Joseph Schmutzer.

You leave the village along the B23 Garnish road from the cross roads, but soon take a side road which follows a low ridge and offers once again impressive views of the great Alpine ridges of the Lechtaler and Ammergauer Alps to the east and south, before reaching the Steingaden road. A meadowside path, which eventually dips under an underpass, leads into the little farming village of Wildsteig, which is a scatter of cottages and small houses, including a Gasthof, built round that inevitable little Baroque church. There is a surpringly good range of accommodation in Wildsteig which makes it a good place to halt overnight.

Day 4

Day Four offers a difficult choice. The direct 'main line' route to Buching or Berghof is a pleasant 18km (11 miles) of easy walking, with one or two notable highlights. The Steingaden alternative with a number of dramatic features, including the Lech Valley, is 7km (4 miles) longer. Both are good walks.

Both take the same route from Wildsteig along the lane to Unterbauern, with its intriguing Baroque chapel, before leaving what is still marked on the maps as the King Ludwig Way, to cross low meadows and marshland rich in orchids and other wild flowers to the Schwarzenbach forest. A track emerges at the local District college, from where a field path crosses to Wies Church. The Wies, as it sometimes is known, is a church of great beauty, an acknowledged masterpiece of Baroque architecture and one of the finest examples in Southern Germany.

How it came to be there is a remarkable and moving story. In the later Middle Ages two monks from Steingaden made a figure of the Scourged Christ from a number of older wooden figures, wrapped it in linen and painted realistic wounds and bloodstains onto it. The result was so effective that when it was carried in the village's Good Friday Procession, it upset people and so it was put away and

forgotten for generations. Many years later it was found by a pious local farmer's wife and taken to her house in *die Wies*—'the meadow'. In 1738 the statue was discovered to be weeping and pilgrims came from many lands to witness the miracle. It is this same figure,

Set in the Bavarian foothills, Neuschwanstein seems like a fairy-tale castle. (Photo: Walt Unsworth.)

Hohenschwangau, built by Ludwig's father contains the Hall of the Swan Knights. The swan was the symbol of the Wittelsbach family, rulers of Bavaria. Hence Ludwig's natural affinity to *Parsifal* and *Lohengrin*. (Photo: Colin Speakman.)

Facing page:

Top left: **The view over the Bavarian Lakes and hills from the windows of Hohenschwangau is justly renowned.** (Photo: Walt Unsworth.)

Top right: **The castle gate at Hohenschwangau.** (Photo: Walt Unsworth.)

manacled to a pillar and bearing the marks of scourging, that now forms the centre piece of the altar of Wies Church.

The church was designed by Dominkus Zimmermann and decorated by his brother Johann Baptist, with superb sculptures by Agidus Verhelst the elder, and is remarkable for its elegance and lightness, and the sheer virtuosity of its design and execution, a highpoint of the German Baroque tradition.

The direct path from Wies follows the farm road southwards by forest, to the Upper Landegger Lake and the hamlet of Resle. It then turns westwards to Schober, and crosses the little river Ach. It is possible to take in a superb little nature reserve around the Buchsee by Hainzenbichl, site of a Celtic settlement, before rejoining farm roads north of Trauchgau. Just beyond the Stockingen Paint Factory a path leads to the riverside and by turning right, upstream, you can reach the Rossweg Bridge and a delightful fieldpath, No 118 (not shown on the map). This cuts directly across the field to Berghof and the little Chapel of St Peter and offers a quite breathtaking viewpoint of the ever more dramatic Alpine peaks, now tantalisingly close and, at most times of the year, with high snowfields that glisten in the afternoon light.

Both Berghof and Bayer-niederhofen have plenty of guesthouse accommodation making either a good choice for the penultimate day on the King Ludwig Way.

For those wishing to take the Steingaden loop, this begins at Wies at a boardwalk footpath by the Gasthof Mosen. It passes over a stretch of heathland, with magnificent views back over to Wies church, before turning northwards through forest by Haarseck to Steingaden, an attractive town whose church has been described as an 'illustrated textbook' of Bavarian church architecture from Romanesque to the Baroque. The Way then leaves the tourist office on the Urspring Road, soon crossing to the hamlet of Steingadele, bearing southwestwards, and over another area of heath across to the village of Prem. It then goes along the banks of the Lech Premer lake before taking tracks and fieldpaths by Küchele, Zwingen and Hans to rejoin the main line of path from Trauchgau to Berghof near Achmühle.

Day 5

The last day of the King Ludwig Way is an easy 18km (11 miles), but if you want to visit the two castles of Neuschwanstein and Hohenschwangau, it is worth getting the main part of the walk completed before lunch to have the afternoon free for sightseeing.

From Berghof the path follows the back road via Bayer-niederhofen to join the main road to Pfefferbichl, before taking the quiet lane southwards through the village of Greith and past the little Hergratsried Lake. Here, easy, pleasant walking on tarmac which you share with cyclists (no other traffic allowed) gives you views of the fairy-tale turrets of Neuschwanstein Castle set against the forest. The lane passes the edge of Lake Forgensee towards Brunne, before the King Ludwig Way leaves it along the embankment of a mill stream, the Mühlberger beck. You follow this through to the busy main road but, ignoring the map which is incorrect here, cross over to the far side of the bridge along what is now known as the Lußbach, along the left side of the stream. Keep ahead by willow trees, ignoring crossing tracks to reach the old Plaster Works (now a saw mill) directly behind which the path climbs up the Pöllat Gorge, a tremendous chasm which climbs literally underneath the battlements of Neuschwanstein Castle. You climb past the mill races onto a path with steps and handrails, soon seeing the 90-m (300-ft) high Marie Bridge which cuts across the top of the gorge to and from the castle. Follow the path and steps which eventually climb a narrow ravine to join the main track leading to the entrance into Neuschwanstein.

Before going into Neuschwanstein itself, it's worth taking the path to the left which leads to the Marie Bridge to enjoy the quite sensational views down the gorge and across to the castle.

But be warned. There, and at the castle, you are suddenly in mainstream tourist Bavaria. Unless you come outside the main season, expect queues, guides that give a set speech to you in unrecognisable English, and a quick shuffle around those richly decorated rooms, with their astonishing mixture of styles.

But it's worth it. The castle is a *tour de force* of both architecture and engineering, perilously perched as it is on its high rock. It is a mixture of medievalism and sheer fantasy; a folly on a gargantuan scale. It's like a gigantic theatrical set. You'll see the great throne room, Ludwig's desperate fantasy of his kingly power already quite out of date in the age of the steam train and mass production. You'll be taken into the Minstrels' Hall, based on Castle Wartburg, the setting for *Tannhäuser*, but decorated with scenes from *Parsifal*. You'll see the ornate bedroom furniture that took 14 woodcarvers four years to complete. Little wonder that the castle was incomplete at Ludwig's death. A man called Julius Hoffmann was brought in in 1886 to complete what has since become a top tourist attraction.

Interestingly enough, in the kitchen, is a modern heat-saving central heating system devised by Ludwig himself (who took close interest in all details of the castle) proving that if it was madness, then there was method in it.

The well-peopled drive down from Neuchswanstein to Hohenschwangau will take about 15 minutes—horse drawn charabancs are available for the footsore. A path from the

Above: **Designed by the Zimmermann brothers, Wies Church is a highpoint of German Baroque.** (Photo: Colin Speakman.)

garden of the restaurant by the crossroads leads up steps to the entrance of the ochre yellow castle of Hohenschwangau.

This castle was built by Ludwig's father Maximilian, and is, in many ways, on a much more human scale, more of a royal home, than Neuschwanstein. The Hall of the Swan Knights recalls the family symbol of the Wittlesbachs—Ludwig's royal line—and of course the Lohengrin legend which pre-dated Wagner's opera, which helps to explain the obsessive interest of Ludwig with the world of Wagnerian heroes and opera. The knightly theme is taken up by the King's study with its scenes from the life of a medieval knight, whilst the Queen's boudoir is decorated with illustrations of the life of medieval court ladies. You'll see the piano where Wagner performed themes from the operas for his patron.

But perhaps the most glorious aspect of Hohenschwangau is the views from the windows across the spectacular Alpine scenery, including the Alp See and the Schwan See, and, of course, back to the magical Neuschwanstein itself.

The official last part of the King Ludwig Way could hardly be more of an anticlimax along the busy main road to Füssen. Infinitely better is the Alpenrosenweg, a footpath which actually begins from the top of the drive to Hohenschwangau, and, clearly waymarked, soon climbs a rocky, wooded knoll above the Schwansee, before following a beautiful terraced path through the woods above the lakeside. Keep ahead along the path, taking care to avoid stonefall from the steep crags above, for a couple of kilometres before, almost at the Austrian border, taking a path which turns right, signed for Füssen. Keep ahead on this path, now, avoiding crossing paths, over a shallow valley, joining a track which eventually joins the main road into Füssen just above Lech Falls. Walk ahead now to cross the bridge into this lovely old walled border town.

Füssen is an excellent place to complete a long distance footpath. There's a good choice of inns and guesthouses, shops, cafes and restaurants. It's a town with character, one worth lingering in. There's also a railway station, albeit on a branch line which connects with the main line to Augsburg and Munich.

So that is it—not the longest, nor the grandest of European long distance paths, but one of great character and interest, offering a rewarding experience of some of Bavaria's finest countryside and a rich cultural inheritance together with a glimpse, however fleeting, into the personality of an extraordinary monarch.

Walk 5 ITALY: Alta Via 1 by Martin Collins

The Classic Traverse of the Dolomite Mountains

As long ago as 1789, the extraordinary qualities of rock and mountain scenery near northern Italy's border with the Austrian Tyrol were being written about enthusiastically by a certain French geologist—the Marquis de Dolomieu—following a visit there : the Dolomites were to take their name from this early traveller. They have since witnessed many key stages in the development of European rock climbing, from steep wall ascents, already in full swing before World War I, to the evolution of 'artificial' climbing techniques, subsequently applied to the great faces and buttresses of the Western Alps during the 1920s and 30s.

The Dolomites have inspired and tested each new generation of climbers. Today they are a

Typical Dolomite scenery: the spires of Monte Tamer. (Photo: Martin Collins.)

43

The start of the Alta Via 1 at the Lago di Braies, a turquoise lake cradled in the mountains. (Photo: Martin Collins.)

premier location for rock climbing of all grades, with limestone peaks soaring to well over 3,000m (10,000ft) as well as being an excellent venue for winter skiing.

This sensational, landscape of rock spires, beetling cliffs, mountain lakes and plunging, forested valleys, far from being the exclusive domain of climbers and 'hard men', offers unparalleled scope for mountain walkers too. An intricate web of paths covers not only the inhabited valleys and lower slopes, but reaches into the highest massifs. Undaunted even by steep rock, the trails turn into *vie ferrate*— exposed routes aided by metal cables, rungs and ladders, enabling those with a good head for heights to make airy ascents and traverses.

A welcome feature of mountain travel in the Dolomites is the frequency with which huts are encountered; except in a few more remote areas, they are seldom more than an hour or two's walking apart. With towns and villages lying well off route, walkers on the 'Alta Via' can purchase food and drink at the huts and use them for overnight accommodation as an alternative to backpacking.

Seven long-distance high routes—'Alte Vie'—have been established in the Dolomites region, linking together stretches of footpath, ancient mule-tracks and old military roads. They were conceived with the experienced mountain walker in mind and thread their sinuous courses through dramatic and consistently high terrain. Underfoot conditions are unequivocally rough and stony, the trails a mixture of dusty tracks, steep traverses on scree and snow, ascents in pine forest and occasional scrambling, clipped onto anchored metal cable or rungs using a simple protection kit of sling and karabiners.

Alta Via 1, the first to be set up, is still considered the finest and a classic of its kind. Although precise distances are hard to determine across such contorted country, Alta Via 1 is about 120km (75 miles) in length, running on a north-to-south axis from the southern Tyrol, through some of the most exhilarating Dolomite scenery to Belluno, near the edge of the Venetian plain.

Stage 1: 2 to 3 days

The great north face of Croda del Becco dominates Lago di Braies, a turquoise lake cradled in a deep, forested bowl of mountains at the head of Valle di Braies. Delectably picturesque and much visited by Italian families, it has thus far managed to resist excessive tourist exploitation. With its pervasive scent of pines, its little shingle beaches and the unsullied reflections of surrounding peaks, it exudes an essence of the wild mountain environment we all find so alluring.

Alta Via 1 heads for a wooded ravine above the lake's south shore, zig-zags mounting first in thin forest, then out across screes. A rim of elegant, snow-capped peaks—the distant Tyrol—unfolds along the horizon as height is gained and the trail threads up beneath striated cliffs and ascends a rocky valley to the first col (usually *forcella* in Italian).

Porta Sora 'l Forn, almost 900m (3,000ft) above the start, is a sudden and magnificent panoramic viewpoint; it introduces the walker to mountains that will become familiar profiles on the journey south—the glaciated Marmolada, highest Dolomite peak and the climax of a parallel route, Alta Via 2; the imposing wedge of Monte Pelmo; and Monte Cristallo's buttressed pyramid to the south-east.

Rifugio Biella, the first of many huts encountered along the way, lies below the col on a jeep track. This one-time military road is followed round the flowery Alpe di Sennes and down to Rifugio Sennes, less than an hour away. Alta Via 1 continues to make use of the rough road over Pian di Lasta (*pian* means stretch of level ground), winding steeply down to Rifugio Pederü, which is connected to Val Badia by a motorable road.

A 4-wheel-drive shuttle will carry passengers who are prepared to pay for the privilege up the dusty and tortuous Vallone di Rudo. With good motor access, this is prime day-trip

Walkers near the Rifugio Biella.
(Photo: Martin Collins.)

country and long-distance walkers will be forgiven a twinge of resentment at being covered in dust by the occasional passing jeep en route for the Fanes and Varella huts! Not far beyond them, the waters of Lago di Limo attract many visitors on a fine summer's day, but wilder country, already encroaching on all sides, beckons ever more insistently for travellers on Alta Via 1.

A mule-track is joined at a mountain farmstead (*malga*) and a junction is soon reached with one of several official route variants. This one climbs Vallon Bianco to the ridge between Monte Castello and Monte Cavallo, a ridge heavily fortified during World War 1 and still bearing the remnants of timbered trenches, tunnels and artificial ledges clinging to the shattered rock. But the ascent is arduous and the subsequent drop into Val Travenanzes dangerously steep, making the traverse potentially quite hazardous.

Most walkers stay with the main route across the rough eastern flanks of Val di Fanes, climbing screes to the conspicuous notch of

45

Facing page, top: **The first climb on the Alta Via 1.**

Facing page, bottom: **Marmolada, the highest peak in the Dolomites,** seen from the Rifugio Lagazuoi. (Photos: Martin Collins.)

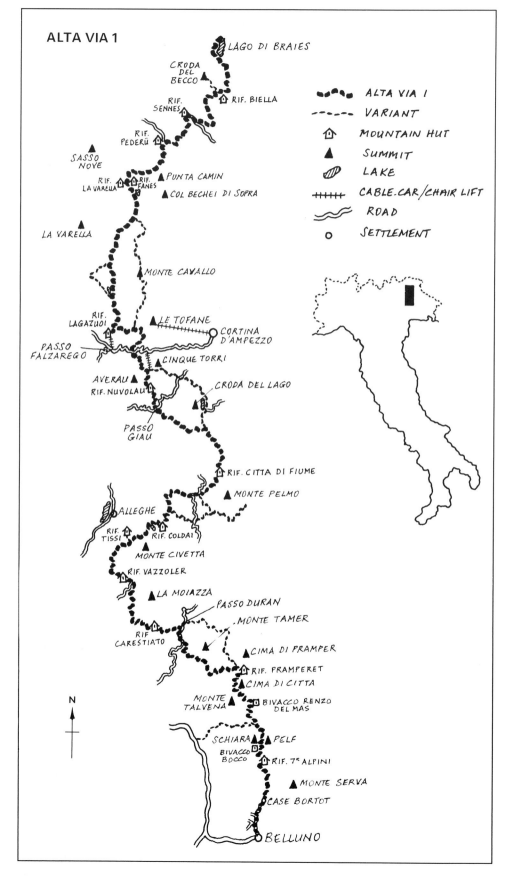

ALTA VIA 1

LAGO DI BRAIES

CRODA DEL BECCO ▲

RIF. BIELLA ⌂

RIF. SENNES

RIF. PEDERÜ

SASSO NOVE ▲

RIF. LA VARELLA ⌂ ⌂ RIF. FANES

PUNTA CAMIN ▲

COL BECHEI DI SOPRA ▲

LA VARELLA ▲

MONTE CAVALLO ▲

RIF. LAGAZUOI ⌂

LE TOFANE ▲

CORTINA D'AMPEZZO ○

PASSO FALZAREGO

CINQUE TORRI

AVERAU ▲
RIF. NUVOLAU ⌂

CRODA DEL LAGO ▲

PASSO GIAU

RIF. CITTA DI FIUME ⌂

MONTE PELMO ▲

ALLEGHE

RIF. TISSI ⌂   ⌂ RIF. COLDAI

MONTE CIVETTA ▲

RIF. VAZZOLER ⌂

LA MOIAZZA ▲

PASSO DURAN
.MONTE TAMER

RIF CARESTIATO ⌂

CIMA DI PRAMPER ▲

RIF. PRAMPERET ⌂

CIMA DI CITTA ▲

MONTE TALVENA ▲

BIVACCO RENZO DEL MAS

SCHIARA ▲ ▲ PELF
BIVACCO BOCCO ⌂ RIF. 7ª ALPINI

MONTE SERVA ▲

CASE BORTOT

BELLUNO ○

N

Legend:
ALTA VIA 1
VARIANT
⌂ MOUNTAIN HUT
▲ SUMMIT
LAKE
CABLE.CAR/CHAIR LIFT
ROAD
○ SETTLEMENT

Distance: 120km (75 miles).
Time Required: A week to 10 days
Type of walk: Good paths through rugged, high-mountain terrain. Previous mountain walking experience and good level of fitness required.
Base: Val Pusteria, Bolzano Province, north-east Italy.
Start: Lago di Braies.
Best Time of Year: July to September.
Maps: Geografica 'Carta Turistica' series, 1:25,000, nos. 1 and 3.
Guidebooks: *Alta Via: High Level Walks in the Dolomites,* by Martin Collins (Cicerone Press).

Forcella del Lago. The straightforwardness of the route so far, much of it on broad tracks, can lead to the misapprehension that the trail is consistently easy. A descent from Forcella del Lago will rapidly dispel this illusion! Loose scree and rock fall away into space at an alarming angle and the need for steady nerves and secure footwork is never greater. (For walkers deterred from attempting a traverse of this *forcella*, a less steep detour over Forcella Col Locia joins with the main route at another impressive mountain lake—Lago di Lagazuoi.)

Shaly slopes used for winter skiing provide an uninspiring trudge up to Rifugio Monte Lagazuoi, but the effort is richly rewarded. At 2,752m (9,029ft) this is the highest point reached so far, and in good visibility views from the timber balcony are simply stunning. Meals and drinks are served here, but for those who need other provisions and services, or who have time to spare and the inclination to return briefly to civilisation, a cable-car descends to a main road at Passo Falzarego, whence the fleshpots of Cortina d'Ampezzo may be reached by bus.

Stage 1 has seen a transition from well-frequented mountain roads and abundant huts to more challenging terrain. Now fully initiated into the kind of rugged travel demanded by Alta Via 1, walkers can look forward to a fascinating and varied second stage, linking several massifs of great interest.

Stage 2: 3 to 4 days

Until World War 1, the Tyrol belonged to the Austro-Hungarian Empire, becoming annexed to Italy under the Treaty of Versailles. It is still predominantly German-speaking, a land of apple strudel and cooked sausage, of feathered hats and lederhosen, where the Austrian way of life co-exists uneasily with the Italian.

From the Lagazuoi hut, Alta Via 1 skirts the Tofane massif, scene of bloody combat between Austrian and Italian alpine troops during World War 1. Although the relics of war are still clearly visible—scattered timbers, trenches, ruined buildings, barbed wire, even discarded shell cases and boot soles—sites of really significant interest are invisible to the unknowing passer-by. The crest of Piccolo Lagazuoi, beneath the hut, contains a maze of subterranean wartime passages and munitions galleries, open to public exploration by torchlight and leading right down to Passo Falzarego.

The Castelletto, a spur of the main Tofane massif, was similarly used by Austrian troops to dominate Italian positions below and was

Monte Pelmo peeps over the intervening ridges. A view from the Nuvolal. (Photo: Martin Collins.)

the object of fierce direct attacks, culminating in a massive explosion on July 11th 1916, when 35 tons of high explosive blew up the entire summit. Now repaired for visits, the Castelletto galleries rise inside the cliff face, past sleeping quarters, ammunition stores, gun chambers and latrines.

An exposed *via ferrata* leaves from the Castelletto summit to another wartime position on Tre Dita, while others climb across the precipitous rock walls of the Tofane group. These technical routes are for experienced and equipped mountain scramblers and climbers only, some routes being snow-bound until the beginning of August.

There are 'normal' ascent routes to the three Tofane summits, though most require climbing experience and often necessitate carrying ice-axe and crampons. However, a cable-car connects Cortina with the highest top—Tofane di Mezzo, 3,245m (10,646ft)—and there are numerous lower-level paths providing walkers with access to the Dibona and Guissani huts, should a more comprehensive exploration of this area be planned.

When contemplating *via ferrata* climbs, not all of which are seriously exposed and may well be within the capabilities of walkers on Alta Via 1, a watchful weather eye is essential. The last place to become stranded in an electrical storm is attached to *via ferrata* ironmongery high on a mountain! Not only are ridges, peaks and fissures dangerous places in themselves, but metal cables and ladder systems can conduct the electrical charge from lightning strike to less vulnerable spots. Weather in the Dolomites is generally drier and sunnier than in the Alps farther west and north, but unstable episodes do occur from time to time. Weather forecasts are obtainable from most huts and from daily newspapers.

On a grassy alp beyond the Cortina-Passo Falzarego road, lies the main route and an equally worthy variant diverge. The variant passes beneath Cinque Torri, clearly visible to the east. This cluster of five rock towers, the remains of an ancient turreted mountain, is a favourite playground of climbers, with routes of all grades on its flanks and a hut of the same name near at hand. Mule-tracks are followed in and out of forest and round the northern spur of Croda del Lago to Rifugio Palmieri on the shores of Lago di Fedèra. Croda del Lago is a classic Dolomite mountain, tiered with steep cliffs and surmounted by several steeple-like spires *(campaniles*, after which they are named). Rising to Forcella Ambrizzola, the variant rejoins the main route.

Alta Via 1 tackles the ascent over bare rock slopes to Rifugio Nuvolau. Just to the west stands the Averau peak, with a short *via ferrata* of about an hour's duration to the summit; a path passing Rifugio Averau at its base takes an easier line than the main route ahead to Passo Giau. In less than an hour, the Nuvolau hut is reached. This is a hugely popular excursion for day-walkers, for not only is the hut a welcoming one, but its elevated and open situation on the little summit ridge of the Nuvolao at 2,575m (8,448ft) endows it with views of unsurpassed range—in fact, some of the best to be found anywhere in the Dolomites. Behind to the north stand the Tofane, Lagazuoi and the now

diminutive Cinque Torri; to the south, rock towers and ridges lead the eye to the distinctive bulk of Monte Pelmo, while to east and west, valleys and peaks extend to the limits of vision.

An abrupt, scrambly descent, aided by metal cable, leads to shallower gradients before a long, scree-filled gully and some short rocky passages are negotiated. Grassy meadows below give temporary relief to feet assailed by hours of trudging over stones and scree.

The Dolomites region is renowned for its flora and fauna, and valley sides are often clothed in luxuriant vegetation at lower levels. Alte Vie, however, are 'high routes' in every sense, dedicated to losing as little height as possible and shunning those softer areas by remaining at around 2,000–2,500m (6,500–8,200ft). The inevitable result is some limitation in the scope of wildlife likely to be encountered; high-mountain species such as marmot and chamois, along with alpine flowers, are most in evidence.

A grassy carpet of pasture stretches to the Passo Giau road and hut, whereafter the path winds attractively round gentle hillsides—in some contrast to the terrain just crossed. There are marvellous retrospective views to the Nuvolau hut, Ra Gusela and the Averau, as well as continuing glimpses of the Tofane, Marmolada and Sella massifs.

It takes walkers a little over two hours to cross Forcella Giau, skirt Monte Formin's stern southern cliffs and climb to Forcella Ambrizzola. A succession of scree, boulders and pasture beneath shapely Becco di Mezzodi and La Rochetta leads on over Forcella Col Duro, Forcella Roan and Forcella della Puina, gradually losing altitude to reach Rifugio Citta di Fiume.

Between pine trees, Monte Pelmo's north face—a great wall of scree and rock soaring over 1,000m (3,000ft) to its 3,168m (10,394ft) summit—seems to possess a magnetic fascination for long-distance walkers on Alta Via 1. First seen from Porta Sora 'l Forn near the start, its square-cut silhouette has drawn the eye repeatedly from many a viewpoint and now, at last, its imposing presence is felt at close range.

The base of Monte Pelmo may be circumvented on a variant path to the Venezia-de-Luca hut, revealing the mountain's huge southern recess known as the 'Caregón' (armchair)—a feature which identifies it from a great distance. Although valley-dwelling huntsmen are thought to have reached the summit as far back as 800BC, the first recorded ascent in recent times was made in 1857 by John Ball, first president of the Alpine Club and a notable British pioneer of that era.

The normal ascent route is not especially difficult, but does demand some mountaineering experience and is reckoned to be a long, tiring climb.

John Ball only narrowly failed to make a first ascent of the Marmolada, reaching the lower summit—Punta Rocca, 3,309m (10,856ft)—in 1860. Four years later, Punta Penia, at 3,340m (10,958ft) the loftiest Dolomite summit, was claimed by Paul Grohmann of Austria, supported by Italian guides.

Leaving the Citta di Fiume hut, Alta Via 1 drops through forest and crosses a torrent bed, directly beneath Pelmo's glacier far above. From Forcella Staulanza, several kilometres of walking on rough, dusty roads are unavoidable, despite two official alternatives linking Pelmo with Monte Civetta, the next objective. In hot weather, progress is less pleasant than on mountain paths, since passing vehicles are both a hazard and an irritation.

Dairy produce and bread are sold at Casere di Pioda, and there is generous, though rough, car parking here at 1,816m (5,958ft). Herds of cows and goats roam the encircling pastureland, melodious bells and pungent odours marking their territory even in thick mist.

The trail takes to a well graded mule-track up the rugged shoulder of Monte Coldai, an outlier of Monte Civetta. The route is very well patronised, forming a day-walk of manageable length to Rifugio and Lago Coldai. On summer weekends, the path is strung out with walkers of all shapes and sizes, some clearly enjoying the climb, others with resolve and suffering etched onto sweaty faces! Whole families often attempt the ascent, apparently regardless of physical condition, and it is with nothing short of admiration that one sees elderly or overweight individuals willing to have a go!

One disappointing 'false top' follows another until, quite suddenly, the path emerges at the large Rifugio Coldai. This forms a good base for an ascent of the Civetta (3,220m, 10,564ft), the 'Tivan' path from the hut connecting with the normal ascent route (via normale) and with the 'Via Ferrata Alleghesi'.

The Civetta is a magnificent mountain, first climbed in 1867 by an Englishman called Tuckett. Twenty-eight years were to elapse before the great north wall was scaled by two more English climbers—Raynor and Phillmore—who managed to solve the technical problems involved, at a time when steep wall climbing was still in its infancy. Since then, numerous routes have been opened up, earning the mountain considerable popularity. An ascent is, however, for experienced climbers only, since there are long and exposed sections

leading to a serious high-mountain environment.

Not far beyond the hut, the emerald Lago Coldai slips into view over a lip of land. Like other lakes before it on Alta Via 1, its appeal lies not only in its fine setting, but in the counterpoint it creates between rock and water—hard and soft, warm and cool. Wild camping pitches abound in the vicinity, and there are little stony beaches and grassy banks on which to sit and absorb the scenery. Opposite, Torre Coldai and Torre di Alleghe, (northern spurs of the Civetta massif) send down buttresses and towers, while away to the north, across the deep trench of the Alleghe valley, the distant Tofane's cable-car top station is just discernible.

Alta Via 1 crosses Forcella Col Negro before starting to lose height and entering the upper reaches of Val Civetta. The west face of Monte Civetta is an awesome sight—7km (4 miles) of overhanging slabs, pinnacles and peaks towering 1,200m (4,000ft) above the trail : it has been likened to a row of gargantuan organ pipes and dubbed the 'Wall of Walls', unique in the Alps.

Rifugio Tissi is 20 minutes off route, close to the summit of Cima di Col Rèan (2,281m, 7,483ft). Its situation facing the Civetta's west face provides overnighters with unforgettable views, especially at sunrise and sunset during settled weather, when the pale Dolomite rock walls are touched by a low sun and for a while burn with the colours of fire.

During late spring and early summer, Val Civetta is a botanist's paradise, for although still too high for bushes and trees, wild flowers grow in profusion. As Alta Via 1 rises and dips between alp and high, stony places, observant walkers will spot such species as Purple Saxifrage, Spotted Gentian, Pink Cinquefoil, Devil's Claw, Rhaetian Poppy, Dwarf Alpenrose and even Edelweiss, though the latter is becoming ever harder to find throughout most of mountain Europe. On apparently barren slopes above 2,500m (8,000ft) brightly coloured alpines like the Spring Gentian, Alpine Pansy and Rock Jasmine thrive in sheltered little corners and crevices.

The blunt, square-topped tower of Torre Venezia oversees the trail round the head of Valle di Foram, before a short descent in pine forest leads to the large Vazzoler hut; beyond, other peaks—Torre Trieste and Cima della Busazza to name but two—form an exciting backdrop of rock scenery to accompany the route over Forcella di Col Palanzin and the steep little Forcella Col dell'Orso.

The Moiazza massif throws down a spur south to Monte Framont, crossed at Forcella

del Camp. Beneath the Moiazza's imposing south face, the trail passes a junction with the Gianni Costantini *via ferrata*, which takes an audacious line up a deep 'V' in cliffs to an unmanned bivouac hut at 2,601m (8,533ft) thereafter traversing the Moiazza's summit ridge and descending to Rifugio Carestiato.

Walkers on Alta Via 1 use this hut too, arriving at it along a somewhat more pedestrian route through forest!

Fine views, especially down to the town of Agordo and east towards the Tamer/San Sebastiano group on Stage 3, are gained from the Carestiato hut. Within 30 minutes, a broad

The Lago Coldai is a popular tourist goal on summer weekends. The big peak in the background is the Tofane. (Photo: Martin Collins.)

Above: **Rifugio Coldai rests beneath the gaunt rock walls of Civetta.**

Facing page, top: **In the Dolomites distant peaks sometimes appear like castles floating on clouds. The Pale di San Martino seen from the Col Dagarei.**

Facing page, bottom: **Belluno, the end of the walk. In the background is the Schiara (left) and Pelf (right).**
(Photos: Martin Collins.)

track down through more forest and out across pasture brings walkers to the road at Passo Duran and the end of Stage 2.

Many huts in the Dolomites are run by Club Alpino Italiano, but some, like this one at Passo Duran, are a cross between an inn and *refuge* and are privately owned. Lightweight camping is tolerated in the vicinity of most huts—though, it should be said, not all! Continental long-distance walkers make good use of the hut system, on the whole tending to view the bulkier rucsacs of backpackers with a mixture of incredulity and mild amusement, but on the final stage of Alta Via 1, the tables are sometimes turned . . .

Stage 3: 3 to 4 days

The loneliest and most committing stretch of

Alta Via 1 begins at Passo Duran. Unlike numerous other sections which are simultaneously popular with day-walkers, even in places with casual trippers, this final stage is relatively unfrequented as far as Monte Schiara. The trail itself is no more problematic than elsewhere, except over the Schiara, but it is often far from roads and there are fewer huts at which to break the journey. The traverse of Monte Schiara involves an exhilarating *via ferrata* descent of the south face, though this can be by-passed if desired by an official variant.

Walkers are advised to take stock before setting out on this leg—is the weather outlook reasonable? Are adequate food and emergency rations being carried? If the weather breaks, protective clothing will be needed and basic bivouac gear is desirable. The autonomous backpacker is at a distinct advantage!

Starting with a short road walk from the pass, Alta Via 1 crosses a crystal-clear torrent and climbs through pine forest to Forcella Dagarei. Across 30km (20 miles) of intervening lower ground, the Pale di San Martino on Alta Via 2 appears to the west in clear visibility— apparently a ridge of peaks, but in fact a broad, upland plateau, seen edge-on.

The narrow path continues over boulder fields, scree and meltwater ravines, maintaining height at 1,600–1,700m (5,200–5,600ft). Torrent beds are often dry in summer and fresh water is not easy to find in the high Dolomites, but chaotic piles of rock debris bear witness to the enormous volume of water released during the melting of winter snow and ice.

Two hours are spent on these rugged, undulating flanks of the Monte Tamer massif, the trail twisting and turning in and out of trees which provide welcome shade from the dazzle of sun on white limestone. Malga Moschesin, a group of deserted barns surrounded by derelict enclosures, would give shelter of a rudimentary kind; thereafter, a soundly constructed mule-track zig-zags up to a corner and an unexpectedly fine view of Monte Talvena and Cima di Citta beyond the depths of Val Clusa. Both peaks are soon to be encountered at close quarters.

Ruined wartime barracks are passed, and a shallow stream bed followed up to Forcella Moschesin; not especially high at 1,940m (6,365ft), and on easy ground, this is a marvellous spot. Behind rise the tiered, convoluted cliffs and pinnacles of Cima Moschesin, while to the north, Antelao (3,263m, (10,705ft) floats in the far distance above Val Pramper. Following the 'Sentiero Balanzòle', Alta Via 1 drops through thin forest to a track crossroads and Rifugio Pramperet, a blend of old and new building—as huts go, quite remote.

A major official alternative routing from Passo Duran to the Pramperet hut, known as the 'Zoldano Variant', circles the Monte Tamer/San Sebastiano group on its other, north-eastern, side. Re-adopting old forestry and hunting trails at around 1,500–1,600m (4,900–5,200ft), Club Alpino Italiano have recently waymarked this variant, which is more wooded and some 2 hours longer.

Having checked supplies, gear and weather for the last time, walkers head off for the traverse of Cima di Citta. A good track climbs to rocky Portela Piazedel, after which boulders and scree from the Cima di Citta ridge high above are crossed. As height is gained, snow patches may be encountered while vistas

gradually open out over the whole Agordino mountains. Threading through rockfalls and zig-zagging up steep, stone-strewn grass, the gradient at last eases off and Forcella Sud del Van de Citta is reached—a declivity in the ridge connecting Cima di Citta with Monte Talvena at an altitude of 2,450m (8,038ft).

Ahead lies a primordial, other-worldly landscape of denuded rock, scree and boulders—the Van de Citta. Though in places resembling Yorkshire limestone pavement, the scale is altogether greater. In threatening storm or mist, it is a desolate place, a barren wilderness through which the human traveller will pass with hurried steps. In fine weather, there is a quality of savage beauty here and views are memorable, not only of the immediate vicinity but also of adjacent mountains. Sure to catch the eye is a distinctive notch on the skyline between the Pelf and the Schiara to the south. The main routing of Alta Via 1 takes this line—Forcella del Marmol—the final high pass before the walk-out to Belluno.

A relentless descent of almost 1,000m (3,000ft) first down easy slopes then more tortuously through crags and shattered rock outcrops, leads to Pian de Fontana and the Renzo del Mas bivouac hut, named after a climber who died on the Marmolada. This bivouac hut is a converted barn amongst pastures, but many are of metal construction, situated in particularly high or lonely places for those on protracted walks and climbs. Such shelters usually contain only very basic equipment, so food, fuel and sleeping gear need to be carried; since no wardens are resident, cleanliness depends on the habits and conscience of the previous occupants! A cardinal sin is to leave without closing the door, thus exposing the hut interior to the weather and sheep.

Monte Schiara's north face increases in grandeur as the head of Val Vescova is contoured round and a junction reached with the last official variant. Negotiating the big *via ferrata* on the Schiara's south face may be inadvisable for one of many good reasons. Not all walkers on Alta Via 1 will have the experience or inclination for what amounts to a steep 600-m (2,000-ft) aided rock descent; the weather may be unsuitable; fatigue, injury, the supplies situation or lack of remaining daylight may also militate against making the crossing. In such cases, a route using forestry roads down Val Vescova passes Rifugio Bianchet and drops to the main road at La Muda hamlet. Belluno can be reached by bus and, if

desired, the final stretch of route explored by walking up Val d'Ardo to the seventh Alpini hut under Monte Schiara's south wall.

Views towards Forcella del Marmol will have left walkers with no illusions about the effort needed to reach it up the steep ravine separating the Pelf and Schiara; 700m (2,300ft) of stiff ascent is rewarded by arrival at an airy and spectacular perch.

Club Alpino Italiano report that there have been numerous accidents and several fatalities involving people attempting to descend the icy south gully, an apparently obvious way down for the unwary. Paint flashes—the standard medium for waymarking on Alta Via routes—indicates the correct line turning right towards the Schiara summit and soon encountering the 9-place 'Sandro Bocco' bivouac shelter.

Hereafter begins the 'Via Ferrata del Marmol' a dizzy succession of ledges and corners, gullies, buttresses and airy traverses, all well marked and equipped. An enormous cave—the 'Porton'— heralds a transition to easier grassy slopes, upon which stands Rifugio 7th Alpini, an ideal base for climbing and other *via ferrata* routes.

With the final obstacle overcome, Alta Via 1 turns into a pleasant stroll beside the Ardo torrent down to Case Bortot, a roadhead hamlet with an inn, a telephone and limited car parking. Hilly lanes and the first farms and settlements give way to suburban roads, and from Bolzano-Belluno suburb, only the fiercely purist will shun a bus ride to Belluno town centre.

Situated on the River Piave, Belluno is the perfect terminus to a classic Italian mountain journey. It contains all the supplies and services denied to the long-distance walker since Cortina d'Ampezzo—and even that town was well off route! Several hours could be profitably spent seeing Belluno's sights—Venetian and Renaissance buildings, piazzas and monuments, a fine Civic Museum and delightful, shady public gardens.

Farther still to the south rises a long prealpine chain of hills culminating in the Col Visentin summit (1,763m, 5,784ft); it can be reached with little expenditure of energy by a combination of road, chair-lift and easy ridge walk. Views from this isolated vantage point are exceptionally wide-ranging, from the now-familiar Dolomite massifs in the north, to the Venetian Lagoon. Col Visentin has been officially adopted as an optional extension to Alta Via 1.

The view from Monte Tamer
(Photo: Martin Collins.)

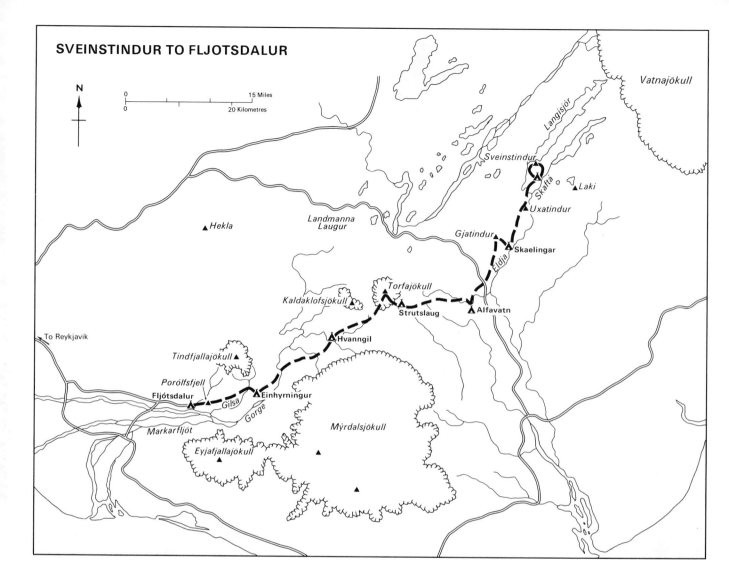

SVEINSTINDUR TO FLJOTSDALUR

Distance: 107km (67 miles). The distance does not include reaching the starting point. If travelling by bus this could put on at least another 22km (13½ miles). Any walking on the free day at Strutslaug is additional.

Time Required: 9 days. (This includes two days at Strutslaug.)

Type of Walk: Remote and uninhabited country yet generally easy walking. River crossings could be troublesome early in the season and it is certainly no place for the lone walker. There is no accommodation other than small, spartan shepherds' huts which cannot be relied on. These huts may be full if your walk coincides with Dick Phillips' groups. Backpacking equipment is essential and all food must be carried, unless you go with Dick Phillips (Whitehall House, Nenthead, Alston, Cumbria).

Base: Reykjavik.

Start: Sveinstindur.

(Continued on facing page)

Walk 6 ICELAND: Sveinstindur to Fljótsdalur by R. Brian Evans

Icy rivers and stony deserts in a Unique Landscape

Iceland is Europe's greatest wilderness and is wonderful country for adventurous walking. It is like stepping back in time to the earth's creation. There are steaming fissures; pools of orange mud which bubble and explode like simmering porridge; green moss which is too vivid and luminescent to be true, slashes the otherwise black mountain sides; sulphurous rivers emerge from icefields which are like huge inverted cracked saucers. It is country to travel through, to soak up the unique atmosphere, for there is nowhere else like it in the world.

If you visit the well known places like Geysir and Gulfoss you will marvel at the phenomena but will share the experience with coachloads of tourists. To sample the real Iceland you must get into the lonely interior. Not too far or you will be trapped amongst the boring ash deserts which surround the central icecaps. These *sandar* are popular four-wheel drive

vehicle routes and are best avoided on foot.

Iceland is a serious place for walking. There are few recognised trails, apart from the vehicle routes which have marker posts here and there. According to the severity of the winter, snow patches linger in the interior. The ash and tephra (cinders) makes for easy walking but if you choose to traverse the fields of lava your boots may be cut to shreds. Potentially dangerous are the river crossings. Any river which bears the word *fjlót* is usually impossible to ford, for it denotes a big river. Beware of any rivers which drain from ice caps for they may be very powerful. Rainfall can swell otherwise fordable rivers and early in the season melting snow adds to the flow. Cross the rivers with great care, preferably in threes, one person moving at a time, and head slightly downstream to minimise the effect of the current.

Weather in summer is generally mild and changeable with more rain along the southern and western coasts than the interior. Surprisingly walking is reasonably dry underfoot, for rain quickly soaks into the tephra and ash,

leaving even the thick springy moss quite dry.

The route described is typical of the type of walking and terrain encountered in Iceland. Many similar routes could be planned which would be just as scenic and adventurous. Hopefully it will encourage travellers to plan their own adventure, not necessarily this one.

The walk lies in south-central Iceland and starts at Sveinstindur, within sight of Vatnajökull, Europe's largest icecap. An intricate route leads south west to the coastal plain at Fljótsdalur. The route weaves between countless peaks of around 1,000m (3,000ft), crosses the small ice dome of Torfajökull and ends along a shelf with breathtaking views of the glacier wall of Eyjafjallajökull.

How you get to Sveinstindur is an epic before the walking begins. There is a special summer bus service which travels the mountain road north of Hekla. You have at least a day's walk from there to reach the start. Then there is the problem of food. You need to carry everything for the trip. The only habitations encountered are a few simple, deserted shepherd's huts, *kofis*, and you will meet few other

Sveinstindur kofi, on the edge of a sandy flood basin, with the peak of the same name behind. The black volcanic ash is relieved by patches of green moss. (Photo: R.B. Evans.)

/continued

Best Time of Year: Late June to September, although early in the season it is impossible to reach the start by vehicle.
Guidebook: None. The most useful general advice to independent travellers is found in *Iceland. An Expedition Handbook* by Tony Escritt.
Maps: Iceland Geodetic Survey. The entire route is shown on the 1:250,000 Sheet 6, Midsudurland, although it would be difficult to navigate by this alone. Better detail, although sometimes unreliable, is shown on the 1:100,000 sheets—67 Langisjör, 68 Skaftártunga and 58 Eyjafjallajökull.

people. Lightweight backpacking equipment is advised.

So the logistics of mounting a fortnight's holiday walk are great, unless you take the easy way out with Dick Phillips. For over twenty years, Dick has been organising trips in Iceland which appeal to genuine walkers. With his small groups it becomes economical to hire a special mountain bus which takes the party far into the interior. Food depots at key places cut the load carrying to a minimum. Thus a masochistic expedition is transformed into a pleasant holiday walk.

Day 1: Getting There

No apologies for including the bus journey for it remains an unforgettable experience. A battered old cut-down Mercedes picks up the group at Reykjavik where you have spent a day assimilating some of Iceland's surprises. First surprise is the sky-high cost of food. The rain is no surprise for doesn't it 'always rain in Reykjavik'? You wonder what on earth you have let yourself in for as the bus traverses a gloomy landscape of riven lava. So this is what Hell looks like! No wonder the moon astronauts practised here. Dropping to more civilised country you pass Selfoss and the lush coastal plain to leave the main road near Hella. The ensuing road would be classed as a rough track in most countries as it traverses a black plain of tephra close to the powerful Pjórsá river. You can continue in this vein, but the driver may decide to take a more scenic way on a minor route which skirts the lava flows from Hekla, one of Iceland's most active volcanoes.

Tyre tracks mark the road. Near Landmannalaugar the more regular route is regained and the jeep track rises around the edge of a lake to a col where the justly famed unreal colouring of the mountains is revealed. Around this area, the mountains are composed of rhyolite, its colourful ochres, reds and browns contrasting with the surrounding slagheap grey of the basalt. This is a honeypot and you will see plenty of tents and people. There is an invariably crowded hut.

One road turns into a steep-sided valley with no trace of a route—until the driver boldly heads into the river and forges upstream. Icelandic maps are misleading for the 'roads' are merely driveable ways. Soon we turn off the 'road' into apparently trackless desert where the driver needs to halt to peer for faint signs of tyre tracks. We bump down snow slopes into a river which is followed for a while before clawing out up the bank to make painful progress into the wilderness. Rivers seem to be favoured routes and one is followed downstream for a mile or so, then up a tiny tributary to emerge on a shoulder. We are there.

Day 2: Sveinstindur

The bus stops on a rise overlooking the Skaftá river. A flood basin just beyond would be dangerous to drive. Often deep snow patches make it impossible to drive so far and the walk in takes several hours. Across the basin it takes all of five minutes to reach the tiny *kofi*. Tents are pitched by those who had the sense to bring them, others peer into the gloomy interior to see an earth floor, rough stone walls and a roof of corrugated iron topped with turf. A shepherd's hut with not a sheep in sight.

Behind the hut rises the peak of Sveinstindur, a prominent landmark which has the honour of a name amongst its anonymous courtiers. A winding route leads over a col to reach the narrow, crumbly, west ridge which is scrambled to the summit at 1,090m (3,576ft) Langisjor stretches its watery finger north to the ice skirt of Vatnajökull. A narrow pimply ridge, the Fögrufjöll, separates the lake from the silvery braids of the River Skaftá, across which lies the most extensive lava flow in the world. The eruption of the Lakagigar fissure began in early June 1783 and lasted for eight months. Part of the resulting lava flow, now largely moss covered, is visible across the Skaftá like a textured carpet. The line of the fissure is marked by a row of craters 25km (15½ miles) long.

Small rocky pyramids thrust through the lava plain whilst the steep scarp of Kambar blocks the view south east. The sulphurous smell from the river suggests thermal activity in its birthplace under the ice of Vatnajökull. Every five years or so there are glacier bursts, when meltwater under the ice surges forth and creates floods; a situation which makes building of permanent bridges on the flood plains a costly exercise.

Day 3: Sveinstindur to Skaelingar

Skaelingar lies about 16km (10 miles) downstream but riverside cliffs bar a direct approach. The way lies round the back of the Uxatindar whose wedge-shaped summit provides the day's landmark.

South-west from Sveinstindur hut cross a small col to join the bus route which is followed down to the small river. Watch out for traffic as you ford the stream, there must be at least three buses per year! Ahead lies an ash desert—and every traveller in Iceland must sample one. It is easy underfoot; a colourless landscape of dereliction which at home would qualify for urban renewal subsidies. Here it is part of the unique Iceland character. To scale the surrounding peaks would be suitable penance for miscreants because the slopes are either steep and unstable or crests of crumbling wafers. Definitely country for the traveller rather than the mountaineer.

The route drops into the Rótagil gorge to a beautiful turquoise jewel of a lake trapped at its foot, and traverses the sandy edge between the deep water and the black cliffs to enter the narrowing gorge. It is like a black Gordale, with a rushing stream, its crystal clear waters appearing as black as its bed. As height is gained a ribbon of snow leads to a stony col. A long descent over stones and moor regains the Skaftá at the lush grassy haven of Skaelingar where there is another *kofi* of humble proportions. Nearby the tents are pitched on a deep mattress of moss.

Skaelingar is situated amongst a wierd collection of stone mushrooms, 2-4m (6-12ft) high, where the Laki lava flow has encroached across the river. A fascinating hour or so can be spent exploring the area amongst little lava tunnels, pinnacles and blocks. Golden plover poke about the river edge. The sheltered grottos amongst the blocks host a rich flora of arctic plants and ferns amongst the moss, whilst there are plenty of trees—if you look hard enough. Birch and willow with trunks at least 2 inches high grow in profusion, their branches spreading along the ground.

Day 4: Skaelingar to Alfavatn

A tiny side valley with a fringe of lava makes a pleasant start, thence a smaller stream on the left is followed into a twisting ravine. Height is gained with interest before emerging onto a mountainside of stones. The route heads across the flank of Gjátindur to its southern shoulder where a dramatic view explodes.

You are on the edge of Eldjá, one of the world's largest volcanic rifts. At its head stands Gjátindur, well worth ascending for an even more dramatic view. 300m (1,000ft) below is the flat rift bed which stretches into the distance, backed by a hint of white where Myrdalsjökull humps into the sky. One of Iceland's most active volcanoes, Katla, lies under the glacier in line with the rift, like a time bomb expected to erupt any year now—and when it does there will be enormous glacier floods which will destroy the coastal road.

We return to the shoulder and enjoy the 200-m (650-ft) descent of the steep rift side, for after an initial careful pad across slabs coated with ball-bearing-like gravel, you can swoop down the billowy ash like an off-piste powder freak. If it wasn't so far you would love to do it

again . . . and again. The tephra of this area is different, for it is composed of tiny colourful stones—purple, blue and red. The way crunches down the valley towards the source of an ever increasing noise of thunder; Ofaerufoss.

This is one of Iceland's renowned waterfalls, where a river jets over the side wall of Eldjá and in a double leap has carved through a natural arch. A path mounts the steep right bank to a spray-fresh viewing platform—then you can cross the exposed arch, like a narrow packhorse bridge with no side walls, and a scrambly descent regains the main valley floor. You may meet tourists here as it lies only 4km (2¹/₂ miles) from the 'road'.

A lesser continuation of the Eldjá rift is followed for a while past a curious 15-m (50-ft) volcanic blowhole with treacle toffee sides, and later a deep blue lake which may have its resident harlequin duck if you are lucky. A small path winds round the right side of the lake and crosses into a broader valley where sheep graze. A track ahead is spurned for a narrow ash-walled gorge. So often in Iceland the best route is not obvious. It is possible to touch either side as you tread the dry cinder floor and twist cave-like up the hillside to a col overlooking the Ofaerudalur. The river looks ominously powerful, but if the water level is low enough you can cross dry shod, across a natural rock bridge, where the river thunders over a fall to sink under a rock shelf and emerge below. The *kofi* lies just round the corner, in a delightful setting. A steep walled cirque with its gorge and waterfall, form a backcloth to the circular turquoise lake called Alfavatn.

Day 5: Alfavatn to Strútslaug

Across the natural bridge, the route follows the riverside upstream. The valley widens into grassy meadows where whimbrels float in the air and skuas wheel. The river must be crossed again, this time a cold, deep wade. A little further along there is more dramatic river scenery where a cascade drops into a pool and some of the water sinks into a lava tunnel.

A long ascent is made to a shoulder with the steep ramparts of Svartahnúksfjöll on the left. The way descends a small valley to regain the main Ofaerudalur, now wild and lonely, with a tumble of peaks ahead, one a dome of ice, Torfajökull. The main valley forks away right but we keep straight on to the foot of a long spur which descends from Torfajökull. A short way up this spur a small track left cuts across the steep hillside, across several ravines to a tiny triangular tin hut, like a solid ridge tent pitched on a dug-out platform high above a

Above left: **Ofaerufoss, one of Iceland's many impressive waterfalls, flows under a natural bridge.**

Above right: **High on the slopes of Torfajökull is this hole melted in the ice by thermal activity.** (Photos: R.B. Evans.)

braided river plain. This is Dick Phillips' Strútslaug hut, a refuge built in a key position to service his walking groups, but open to travellers in need. Groups who wish to use the hut should contact Dick Phillips as space is limited to about 16 people.

Building the hut was an epic feat, as it is only possible to approach by landrover towards the end of the summer when lingering snow patches have melted sufficiently. After an arduous approach with the vehicles getting stuck in tricky places, the spur was reached, the timber and materials unloaded, slid down the hillside and where it came to rest the platform was excavated.

The view from the hut is remarkable, across the striated flood plain where a silver web merges into the Holmsárlón lakes. Strútur's proud pyramid juts above other lesser peaks and the snows of Torfajökull beckon across the way. South and east, black predominates, below and west are the more attractive rich

colours of the rhyolite, a welcome change. At the western edge of the flood plain, between two streams, is a green oasis of lush grass, a sure sign of something, in this case hot springs. Boiling water bubbles from the hillside and surges down to an excavated basin. Sinter, a curious brittle, plaque-like growth edges both stream and pools. The water is almost too hot to bear and a quick dash is made to the far side away from the current. I have fond memories of sitting neck deep in the hot water in a cold shower of rain with a rainbow arcing over the black edge of Svartahnúksfjöll. A German in the party periodically had a roll in the adjacent ice-cold glacier stream and tried to convince the others that it was refreshing!

Camping on the soft, rich grass above the springs is idyllic, with underfloor heating too and warm water to wash in.

It is worth staying at least two nights here for there are plenty of interesting places to visit in the high rhyolite with its fumaroles and

snow peaks; or you can just laze in the springs.

Day 7: Strútslaug to Hvanngil

A narrowing ridge leads steeply up the hillside above the springs to emerge on the edge of a stony plateau. Snowfields are soon encountered and crossed, with the ice dome of Torfajökull on the right. Just below the final slopes on a shoulder of the glacier is a curious hole where the ice has melted. It is often possible to slide or kick steps into the base of the hole, although some years this descent would require a rope for aid. In the bottom you are greeted by hissing, spitting fountains of boiling water. You may be glad of the shelter from the wind and can eat your butties from a thermally heated stone seat! Ice cliffs like a layered cake show the snow fall of many years. With luck you can duck under a low arch to explore a passage in the ice, melted by the warm streamwater.

With care the steeper snow slopes above the hole can be ascended to reach the rocky summit of Torfajökull at 1,190m (3,904ft) a fine viewpoint in clear weather when nine different icecaps can be seen in a vast panorama. Pride of place is given to the Mýrdalsjökull whose gentle dome of ice fills the southern horizon. Much further east the edge of Vatnajökull only hints at its extent, the largest ice sheet in Europe. North, in the centre of Iceland is the almost circular Hofsjökull at the southern foot of which are extensive marshes, the breeding ground of huge flocks of pink footed geese.

Back at the hole, for a while the route follows close to the line of the underground stream, which can be seen in places where the ice has collapsed. Across a ridge on the right steep snow slopes are descended into the Kaldaklóf valley, still rhyolite country, confir-

med by the ridged peaks of orange-yellow, and the colourful pebbles underfoot. However we soon enter the grey black world again. A low col between Sléttafell and Einstigsfjall is crossed and then another low col to reach Hvanngil (pronounced 'quanngil'), a much

Above left: **Crossing the River Gilsa can be hazardous—the current is strong and the invisible river bed is full of boulders.**

Above right: **The route traverses the edge of the dramatic Markarfljót Gorge.**
(Photos: R.B. Evans.) 61

bigger and more palatial *kofi,* with the luxury of tables and benches upstairs, and a genuine toilet outside. Much of the shepherding in Iceland is done on horseback, and the rich aroma from the downstairs stables suggests that Hvanngil is regularly visited. It lies on a 'road' and indeed, a little way north is another, Alfavatn, with a busy tourist hut. But here at our *kofi* we capture the local atmosphere, even if it is somewhat powerful.

Day 8: Hvanngil to Einhyrningur

This is a day of river crossings. So far all the streams have been easily crossed, but today we meet several powerful glacial rivers, the first two, the Kaldaklófsvisl and the Bláfjallákvisl, a short distance along the road. The water is cold and deep enough to justify crossing in pairs. Then comes a long trudge over featureless grey desert where you are glad of the easier going that the road affords, to the cold Imri-Emstrua, again born in the depths of Mýrdalsjökull. The river is split into two channels, the first narrow but deep, the second thankfully bridged. You cross with a sigh of relief, for the river below is like the Tees in full flood and hurtles downstream over a carbon copy of High Force, in a striking basalt gorge.

We trudge the road again through miles of desert and reflect that some travellers in Iceland choose to walk days through terrain like this! The road swings down to a valley which carries the ominously named Markarfljót. This is indeed a *fljót* and no way could the river be crossed without the suspension bridge which carries the road. These recent bridge improvements are in readiness for the Katla eruption, thus safeguarding an alternative to the coastal route.

Where the road swings away up the hill, we leave it and follow the grassy edge above the river to a breathtaking sight. Below, and stretching away to the south-west is the dramatic Markarfljót gorge. The river enters it over a waterfall and thunders along a white maelstrom between vertical cliffs of over 200m (650ft). The walk along the rim is impressive. Fulmars nest along the walls, and there is a hanging garden of moss, streaming with rivulets which drop like threads into the main flow.

After this Wagnerian interlude the road is regained west of the gorge and left again at a col near the Einhyrningur. The grass slopes of this strange peak, with its summit like a beckoning finger, encourages you to the night's destination, a yellow red-roofed *kofi* visible amongst the lush meadows below. As we are now closer to the sea, grass is more evident, more luxurious and supports many sheep.

Day 9: Einhyrningur to Fljótsdalur

Rather than follow the jeep road down the valley, there is a much more interesting route to Fljótsdalur over the southern slopes of Tindafjöll, along a high balcony. This provides a grandstand view over the Markarfljöt, its flat floor now five kilometres wide, to the great ice wall which forms the southern flank of the valley. The ice wall is yet another glacier, Eyjofjallajökull, at 1,666m (5,466ft) a little higher than its neighbour Mýrdalsjökull. Glacier tongues stretch from the crater-like summit to lick the valley floor in a tumble of crevasses and seracs which are reminiscent of Mont Blanc above Chamonix.

The day starts by retracing steps along the base of the 'beckoning finger' mountain to reach a broad combe and the River Gilsá at a convenient crossing point above its lower gorges. Tumultuous glacier water confirms that this is the most serious river crossing of the trip; stony underfoot and impossible to see the bed, it is necessary to choose the shallowest spot and a sturdy companion.

A steep ascent restores the circulation, followed by a long traverse of the mountainside, across ravines, along stony shelves, accompanied by the breathtaking glacial views. Ahead is the flat topped peak of Pórolsfjell across a boggy gap, and a steep ascent is accomplished to reach its table top at 574m (1,750ft). Our destination is seen below like an aerial view—civilization again, with a handful of farms and chequered hayfields. The valley floor is flat and scoured by the powerful Markarfljöt. A battle is evident between the river and man, for huge stone defences have been built to stop river erosion and to reclaim useful farmland. In the distance is the sea with the Vestmann Islands just out of sight, but near enough to stir the imagination into visualizing the emergence of Surtsey in 1963.

The promise of afternoon tea and cakes at Fljótsdalur is enough to stir the reverie and commence the headlong descent. A final small river sports a narrow plank bridge but it just isn't worth attempting to balance with permanently wet boots. Journey's end lies just across the meadow at Fljótsdalur Youth Hostel where Judi and Paul Stevens hold a warm welcome for tired travellers and Dick Phillips has his Icelandic base.

Sleep is under a roof of turf in the unique old farm building, before returning to Reykjavik.

Walk 7 FRANCE: Through the National Park of the Western Pyrénées by Kev Reynolds

From Lescun to Gavarnie through the High Mountains

Catching the sun from its slope of lush green pastureland, there nestles the charming little village of Lescun. It's a delightful place in an idyllic setting; simple, dignified, peaceful. A village of unpretentious stone-walled houses and hay barns, it occupies a site of perfection

way above the left bank of the Aspe Valley. As a backdrop it has rank upon rank of bleached limestone peaks that form the frontier between France and Spain. To the west stands Pic d'Anie. Beyond that sentinel all the country rolling off to the Atlantic is Basque land. To the east the mountains grow higher, folding in one massif after another through the central

On a day when three high passes are crossed, the route traverses the valley of Oulettes de Gaube below the Vignemale's North Face. (Photo: Kev Reynolds.)

The gentle pastures of Lescun through which the first day's walk leads on the way to the Aiguilles d'Ansabère. (Photo: Kev Reynolds.)

portion of the range, known here as the High Pyrénées.

The High Pyrénées consist of alpine-style peaks, small glaciers and shrinking snowfields, flower-decked valleys and strings of little tarns to throw the mountains on their heads in a dazzle of rippling light. It's an area of enchantment that is growing in popularity as more and more climbers and walkers discover its splendours. In it lies the National Park of the Western Pyrénées through which this route makes a west-to-east traverse along a portion of that classic 45-day journey, the Pyrénéan High Route.

There are three National Parks within this range of mountains. Two lie on the Spanish side of the watershed: Ordesa, found south of the well-known Cirque de Gavarnie, and Aigües-Tortes, which is much farther east and contains the fabled Encantados. But that which lies entirely on the French slopes, officially known as the *Parc National des Pyrénées Occidentales* (PNP), is the largest and most scenically varied of the three. This traverse effectively explores the very best of that splendid region.

On the traverse there are two nights for which there remains a question-mark over accommodation. The first of these lies at the end of the preliminary stage which leads from Lescun to the Aiguilles d'Ansabère. There is no mountain *refuge*, but it may be possible, with permission, to share the *cabane* of local shepherds beneath the spire of Petite Aiguille d'Ansabère, otherwise you must be prepared to bivouac or camp. Two days later a short stage of the walk will have brought you down into the Aspe Valley a little below the Col du Somport. A trekkers' *refuge* is planned for this area, but as yet no details are available as to when this might come to fruition. Possibilities lie in either hitching down-valley 10kms (6 miles) to Urdos, or up to the Col $2^{1}/2$km ($1^{1}/2$ miles) away to reach hotels on the Spanish side.

On all other nights, accommodation is available in mountain *refuges*. Some of these belong to the French Alpine Club (CAF). British walkers with a reciprocal rights card will be able to claim reduced rates for their overnight stay. Other huts have been provided by the National Park Authorities, while Refuge Wallon in the Marcadau Valley is owned by the Touring Club de France (TCF). During the summer period meals are available in each of these huts, but food to eat whilst on the walk each day should be carried from Lescun, for there are no villages en route at all between Lescun and Gavarnie, journey's end.

The best time to tackle this traverse lies between early July and the middle of September. Naturally, the later you leave it the more likely you are to have the mountains—and the huts—to yourself, but after the middle of September a number of *refuges* will have lost their guardian, so no food will be available and allowances must be made for this eventuality. Attempts to follow the route earlier than July may well be frustrated by difficult or even dangerous snow conditions on some of the higher passes, and the above comments with regard to huts without guardians will also apply here.

In all but a very small portion of the route there are good paths to follow, with adequate waymarking elsewhere in the form of either paint flashes or stone cairns. For a short section only—on day two—the route strays across the frontier into Spain, and here the way becomes rather vague and it is essential to follow the descriptions given in the guide book with care. Other than this warning the trek should be suitable for most mountain walkers whose apprenticeship has been served on Britain's hills.

As for the amount of time required for the traverse, it would be possible for a fit and experienced mountain walker to complete the journey from Lescun to Gavarnie in about seven or eight days. But these mountains and valleys should not be regarded as a mere course for speedy travel. They're a wonderland of colour, grace, majesty. There are flowers to study, marmots and izard (the Pyrénéan chamois) and numerous birds of prey to watch. There are streams to pause by and tarns to dream beside. And there are also several moderate peaks upon which to scramble on 'rest days'. A two-week holiday is well spent wandering along this route without constantly referring to one's wrist watch. Take your time and absorb all the landscape has to offer, for in it you will find the rewards for undertaking the journey. It'll be quite memorable.

Day 1: Lescun to Aiguilles d'Ansabère

The overnight train from Paris arrives in Pau as day is breaking over the hills. Here you change trains to a little branch line for a short rattling ride as far as Bedous in the Aspe Valley. This is the end of the line where the train is met by a SNCF bus which then ferries passengers through the valley and up to the Somport. By riding this bus to the junction of the side road which winds up to Lescun, the walker can spare himself the misery of 6km (3½ miles) of road walking, but there's no escaping the tedious winding tarmac of the route up the hillside. However, it eventually opens to the pastures, forests and encircling peaks of the Cirque de Lescun. And there sits the village, tranquil in its meadowlands; a magical introduction to the Pyrénées and a worthy beginning to a long walk.

A GR10 signpost near the little general stores in Lescun directs the walker out of the village and onto a narrow lane where another sign points to the Cirque d'Ansabère. The way ambles between pastures and streams with here and there a hay barn and ahead the enticement of jagged peaks rising out of forest. The lane gives way to forest track, and this in turn leads to a climbing path out of the forest but dodging among dappled trees with mountains frowning overhead. Steadily the path gains height, but it suddenly tops a rise and looks over a bowl of green hill and scooped meadow, with woodland across the bowl, and above the woodland a slope of dusty scree out of which soar the magnificent Aiguilles d'Ansabère stabbing fingers of limestone into the sky. It's the sort of vision that encourages a halt. It inspires you to throw off the rucksack and to sit there in the grass and simply gaze in contentment. The sort of view to set a climber's fingers itching. A photographer's dream answered.

The route now drops into the bowl, crosses the streams draining mountains that here form a dramatic amphitheatre, then heads up amongst the broad-leaved woods. It's a steep haul, (take care to avoid snagging rucksacks on low branches), and the climb continues after you emerge from the woods among a rough terrain of boulders and scanty grass. A stream dashes down to the left; above, the view of the aigúilles becomes foreshortened as the path rises higher, and the Petite Aiguille assumes a superior pose directly overhead. And there, among the screes and steep pastures, will be found the shepherd's *cabane;* a scene from another period in time, from another world.

Given sufficient energy and time after this preliminary day's walk, it would be worthwhile going up to the Col de Pétragème, seen to the left of the Petite Aiguille, and then to work round on broken slopes to the right on an easy ascent of Pic d'Ansabère (2,377m, 7,798ft) which, despite its modest altitude, affords a spectacular view onto the twin aiguilles set

Overleaf

Top: **Crossing Col de Cuarde on day 2, where a series of gentle ridges mark the frontier between France and Spain. The route can just be seen crossing the green pastures in the centre.**

Middle: **Drying milk churns outside Cabane d'Escouret at what in Switzerland would be called an alp. The path from Refuge d'Arlet brings the walker past this simple hut, half an hour or so from the Aspe Valley.**

Bottom: **Day 3's walk begins with a charming path rising out of the Aspe Valley. At the head of the valley the mountains of the Aspe Cirque constantly demand a halt for 'one last look'.**
(Photos: Kev Reynolds.)

65

before you, and between them to a vast panorama that contains much of the country to be traversed in the days ahead.

Day 2: Aiguilles d'Ansabère to Refuge d'Arlet

The great needle of the Petite Aiguille catches the reflected glow of daybreak in a magical way. The pale limestone appears to have a wash of pink dye poured over its eastern wall, and the colour slowly stains from summit block to scree ankle as the sun rises far off and out of sight. If you're awake early enough to catch this moment, the day will be set fair and full of promise.

A narrow path leaves the shepherd's cabin and works its way round the head of the valley, rising gradually and becoming clearer as it approaches a little jewel of a tarn, Lac d'Ansabère. Behind the tarn to the east rise the crags of a ridge that projects north from Pic de Lac de la Chourique. But this mountain throws out another ridge westwards, and along this runs the frontier. The path continues away from the tarn and climbs directly onto the ridge at about 2,032m (6,666ft). There before you lies Spain.

How different are the Pyrénées from one side of the frontier to the other! Behind lies France with its somewhat savage walls, its tarns and streams, its screes and forests. Ahead lies an empty Spain; a downland-like landscape of rolling hills and charming, yet deserted valleys, leading the eye to blue-tinged sierras that fade in the distance of an horizon that loses itself in the sky. In that view there's nothing made by man. A vision of peace and tranquillity and solitude.

Dropping down from the ridge on a steep slope of treacherous grass, the route leads over a minor ridge to the shores of another lake. This one, Ibon de Acherito, is larger than the last and has a backdrop of fine cliffs that repay a few days' exploration. At its southern end there flows a stream, and it is important to refill water bottles at this point for there will be many hours of wandering to come before another opportunity arises in the shape of a clear spring. This is limestone country, of course, and limestone has a habit of secreting its water underground.

The path now makes a pleasant descending traverse heading south-eastwards. It's tempting to hope that one need only follow this all the way to Refuge d'Arlet, but alas, reality is not like this. Reality is a wearisome struggle up grassy hillsides with barely a sign of the onward route, followed by several hours of undulating ridge path. First, though, to find the true route. The path from Acherito eventually leads to a well-vegetated area in which there are several fragrant clumps of box growing. Here a vague trail will be found leading away to the left and climbing towards a shallow gully of white limestone. Above this, broad hillsides confuse the onward route. At the head of these grassy slopes the frontier ridge is enlivened with rocky crests, and it's a steep pull with a bright Spanish sun beating down, to gain the ridge once more. Up here there are two passes that give access to the continuing path, one on either side of the lump of Pic de Burcq; the Col de Pau to the north and the Col de Burcq to the south. Col de Burcq is preferable.

Emerging through the pass a fresh vista appears before you; French valleys deep below, contained by ridges that thrust north from the frontier. Down there streams are flowing, while in the distance are forests lapping in a wash of green. But rising above intervening crests to the east, the eye is caught and held by the unmistakable signature of Pic du Midi d'Ossau, that lovely dignified peak that has become the symbol of the Pyrénées, and around which the route will lead in a couple of days' time. It's a welcome sight, and the path which now curves a little below the frontier on the French side of the mountain, entices you on. It leads eventually, after the crossing of two or three more minor passes, right to the door of Refuge d'Arlet, a PNP hut perched on a grassy bluff overlooking its own glistening lake.

Day 3: Refuge d'Arlet to the Aspe Valley

A short and easy day's wandering, downhill for most of the way, comes as a welcome surprise after the rigours of the long walk from the Aiguilles d'Ansabère. It's the sort of day that encourages a study of flowers along the path; there's time to sit and gaze at the distant views and to enjoy this most pleasant, if modest, mountain scenery. It's not notably dramatic, not sprinkled with tarns or laced with huge cascades, not lined with big peaks nor cut by fantastic gorges. But it's just quietly lovely, and the route is easy enough to follow so that the mind can wander and the eye stray to the passage of high drifting clouds and the specks of buzzards or eagles or vultures riding updraughts overhead.

There's a curious scattering of pudding-stone not far from Arlet, and a pastoral landscape sliding away in cupped valleys towards the deeper, broader valley of the Aspe. The path eases between scree and pasture, rises over a ridge or two, then drops steeply into the Espélunguère Forest. There's another path

that climbs into the head of a tight little cirque above the forest and crosses into a delightful corner of Spain. Our route, however, ignores this. Having crossed a youthful stream it suddenly climbs over a steep grassy hill and

Crossing Col de Peyreget on Pic du Midi's shoulder, a fresh vista opens up—the onward route to Balaitous (the central peak on the horizon). (Photo: Kev Reynolds.)

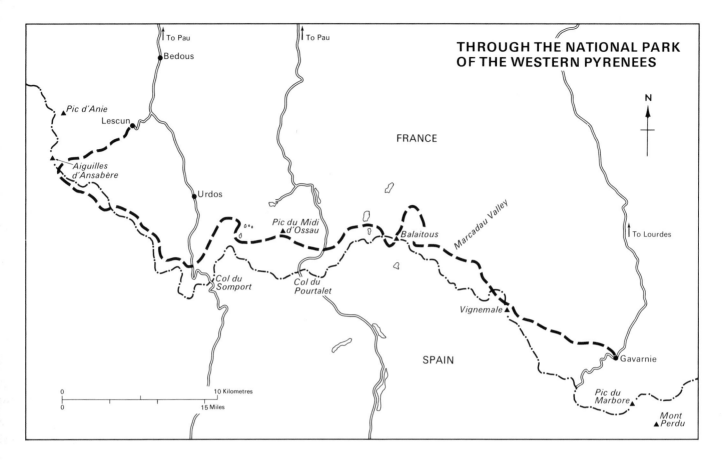

THROUGH THE NATIONAL PARK OF THE WESTERN PYRENEES

Distance: 75km (50 miles)
Time Required: 10 days.
Type of Walk: Strenuous and varied with some very rough sections, but mostly on good paths.
Start: Lescun.
Best Time of Year: July – September.
Maps: IGN 1:25,000 273 *Aspe-Ossau;* 274 *Balaitous-Vignemale;* 275 *Gavarnie-Néouvielle.*
Guidebook: Walks and Climbs in the Pyrénées by Kev Reynolds (Cicerone Press).

dips into the continuing forest. After a while a clearing is reached, and in the clearing, which in Switzerland would be a neat 'alp' with cropped grass and gushing water-trough, there stands a rough peasant's hut. When I wandered through one bright afternoon several milk churns were drying from the branches of a dead tree, and a tangle of pigs were sleeping in the shade of a poor lean-to. Rising ahead were the lovely shapes of the peaks that form the Cirque d'Aspe. Less than an hour later the path comes onto the Somport road where a decision has to be made with regard to a night's lodging. (In the National Park it is forbidden to camp within an hour's walk of a road.)

Day 4: Aspe Valley to Refuge d'Ayous

The setting of Refuge d'Ayous above its cluster of tarns, with a head-on view of Pic du Midi's west face across the empty depths of the valley of Bious, is one of the classics of the Pyrénées, and it is fortunate that it falls conveniently on the line of our traverse. To catch sunrise over Jean-Pierre's shoulder is one of the most memorable sights that the walker can hope for. Jean-Pierre, incidentally, is the popular name given to Pic du Midi d'Ossau by *Pyrénéistes* and those who live in its shadow.

The path which climbs out of the Aspe Valley will be found a short distance up the road from the car park at Sansanet where the trail from Arlet deposited you yesterday. This continuing path heads north among shrubs and the occasional tree, but there is an ever-present urge to pause and to turn round in order to catch one final glimpse of the Cirque d'Aspe that looks so fine from this position. It is almost with reluctance that you turn your back on it and face the onward journey. But this too has its compensations: views down into the valley, views off towards the foothills, the mass of flowers strewn in the grass around you and, at the right time of year, bilberries and wild raspberries to gather as you walk.

Minor spurs are crossed, followed by a downward slope into a knuckle valley inhabited by a shepherd, before climbing again, this time through a little wood before emerging into the sunshine for a traverse of the open hillside of Gouetsoule. Once you pass over the

Col de Gouetsoule the path branches off towards the east, and shortly after reaches the Refuge de Larry, a small, unmanned National Park *refuge* which is rather too close to the start of the day's walk to be of much use except in emergency. Beyond it the path rises through rough country to reach a brace of passes: Col de Larry (2,130m, 6,988ft) and Col d'Ayous (2,185 m, 7,169ft). From the latter, there opens a sudden view of Pic du Midi like a great volcanic plug to the east. It's a welcome sight. The night's lodging, in Refuge d'Ayous, lies a short downhill walk away.

There are those who would advocate continuing as far as Refuge de Pombie found another four hours' away on the south-eastern slopes of Pic du Midi. But for those who care more about the delights of mountain scenery than for the physical pleasures of extending one's exercise to the limit, a night at Ayous will be worthwhile. The hut overlooks Lac Gentau. Beyond the lake, pastures fold into the unseen Bious Valley, and out of that soars Jean-Pierre in a magnificent sweep of rock walls and buttresses to a crown of summits; shapely, regal. A superb piece of mountain architecture. Set back to one side the distant welter of peaks contain a number of 3,000-m (10,000-ft)

summits—the Balaitous massif through which the route will wander in a couple of days' time.

Day 5: Refuge d'Ayous to Refuge de Pombie

The walk between Ayous and Pombie uses a section of one of the finest of all Pyrénéan circuits, the Tour of Jean-Pierre. This circuit may be completed within a day, or extended to make a two-day outing of great charm. For the walker bound upon this traverse of the National Park, a diversion to take in this tour makes an interesting option—time permitting. But Pombie is the best starting place for the tour, and a decision is better left until the completion of this day's stage.

On departing from Refuge d'Ayous the path climbs southward among a jumble of boulders to find Lac Bersau which is set in very gaunt countryside, but around which many plants grow to add colour to an otherwise solemn landscape. Rising to the left, and blocking Pic du Midi from view, is a peculiar lump of mountain, Pic Castérau, seen to better effect from the pastures of the Bious Valley in the north-east. A saddle is crossed, then the way drops into a little valley pitted with limestone *gouffres*. There's a narrow tarn, sheep grazing,

A trekker pauses for breath on the stage between the refuges of Pombie and Arrémoulit, the East Face of Pic du Midi d'Ossau above. (Photo: Kev Reynolds.)

Refuge de Pombie, set above its little tarn, is one of the most popular huts in the Pyrenees, and marks the end of day 5. The original hut is seen to the left of the main refuge, and is used as an overflow. (Photo: Kev Reynolds.)

maybe a few ponies. But above all a sudden view again of Pic du Midi ahead.

Later, having crossed a dashing stream and passed a *cabane* or two, a little knuckle-valley is reached on the right. There's another *cabane* squatting amid a tangle of giant dock at the foot of a steep hillock topped with pines, and it is up this knoll that the route climbs. At the top, where shrubs form a lush foliage, the path branches away to the right, then in full view of the Petit Pic begins the long haul up to the saddle which grants access over the southern shoulder of the mountain to the lake and hut of Pombie. It's a wild crossing. On the western approach to Col de Peyreget there's a section of boulder-hopping through a wilderness of enormous rocks long tossed from the looming heights. But on the eastern descent the path is soon among tarns and grass slopes again, yet always with a view into the recesses of the South Cirque where couloirs hug shadows and daily send their loose stones onto the screes of the *Grande Raillere*.

Refuge de Pombie gazes up at the south face of Pic du Midi across the little lake. A popular hut from which climbers set out for epic routes on the mountain's many walls; from which the *voie normale* is tackled; from which the tour of Jean-Pierre begins. A day snatched from our traverse and based on this hut opens many possibilities. Study the guide for details.

Day 6: Refuge de Pombie to Refuge d'Arrémoulit

For most of this day's walk the route leads through green and pleasant countryside, following streams and enjoying for a while the shade of woods. But towards the latter part it becomes clear that the nature of the mountains is changing. The soft, almost feminine character of Pic du Midi's surrounding pastures, is being traded for a more rugged, masculine landscape. Arrémoulit lies on the edge of the granite wilderness of Balaitous; a wilderness of boulders, screes, chilly-looking tarns and miniscule glaciers. It is, however, a wilderness that has its own distinctive charm.

A much-trodden path plunges down the steep hillside to the east of the Pombie hut and soon enters the woods that clothe the lower slopes of the valley of Brousset. A footbridge eases the crossing of the stream in the valley bed, then it's up the far side with prospects of snacks and sometimes a few basic provisions from a hut shown as 'Soques' on the map. This occupies a spot beside the Pourtalet road. On the other side of the road stands a huge boulder beside which the continuing path heads into woods once more. It's then a steep walk through these woods to gain the tight wedge of valley down which leaps the Arrious stream. The path goes straight through this valley to the left of the stream, climbing higher and higher towards the little col at its head. Behind, Pic du Midi stands on its pedestal to display its great east face; a lovely sight.

There are two options available on reaching Col d'Arrious. The first is to drop down immediately to the north-east towards the large Lac d'Artouste in its great rocky bowl, then to veer off south-eastwards on a steep zig-zag path leading directly to the hut. The second option is to bear right at the pass until you reach a fiord-like teardrop of a tarn, then cross a minor ridge to balance round an exposed but safe path with a sobering drop beneath you, shown on the map as the *Passage d'Orteig*. This was cut by members of the CAF about a century ago, and it affords an entertaining stretch. It leads onto a bleached granite tableland across which a string of cairns indicate the route to the hut.

Of the two options, the second is quicker and more adventurous; the first more suitable for the less-experienced mountain trekker.

Day 7: Refuge d'Arrémoulit to Refuge Larribet

Experienced mountain trekkers will not be deterred by this stage, which contains a section of scrambling to attain the second pass of the day, followed by a steep descent into the hollows of Batcrabere; in fact it could be taken as an extension of the previous day's route by the fit, although it is preferable to break it into two stages as recommended here. However, the

less experienced might consider avoiding it altogether and taking the alternative, which is to cross Col du Palas (as on this stage) and pass into Spain to the south of Balaitous in an eight-hour trek that eventually returns to France over Col de la Fache (2,664m, 8,740ft and descends into the Marcadau Valley, thereby saving on one day's journey and missing what could be a slightly troublesome pass.

This traverse climbs over Col du Palas an hour from the hut, works round the head of a wild cirque and climbs over Port du Lavedan (2,615m, 8,580ft) on the ridge linking Pic Palas with Batcrabere. On the eastern side of this pass lies a savage land, and the route descends steeply on snow, through gullies and over scree chutes to a boulderscape. Then beside blackened tarns and over a ridge to discover, with some relief, the Larribet hut from which a number of challenging routes can be tackled on Balaitous, the first of the 3,000-m (10,000-ft) summits to be met. The hut is basic, but with a good atmosphere. From its windows the world is an uncompromising place, but this is

replaced the following day by a walk that takes you into the magical pastures of the Marcadau.

Day 8: Refuge Larribet to the Marcadau Valley

Balaitous is like a punctuation of savagery between the smiling acres that surround Pic du Midi and those of the Marcadau. Marcadau is an oasis of colour, fragrance and light, trapped between the gaunt walls of Balaitous and those of the Vignemale. The essence of this day's walk lies in its contrasts.

Larribet's rough quarter is soon traded for the winding streams, rock pools and cascades of the lower valley where flowers brighten the way. Then the path turns into a second valley, that of the Gave d'Arrens. It heads south now, having rounded the projection of the Crète Fachon that in effect forms the long north ridge of Balaitous, and begins to smile with little meadows of grass. Higher, the valley narrows. There are a couple of slim tarns, their western edges blocked by steep walls. Ahead, ridges converge on a pass which leads over to

The second of three high passes crossed on day 9 is Col des Mulets. This brings the walker into the presence of the Vignemale. Under normal conditions it is snow free, but a sudden change in weather patterns can bring a good snow fall even in early September. (Photo: Kev Reynolds.)

Spain once more, but our route branches away to work its passage over a hidden col; that of Cambales.

Up there it's a world of rock. There's a good view onto the east face of Balaitous, but nearer to hand the ridge climbs onto Pic de Cambales. Just below lie numerous tarns, and in the sunshine the descent to the Marcadau Valley is one of the best things on this traverse. Every step leads deeper into a wonderland. Tarns, then cascades. Streams and wide views and fragrant shrubs, then soft meadows and delightful easy peaks all round. The Marcadau is a valley to spend time in; not to rush through with an eye on the far horizon.

Day 9: Marcadau Valley to Refuge Bayssellance

The Wallon hut in the upper reaches of the Marcadau Valley looks across the stream to the narrow, attractive Arratille Valley. At its head you can just see the topmost crags of the Vignemale. It's a view that entices. Early in the morning izard often can be seen grazing near the hut, while it's quite probable that the occasional small herd will be found higher in the Arratille on this day's walk.

A good path wanders beside the Arratille stream as far as a high lake. Beyond the lake the route goes up among screes and rough boulders to find a little wild corrie that has trapped another tarn 20m (65ft) or so below Col d'Arratille. This pass overlooks the head of the Spanish Ara Valley, and across this rears Vignemale (3,298m, 10,820ft), the highest summit on the Franco/Spanish border. Our route drops into the Ara, then climbs up the eastern side to cross Col des Mulets before a sharp descent takes you to a little glacial plain with a magnificent view of Vignemale's impressive north face; one of the finest views in the Pyrénées.

There is a climbers' hut here, but the path continues past it, climbs over the third pass of the day, Hourquette d'Ossoue (2,734m, 8,970ft) and leads directly to the ancient beehive of a hut, Refuge Bayssellance.

From this hut, recently renovated and now a comfortable lodging, there are good views down towards the distant Cirque de Gavarnie. Just round the corner lies the largest glacier in the range, the Ossoue Glacier, which makes an interesting and convenient ascent route on the Vignemale. Time permitting, and with adequate equipment to cope with crevassed icefields, the ascent of Vignemale is recommended.

Day 10: Refuge Bayssellance to Gavarnie

The last day's stage on this walk is nearly all downhill. Downhill on a good path, then broad track, then road. But there's always something of interest to see, a good view to gaze at or an unusual flower. There are marmots and izard and mountains that suggest a return another year.

Gavarnie itself has its huge cirque to attract you, as it has attracted visitors for two centuries or more. The village is, of course, the most visited place in all the Pyrénées. Daily throughout the summer cars and coaches pour into the village streets. Then their occupants climb on donkeys, ponies or mules and ride up-valley to the hotel near the *Grande Cascade* in a centuries-old pageant. But at night the tourists have gone and the walker and climber can gaze in some solitude at the great walls of the cirque shining under a starlit sky. Then the place has a touch of magic; like the magic experienced in so many places throughout this walk. The memories will almost certainly ensure a return visit. Soon.

Walk 8 SWITZERLAND: The Bregaglia Circuit by Kev Reynolds

Below the granite spires of the Sciora Peaks

In the south-eastern corner of Switzerland a number of deep valleys slice through the mountains and drain off to the warm vineyards and orchards of Italy. These valleys have about them a flavour of Italy, too. Their villages may have the neat orderliness of Switzerland, but the architecture is distinctly Italian, with Italian names and Italian voices in the streets and surrounding meadows. Soft Italian breezes stir the trees, drawn from the distant plains of Lombardy, and there's an essential Latin romance in the air as you sit of an evening beneath lights strung in the chestnut trees, and watch a game of *boccia,* a glass of deep red wine in your hand.

It doesn't feel alpine. Not down there in the valleys. Even though the walling mountains that soar overhead wear winter all year round on their summits, and glaciers curl from their jagged crests. Even though up there you'll find permanent ice and snow and scree slopes and boulder fields and tiny alpine flowers that inhabit virtually inaccessible crevices. But that's where the charm lies; in the contrasts.

The Bregaglia is one of these valleys. Perhaps the very best. It begins at the Maloja Pass which links the Upper Engadine with this sudden taste of Italy. The Engadine, however, is high, broad, dazzling with lakes and in some of its small towns, the very essence of Swiss

The Sciora Hut is set precariously below the lovely granite peaks that enclose Val Bondasca, a wilderness of moraine and granite boulders. (Photo: Kev Reynolds.)

73

THE BREGAGLIA CIRCUIT

Engadine Valley — Inn — Sils
Lunghin Pass
Septimer Pass — Piz Lunghin ▲
Maloja
Val Maroz
Casaccia — Maloja Pass
V. da Cam
Lägh da Cavloc
Piz Duan 3131m ▲
Plan Vest
Maira
Tombal
Soglio — VAL BREGAGLIA — Vicosoprana
Piz Casnil ▲
Promontogno — Forno Hut
Bondo
Casnil Pass
Val Bondasca
Albigna Hut
Cacciabella Pass
SWITZERLAND
Sciora Hut
Sasc Fura Hut — Sciora Dafora ▲
Piz Trubinasca
Piz Cengalo 3370m
Piz Badile 3308m
ITALY

0   3 Miles
0   4 Kilometres

Distance: 55km (40 miles).
Time Required: 6 days.
Type of Walk: High level mountain walking with strenuous sections. Several high passes to be crossed that require care.
Start: Maloja.
Best Time of Year: July – September.
Maps: Landeskarte der Schweiz 1:25,000 1276 *Val Bregaglia*; 1296 *Sciora*.
Guidebook: *Walks in the Engadine— Switzerland* by Kev Reynolds (Cicerone Press)

super-sophistication. How different, then, is the Bregaglia! As you twist down the countless hairpins of the Maloja Pass you know at once that you enter another world. Down there the valley is much more narrow; it's lower, more ancient, simple. Basic, perhaps. The vegetation is rich and abundant, with woods of chestnut, beech and walnut. Ferns grow waist high in an almost sub-tropical liquidity of light. The air is soft and warm. There's an atmosphere of calm, of timelessness, that in Spain would be put down to *manana* indolence. There's colour glowing in the very air, in the woods, in the pastures and at almost every window of every grey stone house. The Val Bregaglia is different; but delightfully so.

The right-hand side of the valley, the northern side, consists of steep pastures dotted here and there with 'alps' and tiny villages. Woods grow in dark green patches to an advanced elevation. Between them, on natural shelves, are perched the alp chalets; stone-based, wooden walls, with slabs of stone on their roofs. They're deserted in winter, but in summer goats are grazing up there, and cattle too. But the meadows are mostly put to hay and throughout the bright summer months peasant farmers are seen scything with that ancient rhythmic movement that owes more to the Old Testament than to the twentieth century. And when the hay is cut and dried it's raked together and carted away in huge wicker baskets on the backs of men and women for storage in the barns spaced along the mountainside.

Above the meadows and woods the mountains here become more rugged, yet facing south they have no permanent snowfields or glaciers. These are mountains that have little appeal for the climber, but between them are notched passes where walkers can stray on journeys linking one valley system with another, following mule trails of old and sharing the mountains and upper basins with marmot and chamois. And, from the belvedere of these lofty slopes, enjoying the magnificent views that overlook the Bregaglia's southern side.

Along the southern side of the Val Bregaglia its wall is broken by wonderful shafted glens; Forno, Albigna, Bondasca. At their head rise granite spires, massive walls, glaciers that throw down cascades and leaping torrents. A line of serration that holds the walker spellbound with wonder, and fills the climber with temptation and ambition. The Bregaglia Circuit explores this wonderland. It begins by tracing a route along the high alps of the northern mountains, then drops down into the valley itself before climbing up into the southern glens and crossing from one to the other in order to experience the full flavour and contrasts that the Val Bregaglia so generously displays.

This walk is a constant delight. In places it's a little strenuous with some extremely rugged terrain that has to be traversed. Clear conditions are essential for the crossing of at least two of the passes, and for working a way below some of the glaciers. But the rewards are memorable for those who undertake this outing.

Day 1: Maloja to Casaccia

Whilst Maloja is geographically an Engadine village, politically it belongs to the Val Bregaglia. It sits at the south-western end of

the Lake of Sils with a charming view along the lake towards Piz Corvatsch and the hinted valleys of Fex and Fedoz. There are many fine day-walks and easy ascents to be made from this village, and with the Maloja Pass dropping into the Bregaglia behind it, Maloja would make a convenient base for all sorts of mountain holidays. It is easily reached from the railhead of St Moritz by post bus, and this walk begins on a path that strikes away from the main road some 200m (6,500ft) north of the post office where the bus from St Moritz pulls in. The path is signposted to Pass dal Lunghin, which marks one of the great watersheds of the Alps.

It's an easy path at first, made and marked with Swiss efficiency, and offering good views early on, over the Engadine lakes to snow

The Lunghia Pass is a bleak, barren place from which a number of paths lead to distant villages and valleys. It also marks a major alpine watershed. (Photo: Kev Reynolds).

Above left: **Soglio is one of the loveliest villages in all the Alps with one of the loveliest views. The path from Tombal leads directly into the village, and a night is spent here with this glorious view spread out as a backcloth.**

Above right: **Like a scene from** *Heidi* **the goats from Tombal form a foreground to the magnificent peaks of Val Bondasca.**
(Photos: Kev Reynolds.)

peaks, beyond which rise the giants of the Bernina group. Piz Bernina is the easternmost 4,000-m (13,000-ft) peak in the Alps, and the Bregaglia group forms a western extension of the Bernina Alps. For the first part of this circuit, however, a very different landscape will be explored.

After wandering initially up rough pastures among shrubs and a few trees, the route enters a region of grey rock and scree, and then reaches the cold-looking Lunghinsee; the tarn which marks the birth of the great River Inn. Half an hour above it you come onto the bleak Lunghin Pass and gaze out to a curious broad basin of poor grassland that slopes off northwards to the country beyond the Julier Pass. Ahead, though, lies the Septimer Pass that has been used as an important trading route for centuries. Up here the winds always seem to be blowing cold. It's a bleak, desolate spot. From

it the Inn flows through the Engadine and, via the Danube, into the Black Sea. From it drains the Maira which grows as it enters the Bregaglia, swollen by the glacier streams of the southern Bregaglia, and on to the far-distant Adriatic. A bleak birthplace, this is favoured only by the occasional chamois and a community of marmots.

The path leads round and over the Septimer Pass and then bears south. Immediately there is an improvement in outlook, and the infant Maira stream offers lively companionship. It leaps along beside the path, then takes a more direct route through the steepening valley than even the tight zig-zags of the path can contend with. Then the valley reaches the important Val Maroz, bears off to the left and drops steadily into the Bregaglia itself, at the little white village of Casaccia at the foot of the Maloja Pass.

Day 2: Casaccia to Soglio

This day's walk brings a revelation and marks the finest possible introduction to the wonderland that is the Bregaglia. First, though, it is necessary to retrace the last part of yesterday's walk by wandering back up the valley out of Casaccia to the junction of the Val Maroz with the tight wedge of valley that comes from the Septimer Pass. There is a broad track leading into the Val Maroz, but it soon deteriorates into a narrow path that is aided now and then with paint flashes. It climbs through a lovely region of rock plants; there are bilberries in great clumps, and juniper clawing over boulders, and alpenroses everywhere.

Two hours from Casaccia the path comes to an isolated alp, Maroz Dent, in a delightful setting. Around it the mountains rise steeply, but in the valley bed there are scant pastures and clear streams flowing. There's a dwelling house and cattle byre, and beside it a pentagonal walled paddock that must have taken a lot of effort to build, long long ago.

The route crosses the valley here and then climbs steeply to the south, aiming for the Val da Cam. In the valley bed there's an alternative path going west to Val da la Duana. This also crosses a high pass and later joins our route for the final downhill stretch to Soglio, but it is better to aim for the Val da Cam in order to make the most of the spectacular panoramas to be had along the traverse of the higher alps.

The climb into Val da Cam is a heart-pounding ascent of steep grass slopes, but the way leads over a minor pass where a curious 'family' of tall cairns stands guard, and then ambles gently through a pleasant hanging valley with a short climb at its far end into the upper level of the valley. Then you work a way through a region of broken crags and suddenly the Bregaglia plunges away beneath your boots. It's a dramatic entry into the Bregaglia's embrace, for 1,300m (4,200ft) below, the village of Borgonovo squats in the valley. Beyond, on the far side, great granite peaks burst out of the forests, catching clouds and looking for all the world like a backdrop to some fairytale film set. It is almost unreal. For the next three hours the walker is

Emerging into the first level of Val da Cam, the walker is surprised by a tall 'family' of cairns marking a broad saddle. (photo: Kev Reynolds.)

treated to one of the most memorable strolls in the Alps. The path maintains its lofty belvedere above the 2,000-m (6,560-ft) contour as it picks a way among rampant shrubs, over little streams, across extremely steep pastures, and from one collection of alp chalets to another. And all the time the views across the valley grow more and more enchanting. It has become a walk in the sky. A walk that is heady with fragrance and colour; the air like champagne. Italian champagne, for the soft light floods in from Italy a few kilometres away, but remains crisp from Swiss glaciers over the valley. The valley itself has those great hollow depths far far beneath, mostly unseen as little projecting spurs and shelves get in the way.

Plan Vest is an alpine hamlet that might have strayed from a dream. Tucked against the steep mountain wall it gazes across a slanting pasture and over the depths of valley into the Val Bondasca. At the head of the Bondasca rise the Sciora aiguilles. To one side gleams the great blade of Piz Badile in the Trubinasca glen. On the other side of the Scioras runs the saw-tooth ridge of granite that divides Bondasca from Albigna; spattered with snowfields and glaciers and hung about with tatters of mist; their ankles wrapped in chestnut woods.

From Plan Vest to the Alp Tombal is a knee-juddering descent through extraordinarily steep pine-woods. Every few moments, though, a glimpse through the trees presents you with another view into Val Bondasca so delightful that the utmost concentration is called for to remain upright on the tight zig-zag of path. Tombal is no less a magical place than Plan Vest, and Soglio, the village that marks the completion of our day's walk, shares the same wonderful view and is utterly charming.

Soglio is, surely, one of the loveliest villages in all the Alps, perched as it is on its green hillside terrace with chestnut woods below and those magnificent views ahead. I know of few more charming places in which to spend a night.

Day 3: Soglio to Sasc Furä

The route from Casaccia to Soglio is the longest section of the whole Bregaglia Circuit, yet some of the other days, though shorter in hours of effort, have moments that are more taxing. Parts of today's walk to Sasc Furä are quite strenuous, but it leads into country that was such a feature of yesterday's panorama that the scenery more than compensates for the effort involved. This is a day of exploration that begins easily enough with a descent through the woods that cluster beneath Soglio's churchyard walls. The path winds stea-

dily down, now deep in leafmould, now open to the sun as a little glade is crossed beside a haybarn or along the edge of a drystone wall. It leads directly into the bed of the Val Bregaglia at the village of Promontogno; a village of narrow cobbled alleys and old grey stone houses leaning one against another.

Opposite the Pension Sciora in Promontogno's main street, a quiet road heads off towards Bondo, a neat village which sits in the mouth of Val Bondasca. Shortly before coming to a bridge over the Bondasca stream, with Bondo on the far side, a narrow path branches off to the left. It climbs into woods and emerges after a little while on a rough track. As you wander along this track, with the stream dashing off to the right, views ahead begin to open out. The Sciora peaks look enticing at the head of the valley; certainly no less so than yesterday when they were first viewed from greater height across the valley.

Then another valley cuts off to the right. This is the Trubinasca glen, guarded at its head by huge walls of smooth granite: Piz Trubinasca and Piz Badile. Between them; snow and ice. From them, streams come foaming into the dark shadows of the glen's lower gorge. It's a wild place. Wild, but most attractive. Up there, above the gorge, sits the Sasc Furä hut. Knowing this, you begin to wonder how to reach it.

The track narrows to a path, and after a while the path divides; left to the Sciora hut, right for Sasc Furä. Heading off to the right, then, our path drops down to the river and crosses it on a footbridge. Then begins the real climb, for the hillside rears up before you, lush in its vegetation with trees and shrubs and ferns and wild raspberries all around. The way is clear. If not in path, certainly with paint flashes or cairns. Steeply it goes, so steeply that in places steps have been cut into the trunks of trees to enable the route to continue.

Then it levels, crosses a stream, rises in a gentle traverse and comes round the edge of the spur up which the way has climbed. The trees begin to be spaced out; there's more light, and the hint of distant views off towards the west. The path rises again, not quite so steeply now. There are acres of shrubs all around and a foreshortened view of huge peaks gleaming above. Then suddenly the ground eases once more and there sits the Sasc Furä hut on one of the most delightful mountain shelves that you can imagine.

It has taken maybe 4½ or 5 hours from Soglio and there will no doubt be several hours of daylight left. But what a place to relax in! It would be a sin to scurry away, for life is too short to miss moments of magic such as the

Sasc Furä promontory offers.

Rising directly behind the hut is the sharp knife blade of Piz Badile's north ridge. This forms the eastern limit of the Trubinasca cirque. Then come Cima Santa Anna, Punta Trubinasca, Piz Trubinasca and Piz dei Vanni; a worthy collection of north faces with buckled glaciers at their feet. Round to the left, seen peeking beyond the spur, the wild mountains that head the Bondasca can be studied. But almost better than these fabulous views is that which looks out westwards over the Bregaglia, for out there is a different light flooding in from Italy, and across the valley Soglio appears as a toy village on a green hillside. Above it you look onto Tombal and above that, to Plan Vest; all rich, lovely country through which yesterday's walk had led.

Who could fail to be impressed and deeply moved by such a place?

Day 4: Sasc Furä to Sciora Hut

It would not be outside most fit mountain walkers' abilities to link this short stage with yesterday's walk, but if the plan is to move through a delightful landscape absorbing as much as possible of the mountain experience, then I would opt for this suggestion, making two days of it. Should you find the desire to explore further around the Sasc Furä hut, there is plenty of scope. There will be no shortage of ideas to fill the day.

The route between these two huts really requires good visibility. It crosses a high nick of a pass just below Piz Badile's north ridge, then works its way down a series of shelves of rock to the moraine wilderness and glacial snouts that litter the foot of Piz Cengalo and the Scioras. Much of the way seems lifeless and barren, but if you keep your eyes open you'll find much to surprise you.

Leaving Sasc Furä the route goes immediately behind the hut up a steep smooth slab that bears paint flashes as a guide. There's no real path above it, just a few traces, some more paint markers and a few cairns. It's a steep winding trail that scrambles over slabs and among scanty shrubs. Piz Badile looms ever higher overhead, and every time you pause the mountains impose themselves upon you; smiling, not threatening, for though this is big country with serious peaks, they appear to be benevolent.

After about 45 minutes of scrambling up the promontory the little pass of Colle Vial (2,200m, 7,218ft) is found. All around there's a confusion of great granite boulders, but the pass is marked with cairns and paint flashes, and through it can be seen a fine view of the Sciora peaks looking suddenly very big, while

At the end of an excessively steep approach path, the Sasc Fura Hut comes as a great relief. (Photo: Kev Reynolds.)

nearer to hand is Piz Cengalo. Over your shoulder rears Badile and you have a grandstand view of its magnificent north-east face; one of the classic walls of the Alps, first climbed in 1937 by Riccardo Cassin. But it's also a sobering view which greets you at Colle Vial, for the cliffs plunge steeply away from your feet, and you gaze across a series of moraines, glacial snouts and glacial smoothed slabs and streams, to the little red speck that is the Sciora hut. It looks a long and complicated way off.

There is a path, distinct if narrow, that leads down from the pass. It leads from one narrow ledge to another, sometimes along terraces of grit and grass, sometimes down scrambling steps tight against the cliff with droplets of water splashing on to you. It's an interesting descent, not perhaps for the faint-hearted, although it is perfectly safe enough. At the foot of the initial descent the route is through a boulder field with paint flashes conveniently marking the way, then over moraine cones, and glacial slabs running with streams off the glaciers above. It's an energetic route, but it is not without its pleasures or interest, and there's always a fine view off to the depths of Val Bondasca where the streams converge. But at last the Sciora hut is reached, and it comes as a welcome surprise to find that its surroundings are not so bleak as they appeared from

For most of the way, the path leading from Val Bondasca to Sasc Fura is an exceedingly steep one. When it eases for a short traverse through the trees, the walker gains a brief respite before climbing steeply again. (Photo: Kev Reynolds.)

Colle Vial. In fact in many ways the setting here is even better than that at Sasc Furä; different certainly, and extremely impressive. Another magical place in which to spend a night, and the recently enlarged hut is one of the finest in the Alps.

Day 5: Sciora Hut to Albigna

Another reasonably short day, but one that is worth taking on its own for the contrasts and delights of the two valleys. Bondasca, dropping steeply away from the door of the Sciora hut, is a deep shaft with lush vegetation in its lower reaches. The Albigna glen is a high cupped valley of rock and ice and a large dammed lake. It's a cold, arctic scene by comparison with Bondasca's brilliant semi-tropical outlook. But in each there is charm, and for the mountain lover the contrasts are all part of the attraction.

Separating the head of Val Bondasca from the Albigna glen is the jagged ridge dominated by the Sciora peaks, but north of them the ridge is breached in two places by the Cacciabella passes; the southern at 2897m (9,504ft) the northern one being 2,870m (9,416ft). Neither are particularly difficult for the experienced mountain walker, and there's a well-marked trail leading from the Sciora hut, with paint flashes and cairns all the way to the south pass. This has been used for two hundred years or more by chamois hunters, and is reached by way of boulder-strewn slopes and small snowfields with a straight-forward scramble onto the pass itself. From here the route descends a gully, crosses a ridge projecting eastwards from Piz Erávedar (2934m, 9,626ft) and works through some boulders to glaciated rocks with the retreating Albigna Glacier seen below draining into the chilly-looking waters of the lake. On the far side sits the Albigna hut and above it, the wild ridge that divides the glen and that of Forno beyond. It's a grey scene: grey rocks, grey moraine, grey glaciers.

The path traverses grassy terraces and boulder slopes, working northward to the far end of the lake. Shortly before reaching the dam it is joined by another trail from the left which has crossed the Passo Val della Neve, one of the access routes from Vicosoprano. The way now crosses along the top of the dam wall to find the continuing path leading round to the right, climbing rough slopes to the hut itself, which commands another fine panorama.

Like that of Sciora, the Albigna hut has also recently been enlarged and renovated and offers a good standard of accommodation for a mountain hut. But it's extremely popular on account of its accessibility, for there's a cableway leading from the Bregaglia to the dam, and as a result many non-climbers or high mountain walkers come up for the day to enjoy the wild surroundings from the comfort of the hut.

Day 6: Albigna Hut to Maloja

If time is running short or the weather becomes threatening, an easier retreat from Albigna would be to go down to the dam and descend on a path from its western end, steeply through forest, all the way into the Val Bregaglia. But the completion of the Bregaglia Circuit via the Forno glen to Maloja is a better bet, and a more satisfactory finish if the weather allows.

As with the ridge dividing the Bondasca and Albigna glens, that which separates Albigna from Forno has two passes offering access one with the other. In this instance the northern Casnil pass (2975m, 9,760ft) is preferable. It demands little more than a rough walk occupying about $2^1/2$ hours from the hut to the pass along a cairned track that works among grass slopes and rocky terrain. From this pass it's possible for a diversion to be made along the ridge leading north to the summit of Piz Casnil (3189m, 10,462ft) in an hour. Views from this peak are a little more extensive than from the pass, but there is a pitch of grade II climbing to contend with.

From the northern Casnil pass the descent into the Forno Valley is again straightforward and clearly marked. It goes down the edge of a snowfield below which zig-zags continue the path to the moraine of the Forno Glacier. This now allows an opportunity to visit the hut across the valley, from which a number of fine outings offer temptations to both climber and walker. But the circuit of the Bregaglia here deserts the wild recesses of the Forno glen, and joins the main trail through the valley leading out to Maloja.

Lower, the former glacial moraine that covers the valley in its aura of grey desolation, is slowly but persistently being taken over by vegetation. In between the granite rocks, flowers have managed to plunge their roots into the gravelly soil, and colour shines here and there to give a foretaste of lovely things to come. In how many years time will meadows carpet the glen where now grey rocks and grey moraines dominate? How soon before the apparent desolation is transformed into nature's own garden?

The path works its way down to a junction with the valley that flows from the Muretto Pass seen off to the right. There are rough meadowlands now; trees and shrubs and more flowers. Another world is being entered. Behind now is the world of ice and snow and granite pinnacles; ahead lie pastures and lakes and haybarns. The track leads enticingly into this bright new world. There's a cattle byre, a stone-built alp hut, and stretching ahead, the gleaming tarn of Lägh da Cavloc, or Cavolocciasee. This little lake is surrounded by pines and shrubs, and there are large boulders making inlets and pools around the edge. A popular place for family walkers and picnic parties who gather here on every bright day in summer.

Down then to meadows and hay barns and houses. Maloja lies ahead with the Engadine stretching away to the right. To the left, plunging down, there's the Bregaglia. As you wander across the last meadow before Maloja there's a view half-left into the Val Maroz. It seems a long time ago that we were last there. And stretching far off to the left, the steep hillside along which the upper alp terrace walk took us to Soglio. And flooding through like a soft beam of liquid, that marvellous light of Italy, bathing the hillsides with its afternoon brilliance.

A few moments later the path leads into Maloja's street, and the circuit of the Val Bregaglia is complete.

Walk 9 ENGLAND: Coast to Coast by Martin Collins

The Eastern Fells which have to be crossed on the way to Ullswater. (Photo: Walt Unsworth.)

Across England in the Footsteps of Wainwright

Alfred Wainwright's inspiration for a walk across England, linking rights of way from coast to coast, dates back to well before the publication of his pictorial guidebook in 1972. Cutting west to east against the grain of the land, it is an exceptionally fine walker's route, some 190 miles (306km) in length and passing through three National Parks. There are many ways of reaching the North Sea from the Irish Sea—certainly shorter ones—but Wainwright's remains the favourite and is followed by thousands of long-distance walkers each year. This is an account of one such crossing.

Stage 1: St Bees Head to Shap

St Bees on a bitter mid-March morning: down on the pebbly beach with its dog-walkers and breakwaters, the two of us dipped a ritual boot in the Irish Sea. St Bees Head is a double prow of white-veined sandstone, split by the deep cleft of Fleswick Bay and home to colonies of seabirds. As you walk the grassy clifftops 300ft (90m) above the sea, it is hard to turn a blind eye to the less attractive coast north and south. Sellafield nuclear reprocessing plant strikes an uneasy but distant discord, while nearer at hand, beyond the lighthouse, Whitehaven's chemical works spew smoke downwind from an unexpected industrial sprawl. Only when heading inland past Sandwith, Stanley Pond and Moor Row are backs finally turned on this over-used coastal strip, with its modern installations and abandoned mines.

Cleator village precedes a steady climb over sheep-cropped turf to double cairns on the summit of Dent, the walk's first real hill. The Lakeland tops were ranged ahead, from Skiddaw to Scafell—a panoramic view of snow-capped fells. On the drop over Nannycatch Gate, we passed the first of many dead sheep along the way, weakened by a winter of unforgiving weather. Kinniside Stone Circle, actually a fake, was upstaged by a view of Ennerdale framed between a derelict shed and an old bath, right on the perimeter of the National Park! We pitched at Ennerdale Bridge and it rained all night.

Ennerdale Water gleamed silver in uncertain sunshine; above and beyond, the fells wore hats of dark, lens-shaped cloud. Heavily laden, we kept to the easier north shore, past Gillerthwaite youth hostel and field centre. The metalled lane becomes stony, climbing close to the River Liza for 4 miles (6km) through pine forest—an example of afforestation smothering the land in a way which is less evident in the Forestry Commission's more recent planting strategy.

Across Ennerdale, Pillar reared high and snowy, masquerading as an alpine peak three times its size. Great Gable appeared ahead, but before leaving the shelter of trees, we snatched an early lunch. Black Sail youth hostel stands in such a wild, romantic setting among glacial drumlins and boulders, that one is reminded more of a Scottish glen than an English dale.

Clouds had flattened benignly and the day was fresh-scrubbed as we sweltered up Loft Beck, lingering now and then to gaze back down Ennerdale to the distant sea. Snow patches below were deep, frozen drifts above, as a stunning view unfolded over Buttermere and the Derwent Fells. The Great Gable track is hugely cairned, and thereafter a stony incline tramway from old slate workings makes a bee-line from the ruined Drum House towards traffic on the Honister Pass. Quarries honeycomb the area from times when slate was a valued commodity, and there is still a limited operation on the pass itself.

Seatoller sits snugly at the bottom of the old, overgrown toll-road. Before pitching, we enjoyed a cream tea—the kind of indulgence fostered by a combination of cosy Lake District hospitality and backpacking opportunism!

The night was bitterly cold but morning dawned fine, frost-greyed fields warmed by a

low sun. On the path up Stonethwaite Beck, overnight freezing had thrust the ground into myriad tiny turrets of ice. Past Langstrath valley, on up Greenup Gill, a last glance down Borrowdale and we were out at Greenup Edge on a snowy line across to the head of Far Easedale. Such bright conditions invited the ridge walk over Calf Crag and Gibson Knott, a delightful rocky switchback ending on a new path provided by the National Trust and Countryside Commission which drops before Helm Crag—drastic relief for serious erosion on the south-eastern flank.

Lanes lead pleasantly to Grasmere, that mecca for artists and poets. Wordsworth was a prodigious walker, as was sister Dorothy, and their small home from 1799 to 1808 (Dove Cottage, which sits almost on the lake edge), is not a place for literary pilgrimage alone. De Quincey, who lived there for the next 28 years, was, some say, the initiator of backpacking, spending many nights out in improvised tents, this despite his heavy use of opium.

With sights set beyond Patterdale for the night's halt, we took the country lane from Goody Bridge, crossed the A591 and climbed to Grisedale Hause on an increasingly rough track, running with meltwater in its upper reaches. Although exceeding 1,900ft (580m) in altitude, Grisedale Hause is a natural way through the mountains to Patterdale, an old, much-used road.

Grisedale Tarn, steel-grey under now lowering skies, was cradled by snow-streaked fellside, so that neither the Helvellyn nor the St Sunday Crag ridges held any attraction and we

Above Loft Beck. In the distance is Pillar and the coast. (Photo: Martin Collins.)

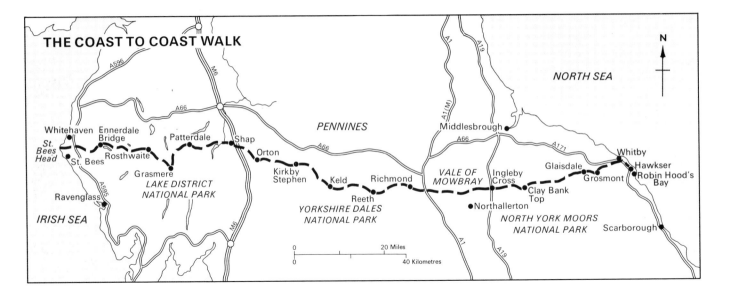

THE COAST TO COAST WALK

N

NORTH SEA

Whitehaven Ennerdale
            Bridge   Patterdale   Shap
St.   Orton
Bees   St. Bees   Rosthwaite
Head   Kirkby
              Grasmere   Stephen   Keld   Richmond
         LAKE DISTRICT
         NATIONAL PARK   Reeth

Ravenglass   YORKSHIRE DALES
                                            NATIONAL PARK
IRISH SEA

PENNINES

Middlesbrough   Whitby
                                           Hawkser
                       Ingleby   Glaisdale Robin Hood's
VALE OF   Cross   Grosmont Bay
MOWBRAY   Clay Bank
              Northallerton   Top
                          NORTH YORK MOORS
                          NATIONAL PARK
                                         Scarborough

0   20 Miles
0   40 Kilometres

Distance: 190 miles (306km).
Time required: 12 to 14 days.
Type of Walk: Varied terrain over mountain, lowland and moor.
Start: St Bees, Cumbria.
Best Time of Year: Any season, but snow cover likely on high sections during winter.
Maps: OS 1:50,000 series—nos. 89, 90, 91, 92, 93, 94, 98, 99.
Guidebooks: *A Coast to Coast Walk* by A. Wainwright (Westmorland Gazette).

scuttled off down the rugged dale head, hardly bothering to notice Brothers' Parting, an outcrop to the right where William and Dorothy Wordsworth bade brother John a last farewell.

Five miles (8km) of descent on improving tracks led to Patterdale in time to re-stock with provisions and climb to Boardale Hause, thereafter squelching through bog and snow to Angle Tarn. The wind had slackened and backed to westerly, with rain forecast; by morning, conditions had worsened considerably and we set off with some misgivings.

Traversing Kidsty Pike proved memorable, not as expected for a final savouring of Lakeland horizons from the loftiest point on the Coast to Coast walk, but for a miserable correlation of map and compass to the rise and fall of ground, seen dimly through driving snow. No chance that day to find the Roman road on its bold course over the tops from Ambleside to Brougham.

The way down Rampsgill Head was almost missed, but eventually we emerged beneath the cloud ceiling and scrambled down to Haweswater for a much-needed brew. This was once secluded Mardale, whose lake was dammed by Manchester Corporation in 1919 to supply industrial Lancashire with water.

Camp was made in a field by the River Lowther at Bampton and an attempt made to dry out. Next morning, the tent was fringed with slush, the sky filled with Turneresque curtains of vapour.

Stage 2: Shap to Kirkby Stephen

The path to Shap Abbey ruins seemed fussy,

but a fascinating packhorse bridge and continuing views west to the mountain barrier were ample compensation. Shap itself, once a travellers' haven where the A6 reaches its 1,400-ft (420-m) summit on wild, exposed moorland, lost its soul in 1970 to the M6 motorway, and now sprawls for a grey mile along the erstwhile main road to Scotland.

The combination of A6, railway, M6, electricity pylons and quarries—a corridor of noise and pollution—comes as a shock to the walker still fresh from Lakeland's romantic and assiduously protected landscapes. We crossed the M6 footbridge, passed fields of granite boulders, paddled through limestone slurry at a vast quarry and reached a wall at Oddendale hamlet as a squall swept over in a great horizontal rush of air and snow. There is a strong and sudden sense of being in different country here, so well defined is the eastern edge of fells, and so distinctive the limestone plateau. Gone are the verticalities and the picturesque, replaced by a rolling expansiveness bearing many signs of ancient settlement.

Near Potrigg barn, we helped a farmer push his car from a morass of mud; he said it had been one of the worst winters he'd known. At a rise, and quite unexpectedly, the Pennines are there to the east. Cross Fell was plastered with fresh snow, caught in fleeting sunshine, and to its right we could make out the valley of High Cup. The Pennines can be seen from Lakeland fells and Cleveland Hills alike, making England's width seem more slender than we imagine.

Sensational limestone pavement and a large erratic boulder lead on over heather moors which, sheep apart, are lonely yet not remote. Up a muddy defile past mis-named Robin Hood's Grave, we were out at the B6260 near Beacon Hill. At the time, the onward route was on tarmac to Orton, our destination anyway for provisioning and a night's stopover. The walk down was distinguished by views to the rounded snowy shoulders of the Howgill fells.

Sunbiggin tarn, a flat marshy pond east of Orton, is frequented by wildfowl and ornithologists. It heralds a section rich in botanical, geological and archaeological interest which is lost if headlong progress is the name of the game. However, even the swiftest walker will notice the low, extensive embankments of Severals Village Settlement, prehistoric in origin, and the so-called Giants' Graves, a rash of 'pillow-mounds' near Smardale Bridge.

With ominously dark clouds piling in from the west, we climbed in a green lane to the undulating top of Smardale Fell and raced down over soggy fields to Kirkby Stephen, beating the storm by a hair's breadth. Kirkby Stephen, like Middleton-in-Teesdale on the Pennine Way, is one of the few towns passed through on the Coast to Coast route, and provides travellers with a welcome array of shops and services. It is also of strategic importance to the eastbound walker, who will pause here and take stock before setting out across the main Pennine watershed.

Stage 3: Kirkby Stephen to Richmond

Beyond Hartley, the way climbs a narrow walled lane until tarmacadam yields to stones and boggy hillside. Gaining height, the Vale of Eden spread out below, the Howgills shining distantly to the west, there was good Pennine walking up towards Nine Standards Rigg and the Yorkshire Dales National Park boundary. At first, only Cross Fell trailed dark storm cloud, but soon we too were engulfed. Old coal workings near the summit were rimmed with snow, peat-hags ice hard.

Nine Standards cairns, so conspicuous from afar, loomed eerily through the sleet, but minds were firmly concentrating on descent and no time was lost setting course down Coldbergh Edge. Our climate is fickle, and if one special viewpoint is spoiled by bad weather, often the next will be blessed with sunshine. The ebb and flow of fortunes on a journey such as this must, of necessity, be borne with philosophical resignation!

Lunch was more than usually comfortable in a shooting cabin shelter at Ney Gill, from where the way drops squashily past shooting butts to Raven Seat at the head of remote Whitsundale. Moorsides were dreary monoch-

rome, but on a subsequent crossing in early summer, marsh marigolds had transformed the dale head with their drifts of vibrant yellow flowers.

Whitsundale Beck is followed past barns and drystone walls, with glimpses here and there into deep ravines. We passed yet another ailing sheep, all efforts to revive it failing, its life fading visibly away. Smithy Holme and its vehicles were derelict, poignant reminders of how quickly habitations succumb to the elements; homes, once furnished and cosily familiar to generations of farmers in their time, are used as barns or left to decay. Changes in farming economics, land ownership and living standards, along with problems of access, have laid low many a hill farm, none more so than in the Pennines.

The Swale, that most delectable of Yorkshire rivers, falls over little shelves of rock to reach Keld. Inscrutable as ever, the hamlet was choked with cars but not a soul was to be seen. We dropped towards the sound of its waterfalls and wandered beneath the trees taking photographs. In summer, midges make everyone's life a misery at Keld.

We reached Crackpot Hall in sunshine. At each successive visit, the old farmhouse, abandoned owing to mining subsidence, seems more abjectly ruinous: its depiction in Wainwright's Coast to Coast book will soon be a fading memory. No homestead could have enjoyed a more wonderful position, looking out over upper Swaledale's lyrical pattern of fields and 'laithes'.

Needing provisions, we camped at Muker and retraced steps next morning. Up behind

Crackpot Hall, a victim of lead mining subsidence, is gradually disappearing. (Photo: Martin Collins.)

85

Above left: **Honister Pass and its slate workings. In the distance is a snow-capped Helvellyn.**

Above right: **Lead mining ruins at Gunnerside Beck.**
(Photos: Martin Collins.)

Crackpot Hall, a path swings north above the steep declivity of Swinner Gill, crossing it at a stone bridge by the remains of a smelt mill. These moors were the scene of intense industrial activity during the 17th and 18th centuries. Veins of lead ore, worked piecemeal since Roman times, were vigorously exploited, first by the landowners and later by all and sundry until, towards the turn of the last century, the best deposits were gone and cheaper foreign imports sounded the industry's death knell.

Its growth and rapid decline has parallels with the ironstone industry of the North York Moors and has left behind a similar legacy of ruined buildings and desecrated hillsides. For the imaginative traveller, however, the intrinsic interest of such relics outweighs their unnatural intrusion and certainly the stretch from here to Reeth is an absorbing one.

Blakethwaite smelt mill is even more impressive, reached by crossing heather moor from East Grain, to drop left off the main track and down beside North Hush, a vast, man-made gash above Gunnerside Beck. 'Hushes' were used extensively in the early days of mining, dammed water being released suddenly to scour the steep slope below of its surface covering and reveal possible mineral deposits.

Farther on, the top of Melbecks Moor was reduced to a stony waste, perpetuated by modern gravel reclamation. We tramped over snowdrifts past a bulldozer and fragments of forgotten machinery. There was an exciting view of the Cleveland Hills far ahead in the cold, hard air.

A rough but motorable track leads down to Old Gang smelt mill, quite the most evocative ruin in these parts—a cluster of old walls and

On the bleak moor of Nine Standards Rigg above Kirkby Stephen. (Photo: Martin Collins.)

gable ends, overtopped by an intact chimney some 30ft (10m) high. Stopping for lunch was excuse enough to inspect the site at leisure and build an impression of working life here, 100 years ago.

Beyond Surrender Bridge and Cringley Bottom, the way lies just outside the intake wall below Calver Hill. Route-finding had so pre-occupied us that a blackening of the sky to our backs went unheeded. Within the space of ten minutes, a full-blown blizzard had developed and we slithered unceremoniously downhill, chancing upon stiles, to Novia Scotia farm. Reeth, capital of Upper Swaledale, lay in a Christmas-card landscape. Across the wide slope of village green, a café was enjoying its first day of the Easter season: Reeth is popular with visitors on wheels as well as on foot.

The Swale is more sedate at lower levels and a sudden interlude of sunshine lent an air of unreality to the afternoon as we wandered along its pastoral valley floor. Another approaching storm detracted from an appreciation of Marrick Priory's 12th-century remains, and as the visible world was obscured by impenetrable veils of large, sticky snowflakes, a farm pitch was thankfully secured for the night.

Swaledale's intricate matrix of fields and walls was delicately drawn: dark lines on white moorsides, seen through bare trees on the way over to Marske. A succession of field paths, sometimes plain, at others the faintest of trods, links farms under Applegarth Scar, Willance's Leap and Whitcliffe Scar. Deep mud in Whitcliffe Woods was the harbinger of worse to come on the ensuing section, though this is not always the case, especially in summer.

Richmond first appears ahead over parkland, its cliff-top Castle Keep a dominating feature. Arrival in the town justifies some celebration, for Coast to Coast walkers have reached a significant milestone: there is, in any case, too much to see for a visit to be rushed. Antiquity has been conscientiously preserved and emanates from every street corner: the cobbled market place and castle ruins are particularly worthy of note. However, in addition to its fine historical ambience, Richmond is the largest and liveliest town passed through on this walk—an opportunity to replenish the rucksack and avail oneself of essential services.

Stage 4: Richmond to Ingleby Cross

A disused railway leaves Richmond in our direction and we were soon doing battle once again with mud. No ordinary mud, this, but a thick, glutinous ooze that clung to boot soles in huge pads, inducing a clumsy skating action!

From here to the Cleveland Hills escarpment, the route crosses an almost flat agricultural landscape. After so much upland walking, it is odd looking out over large arable fields and passing farms whose stock has that groomed, well rounded look from easy living. Some walkers will hurry on, anxious to return to the hills and, indeed, the Vale of Mowbray can be crossed in a longish push of 23 miles

Richmond on the River Swale is a town of considerable interest, with a fine castle and well-preserved Georgian theatre.
(Photo: Martin Collins.)

(37km), much of it on country lanes. But for many, variety adds spice to any journey and with neither gradients nor exposure to the elements to distract, undivided attention can be given to this very rural slice of England.

Past Catterick Camp, largely unseen, the way reaches Brompton-on-Swale and Catterick Bridge, where the busy A1 is negotiated and two thirds of the walk completed. The Swale had grown wider and worldweary, its sullen waters fringed with debris. Camp was made in a muddy farm paddock at Bolton-on-Swale. In the green-lichened church opposite lies a memorial to a Henry Jenkins, reputed to have died in 1670 at the age of 169!

Country life is rarely the oasis of peace it is assumed to be and we were woken early by pigeons, rooks and the milking parlour generator! Large puddles in the roads reflected a sky too clear to be trusted. Avoiding blisters from prolonged road walking is largely a matter of resisting the urge to race ahead when distances seem to pass so slowly; roads are made for wheels and the walker is always disadvantaged. We reached the White Swan at Danby Wiske in time for an early lunch, then plunged out into the chilly air for more muddy farm tracks.

By now, the Cleveland Hills had drawn perceptibly closer—the Pennines were all but invisible behind intervening features—and a plan was hatched to overnight at Osmotherley. Although there is a small store at Ingleby-Arncliffe, we needed more reliable stocking-up for the next long leg over the moors. If no deviation is made from Wainwright's route, there are no more shops until Glaisdale, 30 miles (48km) away.

Stage 5: The North York Moors — Ingleby Cross to Robin Hood's Bay

After the coldest night yet, which had us cocooned in spare clothing and the tent flysheet frozen tight as a drum, a white mist clung heavily to Osmotherley. Wainwright's itinerary cuts up from Ingleby Cross in a big dog-leg through Arncliffe Wood to the dishes and aerials of Beacon Hill television booster station. Thereafter, walkers embark on the most strenuous stretch since the Lake District, a veritable switchback which only relents after the climb to Botton Head some 12 miles (19km) east.

Here at the western edge of the North York Moors National Park, several long-distance and challenging walks coincide: the Coast to Coast Walk, Cleveland Way, Lyke Wake Walk, White Rose Walk and the Bilsdale Circuit. It is no surprise to find the path etched deeply onto the land.

Coalmire Plantation gave shelter from the chilly breeze and the track down to Scugdale started well enough, heavily gravelled but reverting to a 10-ft (3-m) wide ribbon of mud before reaching Huthwaite Green. A stiff pull up brings you out on Live Moor and there are views ahead to the distinctive cone of Roseberry Topping in Captain Cook country. Remains of snowdrifts lined the path along Carlton Moor; the Newcastle and Teesside Gliding Club stood deserted across its broad airstrip.

Throughout much of the year, there is a concentration of activity around Carlton Bank from which the walker will yearn to escape—a hubbub of trail-riding, mountain biking, hang-gliding, and its concomitant traffic. Trail-riders in particular have adopted the old alum workings for scrambling and, permitted or not, seem intent on exploiting the area to destruction. Perhaps it is better that trail-bikes should devastate one small pocket of countryside than roam further afield, though, alas, this occurs too.

As you climb to Cringle End, drop and climb again to Cold Moor and repeat the process to the Wainstones outcrop on Hasty Bank, there may be little energy to spare for the view. Yet all along the scarp a panorama of farmland and villages is laid out below to the north, as if seen from a low-flying aircraft.

Above the crags on Hasty Bank, we raised a few grouse, startled by their late flight and raucous 'go back, go back' cry. These moors support large populations of both grouse and sheep and the heather is systematically burned back to encourage the growth of tender new shoots upon which they graze.

If the weather is wild, paths and tracks can be taken below the escarpment through fields and plantations, or country lanes threaded between neat villages standing back from the hills. Never adopted by the Countryside Commission as an 'official' long-distance footpath, the Coast to Coast Walk is infinitely variable, eschewing the tyranny of one correct line and allowing individuals the freedom to deviate according to inclination or circumstances: on the whole, though, Wainwright's route is hard to improve upon.

The road at Clay Bank Top is the last link with civilisation for 10 miles (16km) and not all walkers will pass up the chance of accommodation by pressing on. For all his extra burden, the backpacker is freer from such constraints and we strode on up the ancient, rutted road onto Carr Ridge, reaching the Ordnance column at Bottom Head on Urra Moor. At 1,490ft (454m), it is the highest point on the Cleveland Hills.

An invigorating sense of freedom and open-ness on these high moor tops is gained at the expense of visual interest, so that occasional punctuation marks in the form of tumuli and standing stones become important focal points—indices against which progress can be measured. Many of the stones mark old boundaries and are inscribed with the initial letters of landowners. Stone crosses such as Ralph Cross (the National Park logo) and Fat Betty (which we shall pass) may have given spiritual as well as navigational guidance to early travellers. Most tumuli date back to the Bronze Age and, despite ransacking by Victorian treasure hunters, have yielded valuable archaeological material.

Bloworth Crossing was once permanently manned to safeguard the passage of man and beast across the Rosedale Ironstone Railway. During its heyday in the late 1800s, several trains a day laden with iron ore plied between the mines around Rosedale and the steep Ingleby incline, connecting with trains to the blast furnaces of Teesside and Durham. It was an audacious undertaking by any standards and indicative of the value attached to Rosedale's high-grade ore. Weather conditions were frequently savage and in bad winters, rolling stock would be snowed in for weeks or months at a time. Even so, small communities of railway employees lived in terraced cottages on the moors at 1,200ft (366m) by Ingleby and Rosedale Bank Tops. Many fascinating relics associated with the ironstone industry remain in this part of the North York Moors and the

Top: **On Carlton Moor, Cleveland escarpment.**

Above: **'Fat Betty', the well-known landmark on the moors above Rosedale.** (Photos: Martin Collins.)

The village of Robin Hood's Bay marks the end of the Coast to Coast Walk. (Photo: Martin Collins.)

area is well worth exploring in its own right.

The cinder track bed is walked for the next 5 miles (8km) through cuttings and along embankments as it snakes cunningly around the heads of Bransdale and Farndale without recourse to bridge or tunnel. On both sides, dark heather and coarse, ochre grasses give way to the green of distant valley fields.

Hopes that the weather might have at last relented were dashed as massive cumulonimbus clouds, already shedding curtains of precipitation out to the west, caught us up: we ducked into the Lion Inn, Blakey, as the first snowflakes began to fall. Dating from 1553 and well patronised by ironworkers and coalminers in the last century, the Lion Inn is possibly the most eagerly anticipated place of refreshment today for the Coast to Coast walker. Like the Tan Hill Inn on the Pennines north of Keld, its isolated position attracts motorists too, and on summer weekends its car park is full to bursting. Tired and hungry, we tucked into a square meal, swapping stories with fellow walkers until dusk fell and it was time to pitch the tent and organise resources for another cold night.

A mile along the road north from the Lion Inn stands Margery Bradley, a monolithic boundary stone and path marker. There were extensive ironstone mines on Rosedale's east flank, and a spur of railway looped round to service them. However, taking the old track bed or a short-cut path will by-pass both Ralph Crosses and Fat Betty—famous landmarks close by the road and not to be missed.

Tiny points of dew glinted spectrum colours from grasses and heather already steaming in the morning sun's warmth. At last the sky shone springtime blue and skylarks sang ecstatically overhead. The way round Great Fryup Head passes Trough House, a substantial stone shooting hut and a welcome haven on many a stormy day. Melting snow added to a generally boggy path, but from Cock Heads, tarmac then the old unmade Whitby Road led unerringly down to Glaisdale.

It is a steep, disjointed village, served by the railway and a scattering of shops. Leaving it past shapely Beggars Bridge, the route undulates through East Arncliff Wood, paved in places with worn flagstones and providing glimpses of the River Esk. Lanes lead to Egton Bridge, and on the old Toll Bar along by the

Esk, original tariffs are still displayed.

A steam train stood at Grosmont station and we were able to look over as yet un-renovated rolling stock in sidings just south of the village. The North York Moors Railway Society rescued George Stephenson's line through Newtondale to Pickering for posterity, and very popular it is too, connecting with British Rail's Whitby to Middlesbrough service. The romance of steam provides Grosmont with a steady influx of tourists during the season.

A road hill of 1 in 3 will need surmounting before an uncertain path through heather, that traverses Sleights Moor can be taken: the reward in clear weather is an unequivocal sighting of Whitby and the North Sea, now tantalisingly close. Beyond the A169, a track drops muddily towards Littlebeck and we shared a farm pitch with a flock of ewes and their lambs.

Sited in the valley of Little Beck, the Falling Foss Forest Trail is waymarked by the Forestry Commission and provided with car parking for its many visitors. Coast to Coast walkers follow the wooded beck up, past Falling Foss waterfall and Midge Hall, continuing alongside May Beck. It is a section of silvan delights, enhanced if there is time to dawdle, but by now there was a scarcely resistable urge to quicken pace towards the coast.

The bridleway marked on our map across Graystone Hills was lost in heather, but the remains of a stone cross acts as a guide to reaching the A171 at a gate. From here it is 2 short miles (3km) to Robin Hood's Bay and journey's end. Had the hour been later or the weather poor, the temptation could well have proved too great: as it was, Wainwright's vision of a grander finish prevailed and a descent was made to Hawsker.

The Cleveland Way coast path is followed south along magnificent cliffs, yet the eastbound walker may be impatient to meet the North Sea on more intimate terms. Robin Hood's Bay village is precipitously steep and traffic is mostly confined to clifftop car parks. It was low tide and we picked a way out over rock reefs to wet our boots beneath wheeling gulls and a sky which soundly proclaimed that spring had finally arrived. Perhaps our sense of timing had been a little out!

Walk 10 WALES: The Pembrokeshire Coast Path by Martin Collins

An Outstanding Walk along the Pembroke Sea Cliffs

Inaugurated in 1970, the Pembrokeshire Coast Path stretches 180 miles (290km) from St Dogmaels in the north, to Amroth, along some of Britain's finest Heritage Coast. The geology of shoreline and islands is absorbing and often stunningly beautiful, as are the prolific wild flowers and seabird colonies encountered along the way.

Promontory forts, *cromlechau*, hut circles and ancient tracks recall Pembrokeshire's links with a past reaching back to the New Stone Age, while relics of more recent history— churches, small harbours, quarries and mineworkings—contrast vividly with modern

shipping and the oil industry at Milford Haven. Fortifications spanning man's known occupation of this region are also conspicuous features of the walk, from Iron Age defences, Norman castles and Victorian forts, to World War II airfields and present-day military installations.

Much of the path follows the very edge of cliff or beach—sometimes precariously—in coastal scenery of exceptional quality. Although in high season resorts are well patronised, tourism is relatively undeveloped: during the rest of the year, the walker will hardly meet another soul away from road access points.

In places, the path is surprisingly strenuous,

Old Red Sandstone at Greenala Point. (Photo: Martin Collins.)

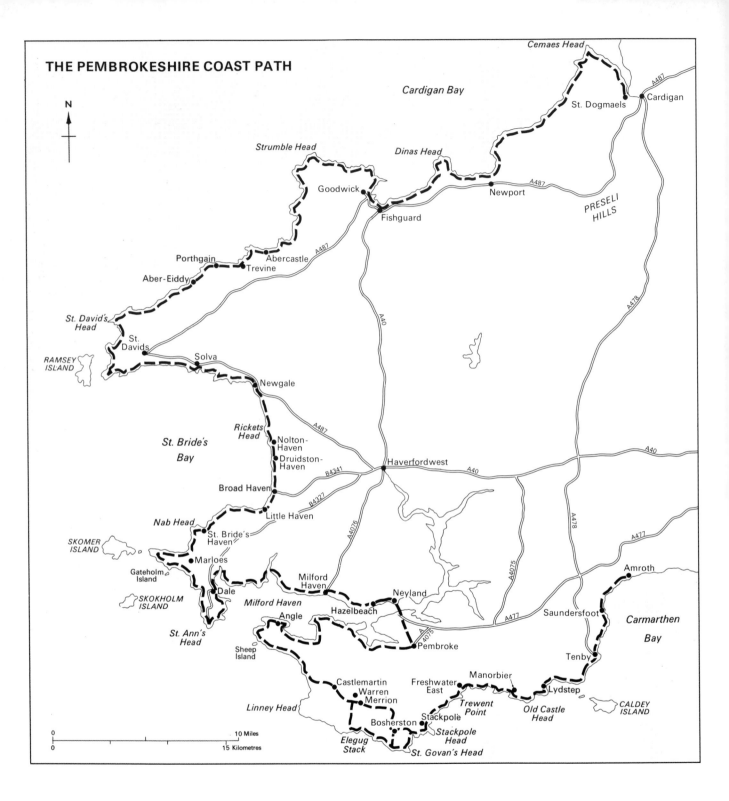

THE PEMBROKESHIRE COAST PATH

N

Cardigan Bay

Cemaes Head

St. Dogmaels

Cardigan

A487

Strumble Head

Dinas Head

Goodwick

Newport

A487

PRESELI
HILLS

Fishguard

A487

A478

Porthgain

Abercastle

Trevine

Aber-Eiddy

*St. David's
Head*

St.
Davids

A40

*RAMSEY
ISLAND*

Solva

Newgale

*Rickets
Head*

A487

*St. Bride's
Bay*

Nolton-
Haven

Druidston-
Haven

Haverfordwest

A40

A40

Broad Haven

B4341

A478

B4327

Nab Head

Little Haven

A4076

*SKOMER
ISLAND*

St. Bride's
Haven

Marloes

Gateholm
Island

Milford
Haven

Neyland

A477

Amroth

*SKOKHOLM
ISLAND*

Dale

Hazelbeach

Saundersoot

Milford Haven

*Carmarthen
Bay*

*St. Ann's
Head*

Angle

A4075

Pembroke

A477

A4075

Tenby

*Sheep
Island*

A4075

Castlemartin

Warren

Merrion

Freshwater
East

Manorbier

Lydstep

*CALDEY
ISLAND*

Linney Head

*Trewent
Point*

*Old Castle
Head*

Stackpole

Bosherston

*Stackpole
Head*

*Elegug
Stack*

St. Govan's Head

0   10 Miles

0   15 Kilometres

Distance: 180 miles (290km).
Time Required: 10 to 12 days.
Type of Walk: Mostly undulating clifftop,
steep and exposed in one or two places,
otherwise straightforward.
Start: Amroth to walk north, St Dogmaels
to walk south.

Best Time of Year: Spring, early summer
or autumn (dense undergrowth on some
stretches in high summer).
Maps: 1:50,000 Landranger Series—145
Cardigan, 157 St David's and Haverfordwest, 158 Tenby.
Guidebooks: *The Pembrokeshire Coast*

Path, by John H. Barrrett (HMSO), *A Guide
to Walking the Pembrokeshire Coast Path*,
by Tony Roberts (Pembrokeshire Hand-
books), *A Guide to the Pembrokeshire
Coast Path*, by Christopher John Wright
(Constable), *Walking the Pembrokeshire
Coast Path*, by Patrick Stark (Five Acres
Press).

in others a gentle stroll. Frequently exposed to wind and weather, however, care is required near cliff edges and while beach-walking during a rising tide. Footwear and protective clothing similar to that used on moorland walks is generally advisable, and provisions should be carried on more remote sections.

Each season holds its unique attractions, but accommodation and refreshment are harder to find in winter, favouring the self-contained backpacker who can ask at farms for permission to camp. Spring is, perhaps, the best time of all: wild flowers embroider the path with a riot of colour, the holiday season is still young, and weather conditions are often more reliable; also, undergrowth which will slow progress in places where the path is not cleared, is not rampant until mid-summer.

Day 1: St Dogmaels to Newport

A colourful, rather old-fashioned fishing village, with shops, pubs and a post office, St Dogmaels lies in a patriotic part of Wales, not

far from the town of Cardigan. At first, the Teifi, one of the best salmon rivers in the Principality, is closely followed on the B4546 for 2 miles (3km) before a plaque installed at the road end, signifies the start of the coastal footpath.

Poppit Sands and Cardigan Bar all but smother the mouth of the Teifi; in rough weather, these shallows push up acres of impressive surf. A sunken lane climbs past the Youth Hostel, and beyond Ty-canol farm a cliff path is joined at last. Rounding Cemaes Head, views extend to Cardigan Island, and on a clear day take in the entire arc of Cardigan Bay, with Plynlimon and Cader Idris visible to the north-east.

Wild flowers grow in profusion amongst gorse, bracken, broom and rough grass as the path rises to 550ft (165m) above the sea on the route's loftiest cliffs. Although some flowers thrive even in mid-winter, springtime brings an explosion of colour as species like wild foxglove, spring squill, sea campion, common spotted orchid, horseshoe vetch and the

Approaching Pwllygranant. Dinas Island can be seen top right.
(Photo: Martin Collins.)

93

ubiquitous bluebell come into bloom.

Walking south-east towards the slanting profile of Dinas Island, gradients are steep and repetitive as the path dips to cross stream valleys, rising again each time to a 200-ft (60-m) platform levelled off by the Pliocene sea 17 million years ago. This wild and windswept coast is distinguished by spectacular rock scenery, with dramatic folding visible past Cemaes Head and a mile farther on when descending from Pen-yr-afr.

Off-season or in poor weather, a clamorous seabird population softens the edge of isolation with noisy calls and aerobatics. Gulls and fulmars abound, and even choughs—those unmistakable crows with red beak and legs which are so rare elsewhere in Britain—are common on much of the Pembrokeshire coast.

A marshy field descends to Ceibwr Bay and in less than a mile, the Witches' Cauldron (Pwll-y-Wrach) is reached, a fascinating sea-cave whose roof has collapsed, forming a tiny bay and several blow-holes, spanned by the path.

Some of the hardest going on the entire walk now follows, with no drinking water or refreshment in sight. As elsewhere on the route, wooden steps are built into the stiffest gradients which would otherwise have long since become muddy scrambles. But summer bracken and brambles are a bigger obstacle, often shoulder high and in need of systematic clearing before children and casual walkers can use the path at all: slow progress on this stretch should be anticipated.

Six solitary miles (10km) high above unseen caves and arches ensue to Newport. Beyond the black recesses of Godir-rhûg and Godir-Tudor, Morfa Head is rounded, and wise is the walker who pauses here before plunging down to Newport Sands, for views are exceptionally fine. Inland, the Preseli Hills draw a knobbly moorland crest across skirts of green fields. Well known as the source of the Blue Stones of Stonehenge, controversy continues over the means by which they reached far-away Wiltshire. The whole region around the Preseli Hills is rich in pre-history from the New Stone Age, Bronze and Iron Ages, including a remarkable hill fort and hut circles on Carn Ingli, behind Newport.

Even at a distance, Newport is a pretty township of grey and white houses, across the Nevern estuary. Closer acquaintance reveals amenities of abiding interest to long-distance walkers—cafés, shops and accommodation—as well as a seasonable influx of yachting enthusiasts amd holidaymakers.

At low water, the Nevern is forded at its narrowest point, opposite the old granary on the Parrog; alternatively, the estuary is followed inland to the road bridge at Pen-y-Bont. Parrog quay was trading with Bristol as long ago as 1566, with coal and culm (anthracite dust) being imported as recently as the 1930s: however, the estuary sandbar was always a hazard.

Day 2: Newport to Fishguard

Past cottages and moored boats, the Coast Path climbs onto low cliffs, seamed with white quartz around Cat Rock. Cwms at Aber Rhigian and Aber Fforest interrupt the levellest walking so far; beaches are shingly and low tides expose wave-cut platforms from more recent geological times, the best examples in Pembrokeshire.

Dinas Island now looms ahead and in its lee, out of the harrying salt wind, hawthorn, gorse and brambles press tight against the path. Only the west wall and bell-tower of St Brynach's sailors' chapel at Cwm-yr-eglwys survived a ferocious storm in October 1859, which sank the 'Royal Charter' and 113 other ships off the Welsh coast. Today, prettified Cwm-yr-eglwys seems preoccupied with sailing and tourism.

Dinas Island became joined to the mainland a mere 8,000 years ago; before then, Cwm-Dewi (now a marshy short-cut along the island's neck) was a tidal channel. Trees give way to steep cliffs as the route ascends past Needle Rocks, a great attraction for seabirds all year round. Species likely to be seen include guillemots, cormorants, shags, herring gulls, fulmars and razorbills, the National Park

The ruins of St Brynach's sailor's chapel at Cwm-yr-Eglwys. (Photo: Martin Collins.)

symbol. Grey seals breed in the sea-caves below.

At 463ft (140m), Dinas Head (Pen-y-Fan) is a magnificent vantage point in clear weather. Behind lie Cemaes Head and Pen-yr-afr, ahead Fishguard Harbour and Strumble Head, while to the west, a shining plane of ocean reaches towards the Wicklow Mountains.

Thirst and hunger can be satisfied at Pwll Gwaelod's pub-restuarant—one of very few places of refreshment actually on the Coast Path. Then from the west end of Cwm-Dewi, cliffs are climbed and, in no time at all, the walking's wild and remote flavour has been restored. Pwll Gwylog, a diminutive, brackeny cove, is typical of numerous idyllic spots on the Pembrokeshire coast, inaccessible except on foot and well off the tourist track.

Ups and downs continue against a backdrop of marvellous cliff scenery, particularly west of Penrhyn, and as Fishguard is approached, underfoot conditions grow rockier. Throughout the route, stiles define an agreed line across private land; they are numbered south to north, the 400th being encountered hereabouts, out of a total of 478!

The little headland of Penrhynychen, with its rows of caravans and tents (and a useful shop), is quickly left behind and, turning left at a disused fort, the A487 trunk road is joined down to Fishguard's Lower Town—Cwm Abergwaun—whose unspoilt and picturesque harbour featured as the setting for the film of Dylan Thomas' *Under Milk Wood*.

Fishguard is one of only a handful of towns on the Coast Path and, with an eye on the long stretch of lonely coastline immediately ahead, walkers will wish to make use of its shops and services.

Day 3: Fishguard to Trevine

From the back of Goodwick Sands, an uninspiring climb is engaged in order to reach a housing estate before the Coast Path proper is resumed. Fishguard Harbour, blasted from precipitous cliffs at the turn of this century, received passenger liners—the prestigious 'Greyhounds of the Atlantic'—for a decade and a half, but by 1918 only the Irish services remained. Since the removal of the Cork trade to Swansea, Fishguard is left with the Rosslare Ferry alone, and a less than secure future.

The coast between Ramsey Island and St David's. (Photo: Martin Collins.)

Stone from the harbour and railway terminus excavations forms the great 2,000-ft (600m) North Breakwater, built in 1908 and clearly visible below.

Ahead lies the bare Pen-caer peninsula. It is a landscape of isolated farms, absentee holiday cottages and eroded rocky prominences—markedly different from previous terrain: Strumble Head itself is composed of layer upon layer of volcanic lava.

Stony moor and cattle pasture lead on, fly-ridden in hot weather, and several stream valleys are crossed. Headland succeeds headland and the going becomes more rugged

Cliffs and a rock arch near Fishguard. (Photo: Martin Collins.)

as Aberfelin Bay is approached, a small anchorage in the lee of Carregwasted Point. It was here that 1,200 French convicts under the command of an elderly Irish-American renegade named Tate, were put ashore on 22nd February 1797, with the avowed intention of pillaging and burning their way to Chester and Liverpool. Drunk from stolen wine, they were rounded up by the Castelmartin Yeomanry under Lord Cawdor and within 48 hours had surrendered on Goodwick Sands without a fight! A stone pillar on Careg Goffa commemorates the landing.

Soon, Strumble Head lighthouse appears, a dazzling white building connected to the mainland by footbridge. Once manned and open to visits, it is now radio-controlled from St Anne's Head. The cliff edge here is a prime site for observing seabirds in passage round the headland.

Another superb stretch of rough walking follows, with Garn Fawr a prominent feature; its summit bears one of Britain's finest Iron Age forts. Atlantic grey seals can be seen at most times of the year along the cliffs around Pwllderi, especially during the breeding season, and many seabirds frequent the area. The nearby youth hostel enjoys a truly spectacular position.

In fine conditions, Carn Ogof is a beautiful climb through blazing gorse and little rocky outcrops, with unsurpassed coastal views and flora: in rain and wind, with vision obscured by low cloud, impressions are of an exposed and unexpectedly hostile stretch. Once over the summit, however, gradients lead downhill to Pwllcrochan's empty sands and cliff folding.

High in the western sky, vapour trails converge, for the coastal walker is now beneath the main air corridor from London's Heathrow airport: 'Green 1' homing beacon lies 2 miles inland, just over the Garn hills.

A mile on, the coast road at Aber-mawr ends abruptly, washed away in recent memory by storm waves which have pushed up a shingle beach in front of exotic marsh plants at the valley mouth. Easy walking above inaccessible beaches on Mynydd Morfa follows the cliffs to Abercastle, a drowned valley harbour which was still trading in the 1920s, but is now just a beach and cottages, frequented by sub-aqua enthusiasts. Above the village stands perhaps the best known of all Pembrokeshire *cromlechau*—Carreg Sampson. Legend has it that the mighty capstone of this New Stone Age burial chamber was lifted onto its seven uprights by Sampson's little finger.

The remaining path to Trevine hugs the edge of farmland, often outside the boundary wall. Turning a corner at Pen Castell-côch, walkers are faced with the most hazardous section of path anywhere on the route, at the time of writing: not only are the cliffs high and precipitous, but cracks are continually opening along the crest to which the walker is tightly confined! Thankfully this is short-lived and a lane is soon reached rising to the quintessentially Welsh coastal village of Trevine, with its tiny shops, pub, B & Bs, youth hostel and campsite.

Day 4: Trevine to St David's

Small bays and headlands lead west for 2 miles to Porthgain harbour, surely the most evocative industrial ruin in the whole of Pembrokeshire. Until 1931, granite quarried from nearby cliffs was crushed and graded in the huge brick-built plant and shovelled down chutes into waiting steam coasters. The semi-derelict crushers, bins and adjacent brickworks invite exploration and provide the walker with a fascinating glimpse of the past: the pub and Harbour Café adding their own attractions!

Moves are sometimes made to 'tidy up' such sites, or else they are left to crumble away from erosion and neglect. Either course threatens the preservation of authentic industrial archaeology, and sensitive measures are called for to consolidate what remains at Porthgain for future generations to appreciate.

The Coast Path keeps to an old quarry tramway along the cliff tops for a while, short-cutting a promontory to Traeth-Llwyn sands. Steps to the shore were cut by Italian POWs during World War II. Quite unexpectedly, the next headland holds another surprise. Porthgain Slate Quarries, unable to compete with those at Caernarvon, closed in 1904 and a connecting passage to the sea was blasted out to form a sheltered anchorage for local fishermen. In some lights, the deep, chemically-blue lagoon is hauntingly beautiful.

Aber-Eiddy Bay is excavated in black Ordovician shales, its sombre grey beach susceptible to marine erosion, the hamlet itself huddled against the west wind. Recent easier going is now interrupted by some sizeable gullies, whilst ahead rears Penbiri, one of the massive volcanic intrusions which have shadowed the coast since the Pen-caer peninsula, and now culminate in the broad thrust of St David's Head. There is a moorland wildness on these seaward slopes; hills seem rugged and high, yet rise to no more than 600ft (200m) above a low, craggy landscape. These volcanic 'monednocks' would have been islands when the sea level was 200ft (60m) higher.

Brambles are left behind for open walking in impressive surroundings as the path approaches Carnllidi. A climb to its stony 595-ft

The silent remains of a once thriving stone-crushing industry at Porthgain harbour. (Photo: Martin Collins.)

(181-m) summit is recommended, for not only is the topography of St David's peninsula laid out map-like below, but in clear weather the great sweep of St Bride's Bay unfolds to the south. When the bracken is not too high, tiny fields of the Bronze Age Celts are discernible on Carnllidi's seaward flanks, contrasting with the acres of plastic sheeting which blight today's agricultural landscape.

Choughs breed hereabouts and an occasional peregrine falcon might be spotted. Wild flowers, too, embroider banks and levels—a delight indeed for the coastal walker. But St David's Head, with its vicious offshore rocks, is an unforgiving place to mariners and has claimed a heavy toll from shipping.

Right on the point itself are eight stone hut circles, served by ancient trackways and guarded by a stone barrier across the Head. Finds from this superb Iron Age promontory fort, including loom weights and blue beads, can be seen in Tenby Museum. It is pertinent to recall that this peninsula was the end of the known world for the medieval English, and a centre of Christianity long before Canterbury. The railway never came to St David's, which remained isolated until the advent of the motor car.

As the south-bound walker descends towards Whitesand bay (Porth-mawr), he is transported swiftly back to the 20th century.

Close by the site of St Patrick's chapel are car park, beach shop and toilets serving a magnificent expanse of sand and surf, and in the summer season, holidaymakers will be out in force. Nearby are a youth hostel and the road to St David's, only 2 miles (3km) distant, but to reach St David's from the peninsula's beautiful southern arm, provides 2 or 3 hours more of magnificent walking.

A broad, grassy path, flanked by purple bog heather, leads round Point St John, and there lies Ramsey island, less than a mile away across the Sound. This restless channel is torn by a tidal race of up to 6 knots, excitingly close to the path. The island's 600 acres of rough grazing are no longer profitable and today, seabirds and seals are the main inhabitants, viewed by boatloads of summer visitors.

The ruinous, overgrown remains of St Justinian's chapel on private land at Porthstinan are eclipsed by a picturesque Lifeboat Station and slipway, dating from 1912 and hugging steep cliffs below the path.

Climbing east to the headland above Mrs Morgan's Cave (who she was, no-one knows!), a major landmark on the walk is reached. This is the northern extremity of St Bride's Bay, a huge bite out of Pembrokeshire's seaboard, almost three sides of a square to Skomer Island and Marloes Peninsula. Peeping incongruously above a pastoral landscape to the south-east are the tall chimneys of Milford Haven's oil refineries.

Thrift, squill, wild thyme, campion and crowsfoot embellish this rugged section with colour and delicacy, while the pungent odour of sheep lies heavily on the air. In spring sunshine, Porthlysgi Bay is a visual feast— yellow gorse against a translucent turquoise sea—but its beach is too rocky and out-of-the-way for most tastes.

Porthclais was once St David's port, and though little was left by the 1800s, steam coasters continued to bring coal for the gasworks (now a car park). There is a good choice of accommodation in which to end the day around St David's—be it campsite, guesthouse or hotel—and with some 20 miles (32km) behind him, the walker will doubtless prefer to leave the delights of this miniscule city to a fresh day.

Day 5: St David's to Broad Haven

St David's is hardly more than village-sized. Set apart from its cluster of shops and tea-rooms is the cathedral, its nave sloping dramatically towards the east end. It lies in a hollow adjacent to the lovely ruin of the Bishop's Palace, and is well worth seeing.

Stone to build the cathedral was quarried from around Caerfi Bay and more of the chocolate-purple Cambrian sandstone is revealed beyond the spectacular Iron Age fort on Penpleidiau, at Caerbwdi Bay.

Coves are inaccessible from Morfa Common, and the eye is drawn to Solva's uppermost houses ranged on the skyline ahead. The high-pitched wine of jets taking off and landing at RAF Brawdy, like bees at a hive, is an unwelcome intrusion, never more so than in its immediate vicinity between here and Newgale.

A big drop to Porth-y-Rhaw, with its disused mill buildings and good Iron Age fort, is followed by high, loose cliffs, home to gorse and rabbits. Two tugs were wrecked here some 5 years ago and have since become jammed tight into jaws of rock by successive tides and storms. A steep way down the sloping cliff has been worn by sightseers, and if conditions are favourable it is a worthwhile scramble.

Despite a tricky entrance, especially in southerly gales, Solva's harbour is the best on St Bride's Bay and in the early 19th century the little port thrived. Today, even if narrow congested streets and a veneer of tourism dissipate its 'Welsh-ness' in summer, Solva is a lovely village and a delight for the visiting walker.

The jagged Dinas-fawr and Dinas-fach headlands herald some hefty down-and-ups over stream valleys, before the vast sweep of Newgale Sands appears, backed by a pebbly storm beach. Shops, cafés and campsites huddle uneasily on low ground behind. At its south end, remains of Trafrane Cliff Colliery are still evident, though it ceased production in 1905. This is the western perimeter of the Pembrokeshire coalfield, yielding best Welsh anthracite; extraction dates back to the 15th century and there are still an estimated 230 millions tons of unworked reserves.

Scenically, the stretch to Broad Haven is less imposing. Until a few years ago, the path was overgrown and dangerously crumbling, but has since been improved. Beyond beaches at Nolton and Druidston Havens are several little rocky bays and sea-level ledges accessible from the path. Settling Nose, a shaly blade of cliff conspicuous from afar, is followed by a fine natural arch known as Haroldston Bridge, and a vast landslip. Thereafter, a well-tramped track leads gently down to sprawling Broad Haven's recently improved sea-front.

Day 6: Broad Haven to Dale

At all but the lowest tides, lanes have to be walked to Little Haven, bracken and brambles giving way to woods of oak, ash, hazel,

blackthorn and even pine along sheltered north-facing slopes near Talbenny—some of the tallest trees on the Coast Path. Borough Head's rock is Pre-Cambrian, the oldest in the world, but a mile or two on, there is a sudden junction with Old Red Sandstone, the re-maining walk to St Bride's Haven being on Devon-red ground above low cliffs the colour of dried blood.

St Bride's Haven, named after a 6th-century Irish saint, is a tiny hamlet and chapel with no amenities for the walker. The extraordinary

Dinas Fawr (middle distance) as seen from the entrance to Solva's natural harbour. (Photo: Martin Collins.)

99

Gothic Kensington Hospital, now a rest home, is surrounded by lawns and gardens, in sharp contrast to natural cliff scenery. A few yards north of the limekiln, 6th to 10th-century stone coffins appear in an eroded cliff.

A substantial boundary wall harbouring plants and lichens is followed round Nab's Head, seaward of the disused MOD. bombing range. Unreachable coves lead on to Musslewick Sands, but the beach is a narrow one and it is easy to get cut off by a rising tide. Marloes village lies just inland, reached up field tracks.

The islands of Skomer and Skokholm are both renowned bird sanctuaries and Nature Reserves, inextricably linked with the naturalist R.M. Lockley, who not only lived on Skokholm from 1927–40, but was instrumental in setting up the West Wales Naturalists' Trust and in mapping out the Pembrokeshire Coast for the National Parks Commission.

Once farmed, but now owned by WWNT, Skomer is reached by boats leaving Martin's Haven on summer mornings. Walkers who circumvent Deer Park (no deer would survive here!) are afforded closer views of bays facing Jack Sound, where grey seals give birth to their pups in late September/October. This tidal race is more dangerous still than Ramsey Sound, Black Stones and The Bench adding to navigational hazards.

Skokholm, too, is famous for its colonies of gulls, petrels, guillemots, shearwaters, puffins and razorbills, but visits are by prior arrangement only. The waters surrounding these islands are likely to become a Marine Nature Reserve.

At low water, the remains of the paddle steamer 'Albion' protrude from the sands, and Gateholme Island is accessible, bearing the marks of ancient hut groups. We have left behind the southernmost horn of St Bride's Bay, and from Deer Park to St Anne's Head is some of the levellest and most pleasant walking on the entire route. Campsites and a youth hostel at Runwayskiln offer several options for a night's halt.

Skirting the foundations of an erstwhile Fleet Air Arm station, a momentary descent is made to the neck of the Dale Peninsula—part of the Ritec Fault, in pre-glacial times a sea-channel and now a short cut to Dale village. Some badly eroded stretches by more disused MOD land above Welshman's Bay are negotiated, and soon St Anne's Head lighthouse is reached.

On the headland itself, gale force winds are recorded regularly and gusts of up to 90mph are not uncommon. St Anne's head is a vital beacon to shipping entering Milford Haven, but it also signifies a change in the character of the Coast Path, which hereafter grows more sheltered and agricultural for a while before penetrating a major industrial complex.

West Blockhouse, a large, disintegrating fort, is one of nine constructed in the Haven against a feared French invasion: they were never used and became known as 'Palmerston's Follies'. Dale Fort Field Centre in a Victorian barracks heads a road down to Dale, a yachting centre of some note, but in other ways an unremarkable place which, nonetheless, will be of interest to walkers seeking accommodation or supplies.

Day 7: Dale to Pembroke

At Pickleridge, old gravel pits from the Dale aerodrome construction provide saltings for waders, duck, snipe and other species. Stepping stones and a slimy wooden bridge are exposed 2 hours each side of low water at The Gann, and walkers are advised to consult tide tables, for another similar crossing ahead could also bar progress. Happily, it is possible to manage both, plus the intervening walking, within the low-tide span.

Monk Haven, a landing place since Neolithic times, precedes more transit beacons and easy walking round Great Castle Head to Sandy Haven. Here, a line of slippery stone blocks is crossed, again at low tide. The Haven's deep-water channel is narrow, the oil terminal jetties correspondingly long, and the whole complex of dun-coloured storage tanks and chimneys which soon dominate the scene form a startling counterpoint to the route so far. As the Esso refinery is approached, the path ducks beneath steaming pipes amid oily fumes right at the edge of the National Park and turns up into Hakin, thence to Milford Haven.

A prime example of a 'ria', or drowned river valley, the Haven was claimed by Nelson to be the finest natural harbour in Europe, but it was not developed until the 1800s. Built on a grid-iron plan by Charles Greville, nephew of Sir William Hamilton, Milford Haven's fortunes have been mixed. With the expected transatlantic liner trade never materialising, and fishing in decline, the oil industry gave a much needed boost to the local economy.

Even some National Park rangers advise taking a bus from here to Pembroke, and some walkers might wish to resume the Coast Path at Angle, missing out the least pleasing section altogether. To reach Pembroke, there is much road walking in a flat, urban landscape, through the unprepossessing town of Neyland and across the Cleddau road bridge. Only afficionados of ships and oil installations will enjoy the way on foot!

Days 8 and 9: Pembroke to Bosherton

Pembroke Dock, in the mould of Chatham or Portsmouth, was a Royal Dockyard until it was closed down in 1926, bringing great hardship to the community. Pembroke itself, appropriately-sited capital of a maritime county, has a fine 13th-century castle—the birthplace of Henry Tudor—which is now maintained by the state.

Overgrown in places and inadequately way-marked, the route follows a miserable course past farms and electricity pylons to Angle Bay. Nowhere else has the spirit of the Pembrokeshire Coast Path been so nearly lost, yet in a few short miles, some of its most beautiful parts are encountered.

Steep undulations relent towards the Texaco refinery and the CEGB's great oil-fired power station at Pwllcrochan, but there is little significant improvement until Popton Fort, occupied since 1961 by BP. Thereafter, a road and the shoreline of Angle Bay are walked, awkward at high tide but a rich habitat for many duck and wader species.

At Angle, the hulks of old wooden sailing ships are juxtaposed with modern dinghies, the feudal grouping of colour-washed cottages with summer cars and holidaymakers. Provisions and accommodation may be obtained here, and the Old Point Inn is a popular watering-hole, suggesting an end to a short 11-mile (17-km) day: amenities at Bosherton are 16 miles (26km) farther on.

Emerging from tunnels of undergrowth above the old Lifeboat Station, there are wide vistas over the Haven. The impregnable Thorn Island just offshore, once matched with Dale Fort across the water, is now an hotel. Steep, open cliffs above big drops, and several fine bays, characterise the Angle Peninsula, but there are wartime relics too: gun emplacements, lookouts and a disused airfield inland.

The same Old Red Sandstone of which St Anne's head and Skokholm are composed will be recognised here in precipitous cliff-face contortions, and soon Freshwater West stretches ahead, an invigorating Atlantic beach with dunes and jetsam. Bathing is quite dangerous, sands to the south giving way to wave-cut rock platforms.

Walkers are denied access from Gupton Burrows round Linney Head by the Castlemartin Army tank ranges, and even the stretch from Flimston Down to St Govan's Head—4 miles (6km) of great interest and quality—is closed during firing practice: Bosherton post office and the local press display advance notice of dates and times.

Hapless walkers arriving at the wrong hour face an 8-mile (13-km) road bash through the forlorn village of Castlemartin, flanked by endless 'Danger Keep Out' signs. During the winter, Preseli sheep graze shabby pastures which in summer support cattle and a voracious population of clegs!

Should the ranges be open, a road south from Warren Camp emerges at Flimston Down opposite the two spectacular Elegug Stacks and the Green Bridge of Wales, a broad natural arch at the start of an exhilarating section. This is limestone country, fashioned by the elements into an exciting succession of caves, arches, inlets, stacks and blowholes. Seabirds and wild flowers abound, and the walking is over flat grass atop the ancient 200-ft (60-m) wave platform. The cliffs are popular with rock climbers.

St Govan's chapel, a tiny 13th-century building on the site of a 5th-century hermit's cell, huddles in a cleft threaded by steep stone steps—an inspiring situation! Above, inland

The lighthouse at St Ann's Head. (Photo: Martin Collins.)

101

Solva. (Photo: Martin Collins.)

tronised and can seem a little tatty: not so the picturesque castle, wherein was born Gerald of Wales and which repays a visit. More military ranges around Shrinkle Camp impose a 2-mile (3-km) detour via Lydstep village and a reunion with the coast at Lydstep Haven; standing with one's back to serried ranks of caravans, it is a pleasant enough place, all shingle between dipping rock strata, and famous for its caves.

Blowholes, discarded shell-cases and round-mouthed snails are all found on open cliffs leading to Giltar Point and a momentous turning into Carmarthen Bay: for the first time, the coast ahead lies beyond Pembrokeshire.

Tenby's long, pebbly strand provides fast walking opposite Caldey Island, where seashells crunch underfoot, until at last the esplanade is reached. Tenby's origins date back to the Middle Ages when it became an important fish market and strategic harbour. There are several fine old buildings, a museum of great interest to the coastal walker, and another 'Palmerston Folly' on St Catherine's Island. The town, however, now relies exclusively on tourism which, echoing fluctuations in the nation's economy, hardly guarantees a secure living for its inhabitants. Most walkers would call a halt here, leaving the final 6 miles (10km) for another short day.

Waterwynch Lane heads quickly for countryside, the Coast Path undulating relentlessly in and out of woods and climbing to 250ft (75m) at Monkstone Point. Idyllic beaches below are subject to treacherous currents. Further ups and downs, much of the way overgrown, bring the walker out at Saundersfoot, once an industrial enclave manufacturing iron, bricks and mining anthracite (the same measures as those in St Bride's Bay), and now geared to tourism and yachting. Coppet Hall colliery tunnel, originally used by the Coast Path, is liable to closure owing to cliff-falls, and a detour forces the route steeply up through woodland.

Amroth beach was the scene of dress rehearsals in 1943 for the Normandy Landings, and for a short while was inundated with troops and military leaders. At very low tides, the remains of a fossil forest are uncovered. Past Amroth's undistinguished seafront castle, journey's end is reached at the border with Carmarthen, as it was once known, but the conclusion of this fascinating walk will be in all probability a wistful glance back towards the western horizon.

from the inevitable car park and picnic area, a lane leads to Bosherton, teeming with tourists in summer but offering refreshment, supplies and limited accommodation.

Days 10 and 11: Bosherton to Amroth

Bosherton's famous lily-ponds are crossed on narrow walkways and the coast is regained at Broad Haven's dunes. More delightful, flat-topped cliffs follow, sculpted into monumental caves and chasms; Stackpole Head juts into the sea 1^1/2 miles (2^1/2km) ahead like a ship's prow. Barafundle Bay is an exquisite spot reached by foot and unfrequented; her white sands and translucent waters are reminiscent of the Mediterranean. Beyond Stackpole Quay, a former limestone quarry and tiny harbour, old red sandstone recurs, with offshore stacks and a marvellous Iron Age promontory fort on Greenala Point.

Lack of co-ordinated planning—even, one feels, of plain concern for the environment—has resulted in visual squalor at Freshwater East, as a miscellany of chalets, bungalows and apartments disfigure the dune hinterland. Swanlake Bay, a mile on amidst much vertical folding, has no motorable access and is unspoilt.

In high season, Manorbier is heavily pa-

Walk 11 IRELAND: Europe's Furthest Point West by Hamish M. Brown

Through the Peninsula from Tralee to Dingle

The Dingle Peninsula reaches out into the Atlantic further than any other mainland spot in Europe and while this gives it a certain romantic fascination it also ensures a close relationship with Atlantic weather, an association which guarantees a certain meteorological excitability.

Nevertheless it is the romance that wins. The peninsula, hoary with legends, peppered with antiquities, bloodied by history, is still part of the *Gaeltacht;* it is rich in culture and literature and its stern quietness appeals to many people. Corkaquiney has spectacular strands, cliffs and mountains. Poets sing its praises. Bran-

don, mountain of saint and sinner, is spellbinding. The Slieve Mish Mountains bear the name of legendary heroes. To walk along these heights is as fine a tramp as you will find in Europe's offshore islands—so long as the weather is fine.

The weather can be diabolical but when it smiles, between showers, or gives a crisp day in autumn or a pulsing summer heatwave, the landscape quality is unique. It has something to do with the light, the vast skyscapes, and the big sea. This is gentle watercolour country, not the harsh world of southern acrilite. It is not going abroad but coming home—to a slower, saner, kindlier world where wind and tide and sun and storm are at the centre of life.

Brandon Mountain. (Photo: Hamish Brown.)

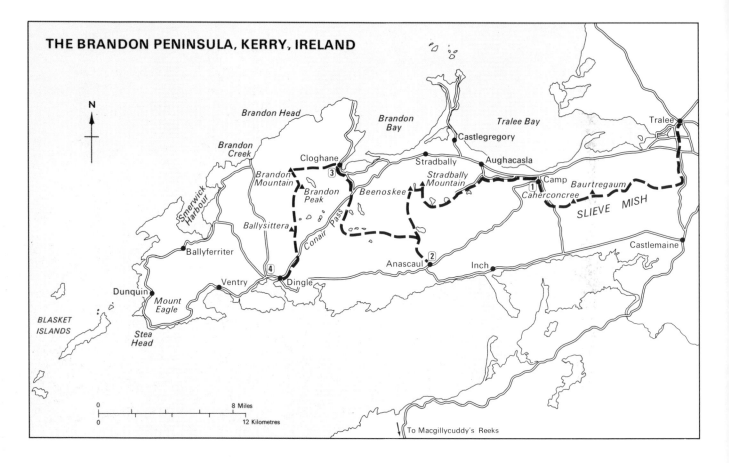

THE BRANDON PENINSULA, KERRY, IRELAND

Distance: Approx 108km (76 miles).
Time Required: 3–5 days.
Type of Walk: Mountain terrain but usually grass underfoot. Good navigational skills essential.
Base: Tralee or Dingle, Country Kerry, Ireland.
Start: Tralee.
Finish: Dingle.
Best time of Year: April–September (July–August less good as tourist season).
Map: OS Half Inch to Mile. Sheet 20. Dingle Bay.
Guidebook: *Irish Peaks*, edited J Lynam (Constable).

Tralee is the principal trading and commercial town of Kerry so has good shops and facilities. It has road and rail links with the rest of Ireland; there is a wide range of accommodation and there is a tourist office. It is the natural place to start, just as Brandon is the natural place to finish. The walk is quite strenuous in its way and the fickle weather combined with some complex country (inadequately mapped) make it unsuitable for the novice, nor would I recommend it as a camping trip. The going is hard enough without a massive pack.

Tralee and Dingle are the only towns. In between there are scattered hamlets and limited facilities. A disproportionate amount of space therefore goes in describing lowland problems rather than the mountains above (if you are going up mountains I assume you can cope with mountains). If you can arrange a friend and car to back you up this would simplify things enormously, doing away, for instance, with all accommodation and transport worries, allowing ample spare clothes to be available and making wet-weather breaks possible. Many people however will be alone or set on self-sufficiency, so for them the details are given as needed. Local information is constantly changing so do write to the Tralee

Tourist Office, Arus Siamsa, Godfrey Place, Tralee, Co Kerry (tel: 066-21288) and obtain the current local guide to visitor services. They stock the necessary maps and can send a timetable of the lifeline Tralee–Dingle bus service (or contact CIE, 066-21211). Three is the advised maximum size for a party but two is probably better if obtaining accommodation en route. It would be advisable to book a day ahead on the walk to ensure accommodation as options are limited.

Two words of warning. The arms of Irish signposts may well be changed by wind or naughty hands so check and double check on the map. The map requires the other warning. The only map of any use is the Ordnance Survey (Phoenix Park, Dublin) Sheet No 20, *Dingle Bay* at an antique Half Inch to the Mile Scale. But even this is inaccurate and out of date, so all your map-and-ground skills of navigation will be needed. Without reducing the walk to a step-by-step Way I've tried to indicate any special problems in the text.

Tralee is a cheerful sort of town. There are few really old buildings (thanks to Cromwell) but there are some notable Victorian municipal buildings (Ashe Memorial Hall), monuments and churches (St John's especially), mostly just off the busy main street. The

The Slieve Mish mountains rise over Tralee at the start of the walk. (Photo: Hamish Brown.)

houses are colourful, there is a fine park, and plenty of entertainment. The Tourist Office is on the road signposted for Dingle, in the Siamsa Theatre building, opposite the Dominican Church (worth a visit). Accommodation on that street ranges from pub to luxury hotel and there are several bungalows/farmhouses offering B & B out on the road we take to the mountains.

Day 1

The walk starts from the Tourist Office to the well-signposted junction. The Dingle road swings right, but ours, advertised by signs for accommodation and 'Viewing Park 4¼' goes straight on. It is fairly obvious on the map. A sign indicates that our road up the hill is 'unsafe for horse caravans'. The view grows with every step and the narrow road wends up above a deep, wooded glen to gain the peat-shorn moors above. There is a last lonely crofthouse and a lonelier new house, then the road goes on over the pass (with a small car park, just before the crown of the pass), giving a fine view back to the Tralee side.

There are two alternatives to this beginning.

One is just to walk up past the Viewing Park (which postpones wet feet by an hour or two) and then turn west along the crest of the hills from a new road from the top of the pass. The other alternative for those keen to leave the road is to drop down into the glen, leaving the road just before a small gravel pit/quarry on the left, aiming for the obvious junction of streams and following the western one up into the hills past Scota's (or Scotia's) Grave, a large slab in the ground, covered in graffiti.

At the top of the pass an unsurfaced road leads off, servicing two new communication aerials and ending at a concrete *kasbah* beyond which one takes to the moor. This building and The Iron Man further on can be seen as you walk out of Tralee. Over the first rise is a row of new butts but after that there is only a great deal of nothing—and soon you are shocked at the map's inadequacies. One would assume a steady rise from the map but there are several sections of downhill going and many bumps to go up and down. I was very pleased to reach the first indicated spot, the 1814ft (553m) top. As it was a bare grassy dome, featureless and without a cairn, I wasn't even sure of that till a

105

break in the cloud showed The Iron Man on the next knoll. (This is the local nickname for a square telephone reflector and the odd poles you may have seen along the northern rim are there to help maintenance staff to find it!) Some brief clearances allowed me to see the limestone-green plains below and Knockauncorragh, 1863ft (568m), ahead across a dip of ochrous autumn bog. Up to this peak the going is generally on easy grass and close heather but thereafter the peaks rise into the bleaker heights over 2,000ft (600m). The bare bones of old red sandstone jut forth in prows and crags and are eroded into deep coombes and corries. It becomes stark and grand, a moated highway fit for heroes.

The scenery steps up a gear after Glanbrack Mountain (2,165ft, 660m), and the final surge up Baurtregaum (2,766ft, 843m) the highest of the Slieve Mish mountains.

Not surprisingly it is one of the best viewpoints in the land, the view reaching north to the Aran Islands and south to Carrauntoohil and the peaks of the Iveragh peninsula.

Baurtregaum means the summit of the three glens. We have just arrived with one, the Curraheen, biting in to the northern flanks, running east and then turning north down to Tralee Bay. The finest is the Derrymore Glen between this peak and Gearhane which holds three paternoster lakes at its head. From the col to Caherconcree (2,713ft, 827m), a bad-weather escape could be made down to the lakes (some boulders and crags). Caherconcree is an even better viewpoint for the view west is no longer blocked. There are several worthwhile ridges and coombes to explore but the most interesting takes you from the small summit cairn down the south-west ridge to visit the prehistoric promontory fort of the same name. It is a natural defensive spur at about 2,000ft (600m) with the open east side barred by a big 1,150-ft (350-m) long wall; a fantastic setting which not surprisingly has acquired a mass of legends. Such iron age forts are common by the sea, rarer inland and astonishing at 2,000ft (600m). It can be seen from many miles away.

The fort was probably constructed about 500 BC but the legends are of the first century AD and, oddly, concerned with the Red Branch heroes of Ulster. Curoi MacDaire was the local king here when Conor MacNessa ruled in Ulster. Curoi fell out with one of King Conor's men (Cuchulainn) over a princess whom they both loved. King Curoi had won the princess as a prize for helping King Conor, but the princess loved Cuchulainn. As King Curoi built a house in the fort for the princess, so Cuchulainn camped below (hence the place

name Camp) awaiting the princess's signal to attack. The signal was that the princess should empty a large quantity of milk into the Finglas river, turning it white (Finglas means white stream). Cuchulainn's attack was successful and he killed everyone but King Curoi's bard who later entertained the lovers on top of a cliff, seized the princess and leapt with her to their death in the ocean below.

Nearby are two stones that are also connected with legends. One is known as Naisi's Grave, Naisi being the ill-fated lover of the doomed Deirdre, Deirdre of the sorrows, one of the most moving of the Ulster stories. The second is Scota's Stone. Scota was daughter of a pharoah, who with daughters-in-law Fas and Mish and many warriors attacked the magical earliest inhabitants of Ireland (the Tuatha De Danann). They won, but at the cost of many lives. Years later, Scota was buried here, Fas was buried in the Finglas Glen and Mish somewhere else in the hills which bear her name.

From these realms of fancy we leave the heights to simply go down the spur below the fort to reach the road over the mountains at Beheenagh. The trees on the map have long gone, so aim for the highest roadside house. (In bad weather, an easier descent can be made following a line of red and white posts from the road. The only low-level alternative is to walk out by Blannerville and along the road—a 'Dingle Way' is planned along the lower slopes of the hills). The walk down to the hamlet of Camp by the road on the western side of the Finglas Valley gives striking views up to the fort and the ragged crest of Caherconcree known as Gearhane.

If you pass that bend where the road bridges the Finglas River and go up the east-bank road 50 yards you'll see the remains of a railway viaduct, part of the Tralee and Dingle railway which opened in 1891. Its tight curves and steep gradients made it slow and accident-prone. Here on Whit Monday 1893 a train carrying pigs and one coach of passengers crashed when its brakes failed. The passenger coach stuck on the parapet but three crew—and all the pigs—perished. There was an outcry about the pigs. The line only ran a goods service after the war and closed in 1953.

You will by now have noticed the luxuriant growth of plants wherever there is shelter. Hedgerows are a tangle of brambles, fuschia, holly and ash and the fields are dotted with flowers. This mild corner has several plants only found in Spain, the Lusitanian Flora as it is called. It also marks the fauna with birds like the chough. The commonest bird on high is the raven but you will put up plenty of snipe and

The Brandon Range from
Stradbally Mountain. (Photo:
Hamish Brown.)

maybe woodcock. Magpies, hoodie crows and garden birds feed lower down. Kerry also has its own species of slug.

Camp is a scattered hamlet. Ashe's Restaurant at the cross roads does bar meals during the day and dinners at night but there are only two local B & Bs, and the only other accommodation is the Tralee Bay Hotel one hour's walk along the coast road at Aughacasla. In some ways the easiest answer is simply to catch the bus to Dingle where there is a wide range of accommodation and an early bus back to Camp next day.

Day 2

From Camp on Day Two we head west to the road up the Owencashla Valley, with Stradbally Mountain very much dominating the view. Off season the 'main' road along to Aughacasla is safe enough but rather dull and I'd recommend the tiny lanes linking the houses at the foot of the hills, especially in July and August. A walk along the main road to a cross roads (not shown on the map) but distinguished by a signpost (often pointing the wrong way) saying 'Anchor Caravan Park' leads to a turn left. If you run your eyes down the left skyline of Stradbally Mountain you can just see it rise in a distinctive spur. That is where you hope to be in a couple of hours. Take care not to head off up into the wrong glen. Visibility can be restricted by the fuschia hedges! Aughacasla has a good shop and the road up from there is further west with a telephone box and picnic place sign at the junction.

Our quiet road up into the Owencashla Valley becomes steadily more dramatic as the hills close in on either side. Stradbally Mountain loses its distant dome-shape and its flanks are seen as sweeping curves of bare strata. The prominent spur now juts out into the head of

107

Loch Slat and Lough Caum from Stradbally mountain. (Photo: Hamish Brown.)

the valley, with a surprising waterfall coursing down its right side. The proper name for the glen is Glanteenassig, the *glen of the waterfalls*.

All the coombes of this valley of lakes have been swamped with forestry plantings (shown vaguely only on the most recent map) and this planting both hinders and helps our route. Where a stream comes down, left, in another sliding fall from between Doon and Gammeen there is a notice saying 'No Through Road' (the track wends on up to a house) but we turn right onto the Forestry Services road which wends its way through the trees of the Glenteenassig Park with various picnic places and walks and views indicated. Loch Slat is passed (but not seen) and the road pulls up to Lough Caum and its feeder, the Doo Lough, with the spur and its flanking fall now just across the water.

The road ahead is marked 'Cul de Sac' and barred, but soon we come to a track signposted to the lake. We skirt the edge of the water, left, to reach the short stream between the lakes and boulder-hop across. Even after wet weather there is usually no problem. Our goal

is the craggy prow opposite where we skirt right, then, above the first crag, traverse left. An easy heather gully runs right to the top. The alternative is to take the road to its boggy end and fight out to escape up the headwall by yet another waterslide; a route I'd only recommend to my enemies. It is *not* an easy option, while the prow is only pretending to be difficult. The only reason to go right up the glen is to make a col-crossing to Anascaul if the weather has turned nasty.

From the prow the route drops to cross the stream of the fall and tackles the bulk of Stradbally Mountain proper. The heathery way up is defined by the curve of cliff to the right and leads to Stradbally's stony summit (2,627ft, 800m). As you reach the flatter summit area look out for odd rifts in the ground. The highest point is actually Beenoskee (2,713ft, 827m) a third of a mile west across a low saddle, but Stradbally is my favourite viewpoint and, as you can see, gives a fabulous view to the whole Brandon range with the dark 'eye' of Lough Acummeen below our feet, backed by the cliffs of Beenoskee, and with the great strands separating Brandon Bay and Tralee Bay edged with Atlantic rollers. In the showery days of autumn the colours and textures are startling.

The route wanders round to Beenoskee, where we study tomorrow's route, and then goes down the big south-west shoulder to pick up the track crossing the saddle, linking Ballyduff and Anascaul. This wends down to Lough Anscaul where it becomes a tarred road. It has largely disappeared on the saddle but is useful and clear on the slopes either side of the pass. The hills beyond Lough Anscaul are full of sites and stories associated with Cuchulainn. He and a giant spent a week chucking boulders at each other from the hills on opposite sides of the lake and when the hero groaned on being hit, the girl involved, Scal Ni Mhurnain, thinking him slain, drowned herself in the lake. The hour's walk down to Anascaul village gives a sample of a countryside that has hardly changed in centuries. It is very beautiful.

(A wet-weather substitute day would be to walk up from Camp and through to Knockbrack and the road under Knockmore and so down to Inch Strand, one of the finest beaches anywhere and a magical spot. Stay at the Strand Hotel or continue through by Knockafeehane to Anascaul, where there is ample guest house accommodation.)

The South Pole Inn (now only a pub) owes its name to local lad Tom Crean who went with Scott to the Antarctic (he was one of the party who found Scott's body) and shared with Shackleton, another Irishman, in the epic boat journey that is one of the greatest of all adventure stories. He set up the inn on retirement.

Those with only three days available could descend to Cloghane from Beenoskee, going over Coumbaun and Beenatoar and off its south ridge to the head of the remarkable Glennahoo valley, or simply descend off Beenoskee to the saddle and take the zig-zag track from it down into the glen.

Day 3

We wander back up the road for Lough Anscaul to start Day Three but before reaching the gate/cattle grid on the road turn up the hillside for Knockmulanane, (1,953ft, 595m). Shortly after the route angles right to follow up the edge of the Carrigblagher Cliffs, that shattered hollow that looks down on Lough Anscaul. It is an easy if steep pull up and, once high, the walking is never taxing and the feeling of space is exhilarating, flagged as it is with greens below, tawny browns around and blue and white overhead—the primary

colours of a gala. A straightforward ridge leads to Banoge North (2,094ft, 638m) and the drop to Windy Gap. There are lochs on both sides of it and lochs seem to be tucked in on all the many levels of the layered landscape to the north.

The necklace of pools—the Paternoster Lakes—on the way up Brandon. (Photo: Hamish Brown.)

A track, built for unknown reasons (it's not a peat/turf road), angles down and skirts the ridge to the north. We climb up from the Gap to Gowlane Beg (2,134ft, 650m) and a huge empty landscape beyond: grassy and littered with decaying peat hags. It is well worth going out to Croaghskearda (2,001ft, 610m) for this is a commanding prow with superlative views. The Reeks show well and Mount Eagle and the Blasket Islands point to the furthest west of Ireland.

In mist this can be confusing country (I talk from experience) but the Conair (Conor) Pass, with cliffs falling to it in wild array, is a fairly broad target. The aim is for Slievanea, (2,026ft, 618m) from which you can just see down to the head of the pass. By skirting the cliffs westwards easy grass slopes lead down to the Pass (1,392ft, 424m).

From there there are several options, but it is best to avoid the tarred road as much as possible. It is narrow and traffic makes it dangerous for pedestrians. Instead about 150 yards/metres down the road careful observation will pick out the tight zig-zag of the old pack-route coming up to the wall supporting the road. This can be followed parallel to, but safe from, the motor road, or it can be left to descend a new bulldozed track down to Cloghane Lough and the quiet road down the west side of the Owenmore River to Cloghane. The outflow from the lake can be difficult so it is best to go round its head and cross the Owenmore near Lough Gal.

On a good day it is possible to stay high and from Slievanea head move east along the coombe-bitten cliff tops. There are some remarkable deep-set glaciated tarns hidden in the coombes below. Turn up the big dome of hill, neither named nor given a height, which has Lough Camclaun below its eastern cliffs, the way then descends its long ridge towards Kilmore Lodge. It is worth a rough deviation to look up Lough Adoon. The valley headwall has a big waterslide. The walk down to Cloghane is no anticlimax: Brandon Peak and Brandon Mountain grab the skyline and the scents and sounds of the sea welcome us to the village, where we spend the night.

Day 4

The problem with Brandon is knowing how to tackle it to gain the maximum interest. It is not a hill you can explore in a single visit but at least a traverse doubles the initial experience. There is a walled shrine on the hillside above Faha, the starting place for pilgrimages up Brandon, hence the Pilgrims' Route for the track we follow on Day Four. It used to be marked with signs such as one sees on a highway, and in the triangle are the words 'Aire. Cnoc Gear.' (Attention. Dangerous Hill.) The dangers are of mishap rather than difficult navigation for there is soon a well-marked track and, though the scenery is spectacular, going astray is much less likely than on the first day over the featureless moors. New red and white posts mark the route and someone has unnecessarily added arrows to indicate a path which is perfectly clear anyway.

The path climbs up through fields almost onto the crest and then flanks along under the East Ridge of Brandon (see below) to gain the inner heart of the great south-east corrie, a glacier-scarred hollow with its sandstone strata bared and glittering with scores of pools. The main drainage tumbles down from lake to lake to reach the Owenmore River which is overhung by the cliffs and prows of Brandon Peak which, at 2,764ft (842m) often appears higher than Brandon Mountain (3,127ft, 953m) for it is a sharp peak against the tamer, rounded mountain. The crags are hung with flowers, among them St Patrick's Cabbage, the wild version of Nancy Pretty or London Pride.

From the back of the corrie the path zig-zags up in dramatic fashion, following the curve of the sandstone strata, to gain a col a quarter of a mile north of the summit. This can be a windy col so it is often as well to eat before popping out onto the exposed upper reaches. On a good day the view, suddenly revealed, is a spectacular mix of land and sea forms. An easy ridge, but with the big cliff on the left, leads to the summit. It too has been needlessly cluttered with posts and paint.

Now for the alternatives, which are all interesting, and harder. From Cloghane you can walk up the quiet road that leads to Loch Gal, south of Brandon Peak. A clear track crosses the pass above (between the peaks of Gearhane and Ballysittera) and is our bad-weather alternative if Dingle *has* to be reached. As this road nears the big cliffs we turn up the road beside the stream which drains Lough Avoonane. It passes a farm and ends at the loch's outflow. By contouring round to Lough Cruttia (Harp Lake) and then up to Lough Nalacken (Duck Lake) we can climb, layer by layer, by slab and scree and squelch and waterfall, to eventually join the Pilgrims' Route in the innermost heart of Coumaknock. This route up is not tracked and gives rough going, but the scenery is on a grand scale.

The most exciting route of all, however, is to follow the East Ridge which is the skyline above the Pilgrims' Route. It starts from Faha but angles up onto the ridge and is followed up to the summit of a peak variously called the

Facing page, top: **Beenoskee seen across Brandon Bay.**

Facing page, bottom: **The col of the Conair Pass from the Ballysitteragh side. Slieveanea is above and the skyline to the left is a good way down.**
(Photos: Hamish Brown.)

East Top, Binn na Port or Benagh, 2643ft (806m). Two walls across the ridge not far below the summit indicate another Promontory Fort, set high on a mountain. This one may be allied with all sorts of pagan rites and rituals that lingered long in Cloghane by being given a veneer of Christianity. The ridge is fine

Lough Cruttia. (Photo: Hamish Brown.)

and narrow and on the descent westwards it begins to look impossible but if you press on the way becomes clear and the impossible is side-stepped. Its jagged silhouette later is the picture to impress friends with! You can drop down into the corrie after all the sharp prows are passed and join the Pilgrims' Route (a band of cliff presents a level traverse) or you can go up to tackle the craggy, exposed flank of the mountain, easiest by a steep, rightward, line. This approach is for those who feel at home on rock, or 'vertical grass' of doubtful adhesive qualities.

Brandon is completely linked with St Brendan, Brendan the Navigator, and he had an oratory on the summit of the mountain. Its outline is still visible as are the circles of old beehive *clochans* and a well. Despite this the mountain probably owes its name to Bran, a pagan figure pre-dating Brendan by many hundreds of years. St Brendan was born near Tralee in 483 and buried 94 years later at Clonfert, one of the several establishments he founded. His rule lasted almost to Norman times. He made evangelical journeys to Britanny, England and the Hebrides. There is a St Brendan's Well on St Kilda, a St Brendan's Creek in the Faroes and from Brandon Creek he supposedly sailed off in a leather boat on a journey that took him to America. Tim Severin built such a boat and set off from Brandon Creek in emulation, quite successfully. Local *curraghs* lie abandoned at the creek now. I can remember them in use only a decade ago. A mountain with this sort of past can't help being a romantic place but, were it without history, it is still spectacular. Brandon is pop of the tops; it is Ireland's highest mountain and better authorities than this wanderer have called it the finest as well.

St Brendan's route, the Saint's Road, is the easiest route off Brandon but if no transport is arranged it leaves a rather long road walk into Dingle. It is the quick way off if the weather has turned vicious. The route, unclear to begin with, more or less descends the south-west shoulder to join a *bohreen* into the hamlet of Ballybrack, five or six miles from Dingle. If you are being met by transport then end with a flourish by walking north to Masatiompan and Brandon Head to finish at Brandon Creek, the end of the tarred road—and what feels like the end of the world.

But the best way is to reach Dingle along the tops; a switchback grand parade over Brandon Peak and Ballysitteragh. Acrobatic ravens often soar on the winds of these cliff faces. Last time I was there I saw snow buntings. I also met the shepherd who has been adding sections of fence to the old wall that runs from Brandon

Mountain to Gearhane in an attempt to stop the toll of sheep falling down the cliffs. All the materials were carried up on his back, a journey every day for 5 weeks!

Generally it is best to keep on the cliff side of the fence/wall. There are one or two prows, one big and grand, that loom over the depths. From Brandon Mountain the rest of the day gives walking on soft grass. Brandon Peak, at 2,704ft (824m) is a superb perch. A huge rockfall lies below it above Lough Cruttia.

Gearhane, at about 2,300ft (700m) is reached along a narrow neck of ridge (which has seen me crawling for safety during a big gale) and is really the last flourish. A new fence heads south east but by following the old stumps of another fence south west along a cliff edge at the head of a valley the eye is led off to Smerwick Harbour, Mount Eagle and the Blaskets. You pass through an area of peat hags, before the ridge down to the col leading to Ballysitteragh.

Ballysitteragh at 2,050ft, (625m) is worth a last push for it too is a good viewpoint, especially westwards at the end of the day. There is only a tiny cairn on its grassy summit and there is a secondary, eastern summit across a hollow. Superb cliff-edge walking follows. Gearhane and Brandon Peak form a spiky 'saddleback' looking behind and Lough Coumeenoughter gives a last dark water hidden in the cliffs. You can follow a fence down to the top of the Conair Pass but I prefer, after rimming that secretive lake and the rise beyond, to cut straight down, over the tarred road and across to walk down the old green road which follows the bottom of the valley. It rises to cross the motor road at Ballybowler on the Sugarloaf col and runs straight down into Dingle. You can also follow the ridge from Ballysitteragh in the Dingle direction and then cut down to the Sugarloaf col, which avoids fields further on. If Brandon was just the right climax to our walk then Dingle is the utterly charming place to finish in.

This corner of the peninsula is incredibly rich in antiquities, such as the Gallarus Oratory or Kilmalkedar church or Reask (Riasc). Ballyferriter has an interesting interpretative centre. There is now a youth hostel at Dunquinn and Slea Head is best known for having been used in the film Ryan's Daughter. A day here is a good bonus following the walk. Cycles can be hired in Dingle so transport is not essential.

In fact time in Dingle can go very easily. There are as many licenced places as there are weeks in the year. You will just have to come again, for after walking from Tralee to Dingle you will only have reached the beginning.

Top: **The dramatic East Ridge of Brandon Mountain makes an interesting traverse.**

Bottom: **Brandon Peak from Brandon Mountain, with Gearhane on the extreme right.** (Photos: Hamish Brown.)

Walk 12 GERMANY, AUSTRIA:
The Jubiläums Weg by Walt Unsworth

Crossing the Nebelhorn massif. The Jubiläums Weg follows the skyline in the distance from left to right. (Photo: Walt Unsworth.)

A Walk through the Limestone Hills of the Allgäu

The little German town of Oberstdorf has surely one of the most idyllic settings in the Alps. It lies at the head of the long Iller Valley, where it divides into the Stillachtal and the Trettachtal, and where it pushes a narrow German salient into the Austrian Tyrol. All around are limestone peaks; sharp crested grey and white towers rising from bright green meadows which in early summer are full of flowers.

Despite its size, Oberstdorf is a place of some importance. It is not only connected to Munich by rail, but there are through trains to the North German coast as well. It is a famous winter sports centre, with a concrete ski jump that looks like a misplaced piece of Mayan architecture or something from an ancient Indian astronomical observatory. The world record jump of 180m (590ft) was made here in 1981 and looking at the fearsome ramp, it is easy to see why. No less famous is the modern ice rink, where world champions Torville and Dean trained.

The town is also a good centre for walking, with a number of named footpaths in the vicinity. Amongst these is the Jubiläums Weg; a high-level route along the Austrian border, constructed by the Allgäu-Immenstadt section of the *Alpenverein* in 1899 to celebrate their 25th anniversary, or silver jubilee. Combined with other suitable paths, the Jubiläums Weg forms the core of a fine circular walk based on Oberstdorf.

Day 1: Oberstdorf to Hinterstein

The Nebelhorn (2,224m, 7,296ft) towers over the town; the highest point in a group of spiky peaks which separate the Iller Valley from the long, wooded glen of the Ostrach. The first day is spent in crossing these mountains, helped at the outset by a cable-car from Oberstdorf to the Nebelhorn Haus, sometimes called the Edmund Probst Haus. An early start is needed for the walk can be tiring for a first day, despite the fact that it is all down hill. A chair-lift continues to the summit of the Nebelhorn, but we don't need it for our walk, although the view from the top is very fine.

There is usually a crowd near the Nebelhorn Haus, but this soon thins out as you follow a rough track past the line of the chair-lift and up a rise which gives out onto a wilderness of scrub and rocky outcrops which roll away until they drop into the Ostrach Valley. In the distance the line of grey peaks making up the route of the Jubiläums Weg can be seen, culminating in the splendid Hochvogel (2,593m, 8,507ft). On the left, close at hand, is the crest of a jagged ridge running from the Nebelhorn to the Gr. Daumen and usually tiny figures can be discerned scrambling along, up and down the gendarmes, like frantic ants. The ridge is one of the Eastern Alps most famous scrambles—the Hindelang Klettersteig.

Our path runs below the ridge to the Engeratsgundsee; a lonely little lake below the Gr. Daumen which bulks over it like Helvellyn over Red Tarn, in the English Lake District. A tempting valley runs down from the lake to the Ostracht but it is not our way, though in bad weather it is probably preferable because it gets onto a surfaced road sooner and is not all that much longer in distance. But in good weather our path climbs steeply up to a distinct *scharte* in the ridge above the lake, where another valley opens out before us, a positive idyll of green meadows, tall pine woods and an old chalet like something from Hansel and Gretel.

The path descends steeply at first, then more easily. If the weather has been wet it is here that you first come across the chief nuisance of these Allgäu hills—clay. Quite a few of the paths seem to be made of slippery clay, and the stuff also gets onto some of the limestone as well—wet limestone is bad enough, as any

Oberstdorf, the start of the walk. The Olympic ski jumps can be seen on the hills behind the town. (Photo: Walt Unsworth.)

walker will tell you, but limestone greased with a film of clay is more slippery still. But for a while at least, all is well as a good track leads past the chalet and into the woods.

At this point several things happen simultaneously. First, the land drops away very steeply through the woods. Second, the path breaks up into raw limestone ledges generously scattered with boulders and scree. Third, the limestone is well greased with clay. All of which makes for a tough descent.

Perhaps I exaggerate; my judgement clouded by memory of a traumatic descent I made a few years ago. The rain was coming down in drenching swathes, and the descent—about a kilometre long—was one of the most heartbreaking journeys it has been my misfortune to make in the mountains. The rock path was like a skating rink, only full of boulders. My glasses steamed up so that I had to continually stop and wipe them, and every step was an unwelcome adventure likely to end in a broken leg. It was the longest kilometre I've ever encountered.

I've no doubt that in fine weather the descent is an utter delight—that's the way these things go.

Eventually, however, the descent ends abruptly at the level valley floor and a pleasant stroll follows through the meadows. A short stretch of road leads to the hamlet of Hinterstein and an inn with the curious name of 'The Green Hat' where the food is good and they are used to mountain wanderers arriving wet through and daubed in clay!

115

Day 2: Hinterstein to the Landsberger Hut

From behind 'The Green Hat' a well graded path climbs up through the woods to Willers Alp. It is a popular stroll for tourists who are attracted by the small cave which is passed en route and was once the abode of some legendary madwoman or witch. It is now decked out with rustic benches for its many visitors.

The woods fall back, giving way to the rough pasture of the Willers Alp where there is a large, rambling chalet which serves as a farm, a cheese factory and an alpine hut. The climb up to it from Hinterstein takes about one and a half hours and if you arrive at the village early on the first day you may prefer to push on and stay the night at the Willers Alp. It is certainly an experience! Food and accommodation is of the simplest and many of the staff are dressed in lederhosen and smoke meerschaum pipes.

From the Willers Alp a path leads across a small meadow then climbs in steep zig-zags up a scree slope to a col in the ridge above, the Geiseckjoch. Stepping through the gap brings you into Austria, for this ridge is the border, and for a while, below the craggy Rauhhorn, the path stays on this side of the line. The view stretches away below the col in green fields and woods to the large and beautiful lake of Vilsalpsee, beyond which, through a gap in the hills, can be seen the attractive Tannheim peaks.

The path is slippery at first but soon improves. It is almost level, and the walking is easy. This now is the Jubiläums Weg proper as marked on the map and it continues all the way to the Prinz Luitpold Haus—though for our purposes we will diverge from it, making a more attractive walk. It climbs to another col between the Rauhhorn and Kugelhorn, called Hinteren Schafwanne (1,957m, 6,420ft) where it steps back into Bavaria. There is a wonderful view across the Ostrachtal to the Nebelhorn group, whilst at your feet the path goes spinning down into a deep cwm with a wild looking tarn, the Schrecksee. The drop from the col to the lake is only 150m (450ft) but it does look a lot more—especially as you have to climb back again on the other side of the cwm!

At the lake the path divides. The one straight ahead leads to the Lahnerkopfscharte but the steeper, shorter route on the left leads to Kirchdachscharte and is the one which is wanted. It takes you back again into Austria on the path to the Landsberger Hut.

Perhaps it should be mentioned at this point that most paths in the Eastern Alps have at least one variant, official or otherwise.

Sometimes these are short cuts, sometimes they are created to make a more difficult route for those who like a touch of adventure in their treks. They can vary from a straightforward path to someting akin to a *klettersteig,* or difficult scramble. On the whole it is a good rule of thumb to assume that all variants are more difficult than the original. Some require a head for heights and some rock climbing ability. (This is never the case on the original routes where any difficulties are protected, except in unusual circumstances as we shall see later.)

There is just such a variant beyond the Hinteren Schafwanne—and temptingly well marked. It seems to avoid the drop to the lake by traversing across the hillside to a col on the ridge from where it obviously joins the route to the Landsberger Hut. At first there are no difficulties except for the steepness of the hillside, but then, quite suddenly, the way is interrupted by a limestone buttress some fifty feet high which has to be climbed. As a climb it is easy, but the rock is loose and the drop considerable. Once this is overcome the path traverses delicately across the lips of steep crags, where a slip would have dire consequences. Exciting though this variant may be, it is not really to be recommended.

However, it does lead across the ridge and follows a delightful rocky path below the crest until it joins the main path to the Landsberger Hut. The scenery here is that of a wide limestone bowl in the hills, with a tiny lake, the Albel See, like a spot of tea in the bottom of a saucer. Our path actually traverses the far rim of this bowl, until it climbs a steep but short series of zig-zags to the aptly named Sattel (1,980m, 6,496ft).

From the Sattel it is an easy stroll down to the Landsberger Hut, perched on an edge of rock, half hidden by pines. Few huts have such a picturesque site. There is a small lake almost at its door and it is overlooked by the limestone towers of the Lachenspitze (2,130m, 6,988ft), which are Dolomite in appearance. From the hut, the view down the deep valley to the Traualp See and the Vilsalpsee is extremely beautiful and if you intend to have a rest day, then this is the place to have it. The attractive surroundings can be lazily explored—and the hut is one of the best you will come across anywhere.

Day 3: Landsberger Hut to Prinz Luitpold Haus

The trip to the Landsberger Hut has been something of a diversion, but a worthwhile one. Now we must retrace our steps for a short way—an hour at most—across the Sattel to the point where our track of yesterday forms a junction with another in a region of rocky outcrops and juniper bushes. The new path is really the main one and is known as the Saalfelder Weg; a fine, high-level route which leads into the fastness of the Kastenkopf (2,129m, 6,118ft). Old snow might be lying here, even in summer, but it is nothing to worry about. The path climbs through a narrow rocky gap and eventually re-joins the Jubiläums Weg below the Lahnerscharte.

Perhaps the most remarkable thing about the Jubiläums Weg is the high level it maintains. It is scarcely ever below the 1,800m (5,905ft) mark, and that is only about 200m lower than the crest of the ridge. It is also very well graded, for except where it crosses the ridge from Germany to Austria and vice versa, it rises and falls very little. This is especially noticeable beyond the Lahnerscharte, where the path sweeps round the head of a long valley: the wild-looking, pine-clad, Schwarzwassertal.

At the Schanzlekopf (2,069m 6,788ft), the path turns a sharp corner and the ground falls away much more steeply on the left side. In recent years there has been a landslide here which has carried away the path and though a new path is gradually being stamped out in the debris, it is still tricky for a few metres, requiring sure-footedness and a steady head.

At last, however, the path reaches the foot of the impressive Bockkarcharte, a deep gash in the ridge between the Glasfelderkopf (2,271m, 7,450ft) and the Kesselspitze (2,284m, 7,493ft). This *scharte* is quite different from anything met with so far on the walk and is often regarded as the most difficult part of the route, though this is nonsense. True, the gully is generally filled with snow and is quite steep and long, but there is a path on the right of the snow if you don't feel like kicking steps, and the only drawback is the labour involved. It really is quite a pull, especially after the easy going of the previous path.

The gap is reached with relief. On the other side a track zig-zags down to the Prinz Luitpold Haus; a huge alpine hut dominated by the fantastically contorted strata of the Hochvogel (2,593m, 8,507ft). From the hut it is possible to climb this popular peak by means of a scramble protected by cables, though you should allow a full day for this.

The Prinz Luitpold Haus is the commanding hut of the Allgäuer Alps. From it all sorts of possibilities open up to the walker, depending on the time available and inclination. Easiest is a descent to the valley of the Ostrach and a return to Hinterstein and Oberstdorf, by an excellent bus service. On the other hand the

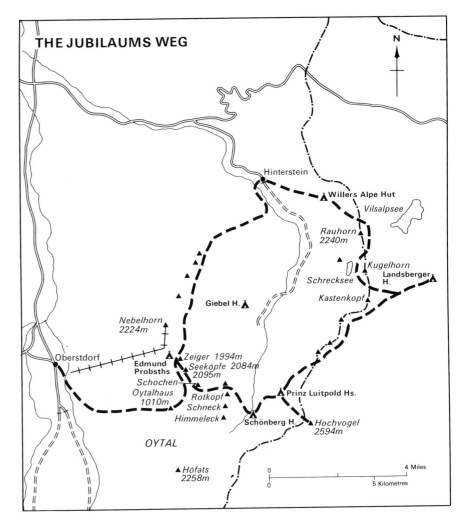

THE JUBILAUMS WEG

adventurous can push further afield, across the Hornbachtal to the Enzensperger Weg or Düsseldorfer Weg, following the route Kaufbeurer Hut – Hermann von Barth Hut – Kemptner Hut, where the famous Heilbronner Weg can be joined. This is a tough itinerary, very exposed in parts and not for the faint-hearted. From the Prinz Luitpold Haus it would take five days to return to Oberstdorf this way.

Day 4: Prinz Luitpold Haus to Oberstdorf

It is now time to close the circle on our tour of the Allgäu. From the Prinz Luitpold Haus a good track traverses round the head of Bärgündeletal, at the top of the Ostrach valley, to cross the Schonberg Alp, where there is a hut of the same name. A stiff climb of some 250m (800ft) follows, up towards the ridge which leads north-west to the Nebelhorn.

The ridge is joined at the Laufbacher Eck

Distance: 53km (33 miles).
Time required: 4 days.
Type of walk: A circular walk along high limestone ridges.
Base: Oberstdorf, Bavaria.
Start: Oberstdorf.
Best Time of Year: July – September.
Maps: The maps fall awkwardly for this walk but Kompass Wanderkarte 1:50,000 K3 Allgauer Alpen—K1. Walsertal and K4 Fussen—Ausserfern cover the area more than adequately. Much more convenient to buy the German guidebook *Heilbronner Weg* which contains an excellent map on the same scale. The map is separate from the book. The guide is a *Kleiner Führer* and inexpensive. There is no English guide to this walk.

(2,177m, 7,142ft); just one of the several summits along the ridge which can easily be visited, because the path runs close to them all, maintaining an altitude of 2,000m give or take a bit. From the Laufbacher Eck the view of the surrounding peaks is quite magnificent, especially of the curiously savage-looking Hofats (2,258m, 7,408ft). This mountain, all organ-pipe ribs and steep grass, is a favourite playground for expert rock climbers.

The onwards path is good and more or less level if you don't digress to capture the various summits. These in turn are the Lachenkopf (2,111m, 6,926ft), Schochen (2,100m, 6,890ft), Klein Seekopf (2,095m, 6,873ft), Gross See-kopf (2,084m, 6,837ft) and the Zeiger (1,994m, 6,542ft). It is amusing to note that the Klein Seekopf is actually 11m higher than its 'bigger' brother!

From the Zeiger, the descent to the Nebel-horn Haus and the chairlift to Oberstdorf is only a matter of minutes, but it is a shame to quit these lovely hills so unceremoniously and as the walk from the Prinz Luitpold Haus has probably taken no more than five hours, there is time for the better descent through the Oytal. The way leads steeply down into a little hanging valley where there lies a charming tarn, the Seealpsee, with a fringe of woods beyond and the Hofats in the distance. The walking is invigorating in such surroundings — even the slight climb up from the lake before once again plunging down steeply into the valley of Oytal where there is the popular Oytalhaus mountain inn.

Of all the many small valleys round Oberst-dorf, the Oytal is deservedly one of the most popular. Looking up towards the valley head is to see a ring of steep mountains which in their form and composition make a perfect re-minder of the last four days. But all good things come to an end and you must turn your back to the mountains and take the easy road to Oberstdorf.

Top: **On the ridge above Willers Alp.**

Middle: **The path keeps a remarkably high level, only slightly below the ridge crest. This section leads towards the Bokkarscharte.**

Bottom: **Rounding the Schanzlekopf, an airy section of the walk.**
(Photos: Pat Hurley.)

Walk 13 SPAIN: A Traverse of The Picos de Europa by Stephen M Lee

A Walk through the Limestone Spires of Northern Spain

The Picos de Europa is a compact mountain range which lies 80km (50 miles) to the east of Santander in Northern Spain. Similar in surface area to our own Lake District, the comparisons end there. Though the Picos are only 32km (20 miles) from the sea, the tallest peaks soar to 2,648m (8,688ft), some of which are snow capped even in the height of summer. The karst limestone rocks of the Picos provide good grip and are a magnet for climbers. For the walker too they have a great deal to offer. The walks vary from 'hands-in-pockets' day-walks to some quite demanding and exposed scrambles on loose rock.

These starkly beautiful and wild mountains are easily accessible from Plymouth by Brittany Ferries in a reasonably priced and comfortable 24-hour journey. Even before you dock at Santander you may well have a sneak preview of the range from a long way out to sea, snowcaps glinting in the sun. Before the advent of electronic navigational aids, the Picos were often the first sight of European land for fishermen returning from the Atlantic and distant parts of the Bay of Biscay: hence the name Picos de Europa.

Add to this the rumours of bear, wolf and wildcat, cheap and friendly local hostels, and people who go out of their way to make your stay in the mountains as enjoyable as possible,

The Pisada de Valdeon is an idyllic spot, warm and friendly. (Photo: Stephen M. Lee.)

A TRAVERSE OF THE PICOS DE EUROPA

Road

==== Jeep track

N

0 _____ 10 Miles

0 _____ 15 Kilometres

1918. It is dominated by the Pena Santa de Castilla at 2,596m (8,517ft).

To the East of the Cornion, beyond the wonderful Cares gorge, lies the central (Urrieles) massif, with half a dozen or so peaks at over 2,400m (7,874ft). It is here that you will find the Spanish Eiger, the Naranjo de Bulnes, at the very centre of the Urrieles massif. It was first climbed in 1904. Though one of the most spectacular peaks (2,519m, 8,264ft) it is not quite the highest, this honour being claimed by the Torre Cerredo at 2,648m (8,688ft). Further to the east, lies the Andara or eastern massif, attaining its highest point at the Lechugales peak (2,441m, 8,008ft). The eastern massif sweeps more gradually down to the river Deva, which flows into the sea at Unquera 32km (20 miles) away.

Although the area is easily accessible from the UK, local travel in and around the Picos can be a little on the slow side. To take a car from the UK when it may spend most of its time parked in the valley is perhaps an expensive exercise, especially when the physical layout of the Picos is such that the three massifs are not conveniently joined by roads or jeep tracks, and you may well find yourself using public transport to return to the car. In these terms then, taking a car is a luxury.

Profile of the Picos Walk

There is no such thing as a 'Picos Trail' as there is an 'Inca Trail' or a 'Pennine Way' with an identifiable beginning and end. But the Picos area, some 50km by 25km (30 miles by 15 miles), contains many interesting if not fabulous walks. Some of these take the walker along gorges, passable only by foot to end up at quite a different road from where they started. A round trip is not always feasible.

I have approached the Picos by car and public transport and have enjoyed both. It would be best to take public transport from Santander, since the most convenient combinations of routes are not circular.

There are many unmissable parts to the Picos. I have strung together an itinerary which takes in the best of the Picos for the non-mountaineering walker. Many of the day stages could be done as part of smaller circuits or even day-walks. The route I have put together includes the best walks which can be done in around a week.

The first decision, then, is where to start. The Picos are accessible from most points of the compass, so it really boils down to personal convenience. My choice of routes includes both Covadonga and Potes. These towns, are such pleasant beginnings or ends to any trip that I have put them at either end of the

Distance: 70—120km (43—75 miles), depending on variations chosen.
Time required: 5 – 9 days.
Type of Walk: Moderate, occasionally strenuous. Rarely over 2,000m (6,500ft) altitude.
Base: Potes.
Start: Espinama/Fuente De.
Best Time of Year: Mid August to late September.
Maps: Mapa Topografico Excursionista 1;25,000 Editorial Alpina, Picos De Europa. I Macizo Occidental, II Naranjo de Bulnes. Federacion Espanola de Montanismo, 1;25,000 Macizo Oriental. These cover the three massifs.
Guidebooks: *The Picos De Europa*, by Robin Collomb (West Col Productions). An essential companion for an area where local mapping can be misleading.

then you can see that the Picos have all the elements for a classic walking holiday.

With the possible exception of winter, when snow may block the highest passes, any time of year is good for a visit. Although Picos rainfall is comparable to the west of Scotland (about 60 inches per annum), there is a tendency for April and May to be fair. But the generally accepted best period to go is the end of August to the end of the September. Even well into October it can stay clear. In autumn one often finds that the access valleys are full of cloud up to about 1,400m (4,500ft) and crystal clear above this altitude. These weather conditions play straight into the hands of the walker who is prepared to make a little effort for his or her pleasures. Whereas the car-bound tourist will mostly see the mists and the green foothills, the walker can find many pathways above this altitude.

The Picos are split by spectacular gorges into three distinct massifs. The Western (or Cornion) massif coincides with the boundaries of the Covadonga National Park, the first area of Spain to be designated as a National park in highlight route.

Potes is perhaps the preferred base since it is also a centre of information about the Picos, a good place to buy plans and maps and to ask local advice about huts, hiring of climbing guides etc.

Picos Logistics

Like any mountain environment, the Picos can vary from the idyllic to the savage. It may be perfectly possible to make a number of treks in these ranges in summer, wearing at most a warm sweater and taking just a mat to lie on, taking your chances at the mountain huts, sleeping under the stars, wearing only running shoes rather than walking boots.

But I prefer the safe approach. Although the access valleys are full of low budget 'simpatico' accommodation and some campsites, when you are high up in the central massifs conditions may quickly become severe. I have had rain, sleet and snow in summer, 90 degrees in late October. You just cannot tell. Also, although there are some new huts under construction, the more popular routes can be quite congested at peak summer times. If the weather is unkind, the lightweight approach might land you in dire straits.

The walking terrain is strewn with loose stones, creating a substantial risk of an ankle twist. Local maps are not noted for their accuracy, and the possibility of getting lost in a suddenly descending Picos mist is ever-present, even in a day walk. The savage stark beauty may not reveal even a blade of grass in the barren *hoyos* of the interior.

You will be better with waterproofs, warm clothes, stout boots, a tent and a water bottle. A camp cooker is also useful; there is no wood at altitude for natural fires, so take fuel too. Although some huts do provide food, enquiries should be made before departing to ensure they are functioning or attended. A water bottle is necessary because above 1,600m (5,250ft) there is no surface water and few springs; it is a wise precaution to carry extra with you. Many of the streams are polluted, especially near villages.

Accommodation and Food

The attractive access valleys to the Picos frequently have basic but good accommodation. Potes, Panes, Cangas De Onis, Covadonga, Posada De Valdeon, Cosgaya, Espinama, Fuente De and Poncebos all have accommodation. There are a number of mountain huts, for which some reductions are obtained on production of reciprocal rights cards. Ask about their availability in Potes.

The local cuisine might have been designed

The view at Fuente De. (Photo: Stephen M. Lee.)

for walkers; it certainly suits the tough independent nature of the hill people. Trout and salmon are caught in the local rivers, and served with bacon. *Fabada* is a great favourite; Asturian beans with meat and garlic. Arenas de Cabrales is home to one of the world's smelliest blue cheeses, Cabrales. Local wine is the Castillo de Arenas, smooth and cheap, and of course Rioja is widely available. The locals favour Magno brandy.

Although Picos residents, like many hill people, are friendly and hospitable, English is not much spoken in these parts. The Picos have not received as many visitors as, for example, the Pyrenees. For asking about routes, note the following: *collada* (col), *horcada* (narrow pass), *vega* (plateau, meadow), *hoyo* or *jou* (circular depression), *lloraza (rainy hollow)*,

mirador (viewpoint), *posada* (inn), *horreo* (barn). The latter, the *horreos*, are a feature peculiar to the Picos. Attractive wooded buildings, they are built on stilts for storing corn safely from vermin. Many of these grace the ramshackle streets of Picos villages.

After all these words of warning, just put your pack on and go; these are magic mountains.

To the Trailhead

A daily bus leaves Santander for Potes in the evening, with an extra one at around 9 am during the summer. I do not give a specific timetable, since in the 'land of *manana*' you have to make many enquiries to be sure. The service gets you to Potes in two and a half hours. Right in the centre of town is a 15th-century tower, called the Infantado. Opposite you will see a photographic store by the name of 'Bustamente'. Here you can buy maps and guidebooks, and get a mouth-watering photographic preview of the Picos. Buses leave thrice daily for the end of the road at Fuente De. There are campsites 3 and 6km (2 and 4 miles) along the road to Fuente De near Camaleno.

Arguably the most luxurious *parador* in the whole Picos region, Fuento De is also the easiest access to the higher regions themselves. From here a small cable car (reduced for holders of reciprocal rights cards) launches you through the mists to a top station. The cables go across a massive amphitheatre of peaks which surround the *parador*. Apart from the *parador* itself, whose polished wood floors are unlikely to welcome big booted climbers, there is unofficial camping in the neighbourhood. This, however, is grubby, unsupervised and without facilities. There is also a hut right at the top of the cable car, intermittently used. From here the barren beauty of the Picos interior is laid out in front of you. It should be possible to reach Fuente De in the afternoon having arrived that morning by boat from the UK.

As an alternative, or if your connections do not work out so well, you will find that the hamlets of Espinama and Cosgaya on the way to Fuente De have a selection of good accommodation and restaurants. A good introductory training walk would be to Sotres from Espinama (see map).

Day 1: Fuente De to the Naranjo De Bulnes

This is quintessential Picos. Although you can walk to the top of the cablecar via Espinama, unless you are an absolute purist you will enjoy the small téléphérique. In summer there can be long queues, but they soon dissipate. Start from the top of the cable car at Fuente De and walk the 1km to the Horcadina de Cobarrobres (1,930m, 6,332ft). Here you have the choice of walking to the Refugio de Aliva, Espinama or Sotres (see map).

Facing page, top: **On the Sotres path, an interesting diversion from the Naranjo Hut to Cares Gorge.**
Facing page, bottom: **Steep ground below the Horcados Rojos.**
Below: **One of the highlights of the walk is the Cares Gorge.**
(Photos: Stephen M. Lee.)

Taking the left (north-east) fork to Horcados Rojos, a further 1½km is possible on the jeep road, across a *jou sin tierra*, translated as a 'depression without earth'. The interior displays a chilling bleakness. At La Vueltona the track steepens towards the pass, and very soon you are able to see the incongruous shape of the Veronica Bivouac Hut (2,325m, 7,628ft). This is the remains of a radar turret from an aircraft carrier, claimed to have been taken there as a joke by Spanish mountaineers. There is space for 4 people to sleep in the bivouac hut. Certainly, through the glare of the bright Picos sun you could be forgiven for thinking it was an hallucination in an already lunar landscape. Following the Sendero Bustamente, you reach the Horcados Rojos in 2½ hours from the cable station.

The descent from the Horcados Rojos is not for the vertiginous, but has been made considerably safer by the erection of a metal cable which walkers can grasp while descending. This has converted an exposed descent into a protected scramble down to the vast high-level rock desert below. After descending into the Jou de Los Boches the path, occasionally waymarked with a red flash on the rocks, keeps to the eastern side of the Garganta de los Boches. It ascends another col, 2,079m (6,820ft) before the Naranjo hut comes into view.

Expect to take a further 2½ hours from the Rojos col. The path is generally good, but the descent from the Rojos col is hard on the knees especially if you are heavily laden. As I said, this is quintessential walker's Picos. For much of the day there is a fine display of rock towers such as the Pico Tesorero and Llambrion on the left-hand side, while from Horcados Rojos you can see the distinctive monolith of the Naranjo gradually increase in stature as you close in on it.

Here you can hardly fail to encounter herds of chamois *(rebecos)* frolicking as only chamois can. Arrival at the Naranjo hut (the Refugio Juan Delgado) is a thrilling experience from any direction. The walk has not been easy and the views are well and truly earned. Only when you are standing insignificantly beneath the west face can its splendour be fully registered and the name Spanish Eiger seems to fit. The hut has space for 40 people, with cooking facilities. Even beer and soft drinks are on sale by the part-time warden. This is where the good climbers hang out, the overflow campsite by the hut resembling a trade fair of climbing technology.

On our last visit, as darkness finally fell and the stars came out, there was one star seemingly brighter than all the others. I realised that this was no star, but the torchlight from a lonely climber bivouacing for the night a few metres short of the summit. He was signalling to us some 450m (1,500ft) below. The sense of excitement in the hut and campsite was such that few of us were able to sleep. Later the next day, the climber returned triumphant. We felt privileged just to have been there.

The Naranjo is known locally as El Picu but its name means 'the orange' and indeed it does have a slight orange hue, even more so when the spectacular west face is warmed by the setting sun.

Day 2: Naranjo Hut to Bulnes

Ascending north-east to the Collado Vallejo, this path has been recently upgraded and is in excellent condition. From the Collado, magnificent views are gained of El Picu. As so often in the Picos, the walker plunges into cloud below 1,400m (4,500ft). Another 2km (1¼ miles) gains the *refugio* and hamlet at Majada de Terenosa, a further 1km to Collado de Pandebano. (From here the walker can descend to Sotres. The path follows the north side of the stream to the north east until the end of the settlement of Majada de Canero. Here the stream is crossed on stepping stones and continues on the south side to Invernales de Cabao. The descent through vegetation is often hard on the legs particularly when rain has made the stones slippery. The Rio Duje is crossed at Invernales. Sotres can be seen perched 1km to the north up a jeep track. 4½ hours down, 6 hours up are the times for this route.)

From Sotres there is a road walk of 12km (7½ miles) round to Carmamena and Puente Poncebos, where access is gained to the magnificent Cares gorge and our main walk.

Head west at the Collado de Pandebano and aim for the hamlet of Bulnes (2 hours). Here there is dormitory accommodation for 20 at the inn. This puts the trekker in a good position to start early for the Cares gorge the following day.

Day 3: The Cares Gorge

From Bulnes descend northwards to the Puente de La Jaya where the path intersects with the Cares path (1½ hours). To the right lies Puente Poncebos, an adequate inn with food and accommodation (Hostel del Garganta del Cares). Cross the Rio Cares and head west on its north side along the gorge. The path follows a most spectacular ravine, through rock tunnels, precariously bridged in places before reaching Cain (460m, 1,500ft). Dubbed 'the divine gorge', the Garganta del

Cares is as impressive a sight as I have seen anywhere in the Alps, or the Americas. In places the chasm is sheer for 1,000m (3,000ft).

Cain is a strange place, with a seeming suspicion of outsiders who materialise from the gorge, but there is accommodation and a bar. It is 12km (7¹/₂ miles) from Poncebos to Cain, 3¹/₂ hours on the described descent, five hours from Cain to Poncebos.

If time allows, I would recommend walkers to try and stay overnight at Posada de Valdeon, jewel of the Valdeon Valley and a most pleasant mountain village. On the way you pass the Mirador del Tombo, a popular spot for day trippers from Posada. Here a beautiful statue of a doe is silhouetted against the jagged peaks in the background. From Cain to Posada is a further 12km (7¹/₂ miles), about 3 hours on a solid jeep track.

This long and wonderful route will take you from Bulnes to Posada de Valdeon in about 8 hours; a tough day but worth every stride. Boasting three hostels and restaurants, the atmosphere is superb in Posada. The Bar Picos, as you might expect, exhibits classic old photographs of the local mountaineers of yore. The ambience in Posada is warm and friendly; it is quite a hard place to leave.

From here you have a choice of returning to Fuente De or heading north east and exiting the Picos at Covadonga, to extend the walk.

Day 4: Posada de Valdeon to Refugio Vega Huerta

From Posada, a fine route can be laid to Fuente De by the Pandetrave pass. Follow the road out of Posada to Santa Marina de Valdeon, where delightful views of the Valdeon Valley and the central massif are gained. When the Pandetrave pass is reached (2¹/₂ hours), turn left on a jeep track. Fork right (north east) after 2km, avoiding the left fork which heads north to the Collado de Valdeon. A 2¹/₂ hour descent from the pass will bring you out at Fuente De.

The preferred route which links Posada and the Vega Huerta is via the road and the Panderruedas col, although access is easier still from the Vegabana hut to the east. However the approach from Panderruedas is gentle, taking some five hours. The hut, which in the past has been in poor condition, has good campsites roundabout, and is in the process of being upgraded.

Day 5: Refugio Vega Huerta to Refugio Vega Redonda

From the Vega Huerta, a spectacular four-hour ramble lies to the north to the Refugio Vega Redonda. The route follows the western side of the Cornion massif, via the Gran Horcada de Pozas and the Alba and Mazada cols. Until the impressive Porru Bolu pillar (2,025m, 6,645ft) is reached, route finding can be a little tricky as the path is not always clear on the ground. A good guide book is recommended (see summary). The original Refugio Vega Redonda has been replaced, in September 1986, by a new hut which sleeps 80 people and provides basic restaurant meals.

Day 6: Refugio Vega Redonda to Covadonga

From Refugio Vega Redonda an hour and a half's walk will connect you with a jeep track leading to the Lakes of Ercina and Enol. In July the local shepherds hold a festival at the lakes which presents a delightfully sylvan scene, with plenty of camping sites, and a

The camp site and hut serving the Naranjo de Bulnes; one of the most popular places in the Picos. (Photo: Stephen M. Lee.)

couple of hostels there if you decide to stop. Sheep graze peacefully with wild horses on the hilly meadows.

From here you may take the road to Covadonga, passing on the way the fine sights of the Mirador de La Reina. You will see the dreaming spires of Covadonga's basilica a long time before you reach it. Covadonga is a peaceful place with a tranquil atmosphere. A place of pilgramage, its local hero was Ramon Pelayo, who led the Spanish reconquest of the Muslims in the 8th century. There are two hostels, one most luxurious, the other quite adequate.

From Covadonga you can easily walk the 12km (7^1/$_2$ miles) to Cangas de Onis; public transport is available too. Cangas boasts a fine example of a Roman bridge over the Rio Sella. If time is short by this stage, you might easily be able to hitch a lift from the lakes to Cangas, for a quick exit to Santander, four hours away by road.

Camping at the Lago Enol. (Photo: Stephen M. Lee.)

Walk 14 SCOTLAND: Coast to Coast by Roger Smith

Go as you will on the Ultimate Challenge

It had been a long haul up from the road to the Bealach Dubh Leac. The first big climb on the first day of a trek, with your boots still finding their feet and your back not yet adjusted to its load, is never easy. But then nothing worthwhile is gained without effort, and the panorama from the South Cluanie Ridge was such as to make the effort required to reach it seem a very small price indeed, especially on such a perfect day.

I was just starting my third west-to-east coast-to-coast crossing of Scotland, and therefore still close enough to the western

seaboard for the view in that quarter to be dominated by islands. Not just any islands, either. The worn gabbro teeth of the Skye Cuillin were unmistakable. To their south, the lesser but still splendid Rum Cuillin, home to thousands of breeding shearwaters and rather fewer sea eagles, struck sharply upwards against the blue of ocean and sky. South again, the weird right-angle of the Sgurr of Eigg stood out.

To north and south of me, range upon range of hills spread to the horizon, folded and gnarled in the way that Scotland's western hills are, through the tearing and scouring of glaciers in ages beyond our imaginings past.

Looking east with 'the thin white line' of the Cairngorm plateau on the distant horizon. (Photo: Roger Smith.)

Many of them I knew, and I reflected again how privileged I am to be able to live and work in this magnificent land and to have the health and fitness to walk its hills and glens, in all four seasons.

Then I turned east, the way I was to travel for the next two weeks. More bright hills and shadowed glens, more superb walking to look forward to. There was something odd, however. The sky was cloudless, yet on the far eastern horizon, at the very limit of visibility, was a distinct white line. It seemed too sharp in outline to be a cloud, yet surely that was what it had to be—cloud on the far distant Cairngorms, 70 miles (115km) away in a straight line and many more than that on foot? Slowly the realization dawned. It was no cloud: it was the high Cairngorm massif itself, the only substantial land mass in Britain over 4,000ft (1,220m) and always the last to hold snow.

It was a moment of pure inspiring magic. My heart, already uplifted by the splendour all around me, soared still further. I felt very humble indeed. How could the next two weeks possibly match the sheer perfection of this first May day?

Of course they didn't. Later that same day, indeed, I was jolted rudely back to reality by the onset of severe stomach cramps brought on, I suspect, by eating dirty snow to assuage my thirst (recent studies have shown that the snow in Scotland is alarmingly acid). I had to drop off the ridge before completing it and camp in upper Glen Loyne. Next morning, after a very cold night, the sun hit the tent at 5 am and another immaculate spring day followed. Fortunately I was recovered sufficiently to enjoy it to the full. By midday I had climbed both hills scheduled for the day and could relax in the sun at the summit of the second, Spidean Mialach, content in the knowledge that it was literally all downhill from there.

Planning the Walk

Crossing a country on foot is surely the best way to see it, to experience it, to begin to know it a little. Scotland is a comfortable size to cross, despite its considerable wildness. Even the longest crossing can be accomplished in a fortnight, and the great joy of such treks is the infinite variety of routes and terrain available.

This simple truth was realized some time ago by the writer and mountaineer Hamish Brown, who used it as the basis for a proposal for an annual event. The event is called the Ultimate Challenge, and all my three crossings have been made as part of this yearly celebration of the joys of walking and of the great cama-raderie that exists within a group of like-minded people doing the thing they enjoy most. The Challenge, which is sponsored by Ultimate Equipment and *The Great Outdoors* magazine, is totally non competitive and is restricted to 250 entrants, who have to plan their own routes and who are entirely self-sufficient for the duration of the crossing.

My own three crossings illustrate the scope available. The first was from Oban to Montrose, camping high all the way—a southerly route accomplished in nine days and taking in 20 Munros (3,000-foot peaks) en route. The second was just about the longest crossing possible, from Ardnamurchan Point to Buchan Ness near Peterhead—300 miles (480km), lighthouse to lighthouse—in two weeks of indifferent weather which kept my companion and myself at low level most of the way. The third is the walk I am describing here, from Shiel Bridge to a tiny and most attractive harbour called Catterline which I had entirely to myself. This trek was also two weeks in duration, with 17 Munros included.

I have never been a great fan of waymarked long-distance paths. They have their place, but for me a truly classic walk is one you plan and execute yourself, not one planned for you by others. Scotland gives infinite scope for such walks, of varying lengths from a weekend to a month.

The logistics of Scottish trekking repay careful study. There is of course the opportunity of camping wild all the way, and this offers the most freedom and can give the best rewards, as I know from experience. I shall never forget the first camp on my first crossing, in 1981. After a very hard day my companion, Cameron McNeish, and I staggered off the second Munro on Ben Cruachan just about on our last legs. The map indicated a small lochan not far down the western ridge. We navigated to it and found a perfect pitch beside it. We had water to hand, a superb sunset to enjoy from the tent door and even a dram of whisky to round off the day and help us to sleep.

At the other end of the scale, Scotland is still lucky enough to possess a goodly number of small hotels in mountain areas which offer the passing stravaiger genuine warm hospitality. Such places as the Tomdoun in Glen Garry and the Ossian at Kincraig, on the western edge of the Cairngorms, have rightly become famous for their welcome. Taking in two or three such places during a crossing is greatly to be recommended.

In between tent and hotel, there is a fine network of youth hostels and also that uniquely Scottish establishment, the bothy. Bothies are simple unlocked shelters made

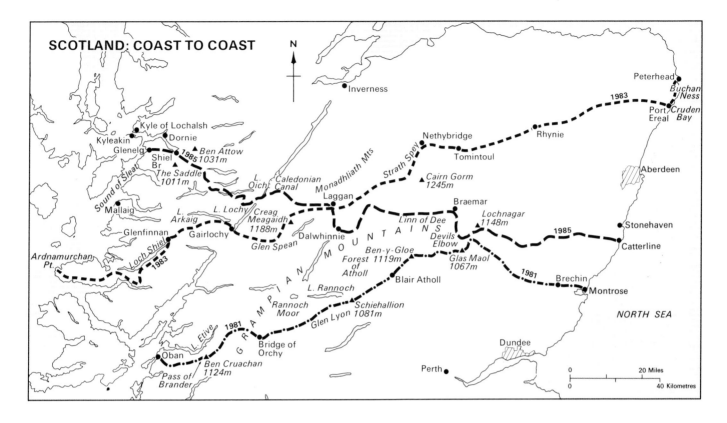

Because the walk across Scotland follows no fixed route, we cannot give the usual fact sheet of maps, times etc.

available to walkers and climbers by courtesy of the estates on whose ground they sit. They have few, or more frequently no, facilities, but a night in a bothy with half a dozen others, with a good fire going, is an enjoyable experience. Bothies are not publicised but one gains knowledge of their whereabouts through experience.

I am not one of those who can happily hump 40lb or more of gear on their back. I find anything over 25lb a struggle, and I have therefore (in common with many others, I may say) developed a fair amount of low cunning in the refinement of weight-reducing tactics for cross-Scotland walks. Parcels of food, maps, etc can be left at stopping places or sent to post offices to await collection. This cuts the amount to be carried substantially. I try never to be carrying more than two Ordnance Survey maps or more than three days' food. Modern equipment is versatile and I use that versatility to the full in reducing the amount of clothing to be carried. I take only a small gas stove and replace its fuel canisters en route. In this way I have cut my pack weight down to little over 20lb. It is great fun working out still further refinements and as I write I am starting to plan my fourth crossing, for May 1987, and wondering how little I can get away with! It is of course very important to stay on the right side of the safety margins, but self-planned treks teach you to do this better than following

marked trails, I believe, and one of the great advantages of planning your own route is that you can adapt it, on a daily basis if necessary, to take account of the weather conditions, your surroundings and your own state of fitness.

But it is time we got back to the walking. The trek I made in 1985 is a good example of its kind and describing it should give a reasonable flavour of what walking across Scotland is like. If it inspires others to similar treks, I shall be very pleased. There's no need to follow my line exactly, but, though I say it myself, it turned out to be not a bad route at all.

To the Great Glen

You left me on the summit of Spidean Mialach, 3,298 glorious feet (1,005m) above sea level. The Gaelic name translates as 'peak of the wild animals' but the wildest animals on view that day were hairy backpackers. This is one of the areas where sightings of golden eagles are not uncommon. I didn't see one on Spidean but while on the summit I recalled the shock my dog and I got the previous year on Beinn Sgritheall, on the north side of Loch Hourn. We were descending from the summit when an eagle got up almost at our feet. The dog stood transfixed, looking at me as if to ask 'what on earth is *that?*' Nor did I move as the great bird soared across the glen at amazing

Above left: **Ray Swinburn leads a group of Challengers on the way out the Great Glen.**

Above right: **The monument to 'Claum Piobhair'.**
(Photos: Roger Smith.)

speed, hardly moving its wings. I felt very privileged to see such aerial majesty at close quarters.

Reflections, and my spartan lunch over (I generally eat very little during a hill day, preferring to stoke up in the morning and at night), I ambled off down Spidean's easy eastern slopes towards the shores of Loch Garry and the Tomdoun Hotel, my night's stopping place. Partway down I stopped for one of the those infinitely satisfying periods of virtual inactivity which the timespan of a long trek allows (weather always permitting). Settling down by a rushing hill burn I spread the tent, still wet from the previous night's frost, out to dry and brewed up. An hour passed very happily before I slowly packed and continued the descent.

As usual during the early part of the Challenge, the Tomdoun was full of walkers on the crossing, including this time Hamish Brown himself. The weather had been kind to us all for the past two days and the only complaints were of blistered feet.

I had hoped that we were in for a really cracking spell of fine weather and indeed next morning it was still fine, but during the day cloud came in from the west and, although we did not know it at the time, that was about the last fine day we would get for a week. Scotland in May can be very unpredictable weatherwise—ranging from full winter to almost tropical heat within a couple of days! It's all part of the attraction of the place.

Day three of my crossing was set to end at Loch Lochy youth hostel. It started with a

pleasant wander through sylvan Glen Garry. Hamish was on the same route so I had the pleasure of his company all day, plus two others who were crossing with him. For part of the time we were joined by Philip Goddard, a regular contributor to *Great Outdoors* and a fine nature photographer. He specialises in the smaller fauna and flora and his enthusiasm for such as lichens and beetles kept us all occupied and involved through the day.

After negotiating some rather unpleasant new forestry—a curse with which too much of Scotland is being visited—we climbed the heathery slopes of Sron a'Choire Garbh ('nose of the rough corrie', 3,066ft, 934m) and delighted in the smooth mossy carpet of its summit ridge. Near the cairn a sudden cold wind blew a dank cloak of mist across us and for the first time on the trip I felt it necessary to wear a jacket. A small box at the summit holds a 'visitor's book' (not common in Scotland) which we duly signed. The book is maintained by Richard Wood, another fine naturalist, and no mean painter either, who lives in Invergarry.

We made our way down a stalkers' path to the Cam Bealach where we paused before tackling Meall na Teanga, which at 3,010ft (917m) just attains Munro status. Stalkers' paths are a feature of many Scottish hills. Built during the last century in the heyday of shooting for sport, they were constructed with great skill and care, and invariably take the easiest route up or down any hill. They had to be capable of taking ponies but today's walker has good reason to be grateful for the labour of those who built and maintained them. It is a great pity that they are now falling into disrepair.

The same is true of many of Scotland's rights of way. These ancient routes, often established as cattle droves or 'coffin' routes leading to the nearest available burial ground, were the subject of frequent litigation during the latter part of the 19th century. The now venerable Scottish Rights of Way Society, set up in 1840, took cases to the House of Lords if need be, and generally won. The wanderer in Scotland enjoys remarkably free access save during the peak of the modern stalking season (mid-August to mid-October) but we still need to safeguard our rights of way, and the best way to do that is to use them.

The Cam Bealach is crossed by a right of way leading from Glen Garry to Loch Lochy, and we used the path for our descent after bagging Meall na Teanga—an easy ascent with packs left at the bealach. We were all pleased to find the homely cafe at Laggan Locks open and revived ourselves with tea before making the last mile to the hostel.

Across the Corrieyairack

We were now in the Great Glen, that massive slash through Scotland created aeons ago by a fault in the rock structure, and were incidentally at our lowest point until we hit the east coast. The Great Glen is steep-sided almost throughout its length and the height we had lost had all to be made up next morning. A toilsome climb it was too, zig-zagging along forestry tracks before a final struggle up the higher part of Coire an t-Sidhean ('corrie of the fairies', which, if they were about, must have been scared off by our heavy boots and heavier breathing as we climbed).

The march to the night's bothy was straightforward, but I diverted to bag Beinn Teallach, which recent resurvey had elevated to a fraction over 3,000ft (914m) instead of a fraction under. (I am trying to climb all 277 Munros, a mountaineering game which has been going on for nearly a century. The achievement is quite common these days, but it still feels like a lot of hills to me.)

The bothy was a very simple one, a former stock shelter with a sleeping area on the first floor gained by a rickety ladder. During the night the wind got up and next morning grey clouds were racing across the hills. Ambitious plans for a traverse of the fine Creag Meagaidh range were abandoned in favour of a simple walk across to the Corrieyairack Pass and down to Speyside, in the process crossing Scotland's main watershed.

For company I had Ray Swinburn, an old stager of the hills with a vast fund of stories. We made our way along the boggy path over the watershed, an almost imperceptible alteration in gradient which nonetheless marks a

The Dirc Mhor on The Fara, above Dalwhinnie. (Photo: Roger Smith.)

very significant point in the journey. Behind us all the watercourses ran eventually west to the Atlantic and ahead of us was the infant River Spey, which empties into the North Sea at Spey Bay, not far from Inverness.

The Corrieyairack Pass, which we joined at Melgarve, is part of the extraordinary road system supervised by General Wade and his successor Major Caulfeild after the Jacobite rising of 1745. Garrisons were established at various points in the Highlands and it was clearly necessary to link them with good roads. For their time they were indeed good roads and many of them are still walkable today. The Corrieyairack was perhaps Wade's finest achievement. Linking the garrisons at Fort Augustus in the Great Glen and Ruthven on Speyside, it rises to 2,500ft (762m) at its summit through a system of zig-zags on either side. It must have been quite a sight to see men and horses—gun carriages even—passing this way.

From Melgarve eastwards the route is now tarmaced and hard miles they seem too. The day had continued dreich and we were glad to reach the welcoming warmth and shelter of the Monadhliath Hotel at Laggan Bridge. I reflected that in five days' walking I had so far used four different types of overnight accommodation—tent, hotel, youth hostel and bothy.

The next night I was to add a fifth option—a private house. I had arranged to stay with friends who were living temporarily in Dalwhinnie, and who were also holding a supply parcel for me (my second—I had left one at Loch Lochy Hostel, and a third was waiting in Braemar). This was to be a quiet and fairly short day, spent on my own for a change. I intended to climb The Fara, a fine and rather neglected hill of just under 3,000ft (914m) so I hoped for reasonable weather.

I was not disappointed, and left the hotel with a light step on a brisk and bright morning when the sunlight had a sharpness that made everything seem new. After stopping to admire a monument erected to a famous piper known simply as 'Calum Piobhair' I left the road and started my wander up the hill. There is extensive new forestry round here too. One of the problems it brings for the walker is that (understandably) it takes time to get onto the map, so the route you planned across open hillside suddenly becomes much more difficult.

Freeing myself from the hump and ditch of the ploughing, apparently an essential part of forestry these days (and isn't it odd how the distance between the humps never matches your stride, however hard you try?), I crossed the delightful wooded glen of the Allt an t-Sluic and paused before making my way further up the hill. Maybe my pause was prescience, maybe not: I don't know. It was certainly rewarded, for I had a grandstand view of a raven trying to see an eagle off.

The smaller bird harried the eagle mercilessly, and I had to admire its bravery and persistence. Its efforts availed it nought, for with a lazy flick of those mighty wings, the eagle could outflank the raven every time. In the end the birds parted and went their separate ways, with each I suppose feeling honour had been satisfied.

I certainly felt satisfied as I climbed towards the Dirc Mhor (big knife), a most odd-looking slash right through the hill, a sharp and stony pass filled with massive boulders. It is well worth a diversion if you're ever in the area. I slanted left from the Dirc and gained the north ridge of The Fara by a sporting scramble up a boulder-choked gully. From here it was easy walking to the massive summit cairn, set by a stone dyke. At 2,990ft (911m) The Fara just misses out on Munro status and is rarely climbed as a result. I prefer it that way.

The descent into Dalwhinnie looked perfectly straightforward on the map but again that wretched forestry intervened and I had to climb two deer fences before gaining the track into the village. Dalwhinnie is an odd place: reportedly the 'highest village in the Highlands' at over 1,100ft (335m) it has the air of a deserted Wild West town. Nothing seems to happen save the regular passing of trains on the Inverness line.

I had the benefit that evening of a look at the TV weather forecast. A dubious blessing it was too. The weatherman confidently predicted a 'high' settling over Scotland, with fine weather assured for the next two or three days. This was great news, for I had two wild camps planned while I bagged hills hither and yon. It was certainly a beautiful evening and having been hospitably received and excellently victualled I went to bed in a happy frame of mind.

Ah that we should be so innocent and trusting. I should learn the read the signs, or smell seaweed or something. Maybe one day I will. I should have known anyhow that Scotland would not submit so easily to a promise of high pressure. As I left Dalwhinnie next morning dark clouds were gathering and on the way up the quarry track leading to Carn na Caim (twisted hill) the rain started in earnest. I gained my 11th summit of the trip easily enough—it is the merest swelling in an undulating ridge—and turned north-east for a traverse I had been really looking forward to, across the high plateau to the dramatic pass of Gaick.

Bad weather to Braemar

Two things became apparent that morning. Firstly, having crossed the A9, Highland Scotland's main north-south road artery, the character of the hills had changed. Gone were the fine sharp peaks and serrated ridges of the west coast, and in their place were much more rounded, smoother and less dramatic hills with extensive areas of high plateaux. I was walking on peat and moss in place of rock and tussock grass. This was especially apparent on the trudge over to Gaick, made worse by the second realisation.

My waterproof—a new model on test from the manufacturer—wasn't. The mizzling wet seeped through my so-called impervious shell, dampening both my body and my spirit. At least it wasn't cold, but the airy promenade I had so looked forward to became a demanding and rather difficult navigational exercise across seemingly endless peat hags and indistinguishable swellings of hill.

All good things come to an end, of course, and eventually I reached the stalkers' path that cuts quite miraculously down the sheer face west of Gaick Lodge. The building looked strangely out of place—a white house set in fields amongst wild mountainscapes. Just before reaching the path I had stupidly dropped my compass in a burn. It probably reached the North Sea before I did. That particular problem was solved by meeting a trio of Challengers on the way down to the Lodge, one of whom kindly loaned me a spare compass to see me to the east coast.

It was raining hard when we four reached Gaick Lodge, keen to find somewhere for a rather late lunch. There was a car parked outside the house so I chapped at the door. The gentleman who answered readily granted our request for shelter by directing us to his bothy, and a superior one it was too with beds and a working stove run from bottled gas. We enjoyed our lunch out of the rain and discussed plans for the afternoon.

My wild campsite had gone out of the window, that was for sure. Instead I resolved to head for the bothy in Glen Feshie and press on over the 'trade route' to Braemar—a much-used corridor—next day. It was a fair pech to Glen Feshie from Gaick and we stepped out at a good rate of knots along the estate track to meet the Allt Bhran and turn east. The turnoff to cross a bealach and find Glen Feshie is much more difficult to spot than it would appear on the map. A plantation of trees is shown but such is the contour of the land that only the very tops of the young conifers were visible. For once I was glad to see them!

From then on to Feshie was straightforward on tracks, and with clearing weather we made good speed. One problem remained. We were on the south side of the Feshie—a substantial body of water—and the bothy was on the north side. We could see smoke rising from the bothy lum so we knew there were folk in residence with a fire going. Wet clothes could be dried, so into the water we went and just charged across at a point where sandspits split the river into four channels. Maybe not textbook technique, but we made it across without mishap.

A fine evening followed with a roaring fire and good chat. From the first floor sleeping area I looked down on the embers of the fire and hoped I wouldn't wake up to find my boots burned and useless! I need not have worried. They were not only safe but dry and ready for the long 25-mile (40-km) day through Glen Feshie and Glen Geldie to Braemar.

I had two hills in mind that dull Saturday. I had climbed neither Carn Ealar nor An Sgarsoch and wanted to add them to my Munro list. Being remote from any road they are best done on a through walk and today seemed an ideal opportunity. I set off early and greatly enjoyed a second breakfast of a bacon roll generously offered by a pair of Challengers camped further up the glen. I crossed the bridge over the River Eidart ready to tackle my two hills—an easy enough circuit they seemed too. But again the capricious weather gods had other ideas.

The heavens opened and I spent a moody half-hour swithering around on the lower slopes of Carn Ealar deciding whether or not to go up. In the end I felt I was so wet that it made no difference, so up I went. I left my pack, covered in the tent flysheet, at the foot of the hill and at the point where I entered the mist at about 2,000ft (600m), took a very careful bearing on my possessions with the compass. I even built a tiny cairn to mark the point.

What's more I found it too, on the way down from the undistinguished summit—merely the highest point on dull heather slopes. I demolished my cairn and set off, keeping the flysheet in view all the way. Picking up my gear I slogged across acres of peat and river flats to the Geldie track then picked up speed, looking forward to the fleshpots of downtown Braemar. At Linn of Dee—the water race swum through by the climber Menlove Edwards in the 1930s—I felt I had earned a break. I lay under an ancient pine and promptly fell asleep, being awoken by the kiss of light rain on my face.

Braemar beckoned and was duly gained

Top: **Shielin of Mark bothy.**

Above: **The Parsonage at Tarfside.**
(Photos: Roger Smith.)

the conditions for a brisk tour of the Munros between Braemar and Glen Muick, my overnight halt. It was a great day. Once you have gained height here you stay high and I ticked off Carn an Tuirc, Cairn of Claish, Tom Buidhe, Cairn Bannock and Broad Cairn—all Munros—in rapid succession. On Tom Buidhe I met David Thomas, an old friend and a regular Challenger. Apart from that happy encounter the day was mine to cherish and I jogged down the tracks into Glen Muick feeling tired but very cheerful.

This must have been a great place for swine in times past—Cairn an Turc is 'hill of the boar' and Glen Muick is 'valley of pigs'. It was this area that Queen Victoria and Prince Albert chose as their Highland hideaway and across Loch Muick I could see Glas Allt Shiel, the lodge she built after he died, and frequently retreated to in the summer months. They were great travellers and climbed most of the hills hereabouts—usually on ponyback but enjoying long hard days for all that.

This, from her own diary, is typical of their early years together. 'The ascent commenced, and with it a very thick fog, and when we had nearly reached the top of Lochnagar, the mist drifted in thick clouds so as to hide everything not within one hundred yards of us. Near the peak (the fine point of the mountain which is seen so well from above Grant's house) we got off the ponies and walked, and climbed up some steep stones, to a place where we found a seat in a little nook, and had some luncheon. It was just two o'clock, so we had taken four hours going up'. Royalty are not immune from the vagaries of Scottish weather, for on the way down: 'the fog disappeared like magic, and all was sunshine below, about one thousand feet from the top I should say. Most provoking!' Ma'am we know the feeling. Yet they did well, did they not, for a royal couple in September 1848?

The connection with royalty is of course maintained to this day, the estate still belonging to the Queen, and indeed a group of us were privileged to have a great crack that evening with John Robertson, who has worked for the family for many years. A kindly and very modest man, his knowledge of the area and its hills and wildlife is encyclopaedic and we learned a great deal from him. In the morning deer came into the yard outside the bothy where we had slept and waited for John to feed them, as he always did.

For me the hills were almost past now and my sights were set on the east coast and the end of my journey. The spectacular country, the very best of Scotland, was all behind me and although there was enjoyable walking ahead,

after half a dozen miles of hard road. This small Highland town, noted for its September Gathering when the Royal Family attend in force, is also noted as a gathering place for Ultimate Challengers. I had won a day off against my schedule and enjoyed meeting the many who arrived or passed through on their way east.

Victoria's Travels

We were all looking forward to better weather and Monday morning was for once auspicious. Not warm but blessedly clear: just

the sea beckoned irresistibly and I felt the need to put miles under my feet towards it. But there was one more highlight to come: another example of the immense kindness shown by so many people towards walkers on the Ultimate Challenge.

The name of Gladys Guthrie has become hallowed in circles where cross-Scotland walkers gather, and her guest house at The Parsonage, Tarfside, in Glen Esk is synonymous with the very best type of hospitality—unobtrusive, genuinely caring, and generous to a fault. That was where I was heading from Glen Muick.

After staying with other Challengers on the climb up to a featureless plateau and round a shoulder to the bothy at Shielin of Mark (a small and unpretentious place but a haven for many tired walkers none the less) I felt the need to be on my own. In this I meant no offence to my companions. Like many people, sometimes I like a bit of company when I'm walking, other times I prefer to be by myself, and although a section in the Mountain Code says 'Never Walk Alone', once you are competent in hillcraft there are many times when your

best company is yourself.

So it was that morning. I wanted to reflect on my journey and on what still lay ahead. I was happy with my route, and with my own performance. With the sole exception of my (non)waterproof, my equipment had all performed well and my decision to go lightweight had been justified. I had climbed splendid mountains, walked through beautiful glens and met and shared experiences with other walkers on the same adventure as myself.

Now it was drawing to a close, but there were still two days to enjoy. Picking up the path on Muckle Cairn, I strode down fair Glen Lee, past Loch Lee and the ruined Invermark Castle and into upper Glen Esk. Rather than tread the road to Tarfside I took the old hill path over Hill of Rowan with its tall monument (about which I know nothing, shame to admit) and past a very ancient cross half-buried in the heather.

My welcome at The Parsonage was all that I could have expected, and the same applied to everyone else staying there. No-one on the Challenge is ever turned away. When the beds are all taken up you can pitch your tent on the

Crossing a bridge on the way up to Shielin of Mark. (Photo: Roger Smith.)

lawn or bring your sleeping bag inside. A large trolley appears to become miraculously restocked with cakes and a large pot of tea and at mealtimes everyone fits cheerfully into a two or three-sitting system. No wonder one Challenger wrote in the visitor's book: 'High point of the crossing—seeing a golden eagle. Low point—leaving The Parsonage'. That's the effect the place and its hostess have on you.

Alone to The End

From Tarfside to the coast I was on my own. I had deliberately not told anyone where I was finishing—a selfish but I felt justified touch of idiosyncracy. I wanted that last section all to myself, so that in the end it became my trek. Besides that, it was all new country to me and I am always very curious to see how a bit of land seen on a map works out when you walk over it.

For a while I had to struggle. For some reason my pack, after almost becoming a part of me, suddenly felt most uncomfortable. The only way I could improve matters was by putting my sleeping mat up my back and lifting the pack clear of my body. It looked a bit odd but it helped so I left it. Then of course the route which looked so simple on the map, with path and track all the way, was not so simple on the ground. As I got on to Hill of Turret rain started, mist came down and the path vanished. I was lefting casting around for the way over into Glen Dye and suddenly feeling very much alone.

It only lasted a few minutes. The compass was again put to good use, the head of Glen Dye was gained and I was on course again. I prefer to draw a veil over the rest of that day. It was not Scotland at her kindest and without the respite afforded by a blessed cafe at Clattering Brig it would have been even worse. I struggled on to the village of Auchenblae, very wet and feeling more than a little sorry for myself. My selection of overnight accommodation was a lucky one: a small pub which gave shelter, good, simple food and was by no means expensive.

Now all that was left was a morning's walk to the coast. People on the crossing are permitted to finish anywhere between Arbroath and Peterhead—a vast stretch of fine coastline—but most prefer to head straight for Montrose, where a finish 'control point' is set up in another very welcoming place, the Park Hotel. I felt such a very special walk deserved a better finish than that, so I studied the maps with some care and finally settled on Catterline. It looked a nice place on the map and I'd never spoken to anyone who had been there. That would do for me!

I could of course have been utterly wrong. I am very happy to report that I was in fact entirely right. Catterline is delightful, a small natural harbour set amongst low cliffs and with an excellent pub in the village. I recommend it as a very adequate finish to a walk across Scotland. I sat on the quay and let my mind roam back over the previous two weeks. I could hardly think of a better walk than this one: by that I don't mean the exact route I followed but the concept, which is immensely satisfying. Sea to sea through mountains and glens: what could possibly be finer?

Montrose was 15 miles (24km) or so to the south. I had no idea how I would get there but I was sure something would turn up, and scarcely 200 yards from the pub a car stopped and the driver asked if I wanted a lift. Having completed my trek I was, for the first time in two weeks and 200 miles (320km) able to say 'yes please'. He was, inevitably it seemed, going to Montrose.

Whatever the future holds I am deeply grateful to have had this opportunity to make my three treks across my adopted homeland. I hope very much to make that four in 1987 and have already identified another 'secret' finish point that no-one has used before! We need to play these games, I think, as we need to get out and be ourselves in the hills a little more than we usually manage in our working lives. As far as I'm concerned, Scotland is the perfect place to do it and the crossing of that splendid land is the most Classic Walk I know.

Walk 15 AUSTRIA: Schladminger Tauern, West–East Traverse by Cecil Davies

A Crossing of one of Europe's Rare Unspoiled Places

East of the Hohe Tauern (the High Tauern) dominated by Austria's highest mountain, the Großglockner, lies the Niedere Tauern (the Low Tauern) whose central and most beautiful area is the Schladminger Tauern. Taking its name from the town of Schladming in the Enns Valley, the Schladminger Tauern is bounded to the north and south by the Enns and Mur valleys, and to the east and west by the Sölk Pass and the Radstädter Tauern Pass. This 'gigantic jewel', lying almost exactly at the centre of Austria, is one of the few remaining areas of unspoilt nature in Central Europe. It

has no east–west or north–south through roads, is untouched—as yet!—by hydro-electric schemes and is unscarred except at its very periphery by the obtrusive paraphernalia of commercialised downhill skiing. No wonder that ever since the 1950s efforts have been made to have the Schladminger Tauern declared a National Park!

The West–East Traverse of this mountain group (part of the Tauern High-level Path No. 702, which runs through the whole Hohe and Niedere Tauern) is without question the finest unglaciated walk of its length in the Austrian Alps. Because the principal explorer of the area, Hans Wödl, worked and wrote his

The view north west from Hochgolling's summit. (Photo: Cecil Davies.)

celebrated guidebook (1924) from east to west, this tradition has persisted in the later guidebooks and most walkers follow the route in that direction, though the reverse, described here, is, as local hut wardens confirm, superior both aesthetically (in that the scenery becomes steadily more beautiful) and practically (in that the steep morning ascents are made in shadow).

There are several convenient places to 'escape' from the traverse if, for example, the weather breaks, and where it can easily be rejoined. To the north these routes converge on Schladming, where there is a good campsite, Camping Zirngast, whose proprietor gives fair discount when walkers leave empty tents for a few days—provided he is told in advance.

Day 1

The start is unpromising enough, as the walk begins at Obertauern, a gracelessly developed ski resort lying bleakly on the Tauern Pass (c 1,700m, 5,580ft) on the main road from Radstadt to Mautendorf. This may be reached by Postbus or by car. If by the latter, turn left in the village as you come from Radstadt and drive past the Tennis Hall to the Seekarhaus (1,797m, 5895ft) where as a guest you may park and leave your car—to be retrieved after the walk using very convenient trains and postbuses. If walking to the hut, you may prefer to take the traffic-free path on the other side of a little lake: left near the Tennis Hall (signpost). This comfortable hut, originally belonging to the former copper mines, was rescued from ruin in the 1920s by the 'Austria' section of the Alpenverein. You will have a pleasant night here.

Although admittedly the first waymark after leaving the hut is actually on a ski-pylon, the walk is pleasant up to the Seekarscharte (2,010m, 6,595ft) where you really take leave of the ugliness of Obertauern.

(An alternative route to the Seekarscharte from the Enns Valley, little used, but very beautiful, is via the Forstautal, which runs due south into the mountains from Forstau. You may drive up this as far as the Vögel Alm (the latter part at your own risk) but will be faced with the problem of how to rejoin your vehicle later!)

From the Seekarscharte the Tauernhohenweg (Tauern High-level Path, No. 702) leads east delightfully through hillocky country interspersed with tarns and outcrops, rich in flora and slightly reminiscent of the Lake District, to a second pass, the Klammscharte (not named on maps). Due north (left) of this the Sonntagkarhöhe (2,245m, 7,365ft) offers an easy, though pathless, ascent to good views,

if you feel confident enough to make a detour so early in the day. From the Klammscharte you can see the skyline of the Steirische Kalkspitze and the Lungauer Kalspitze, with the Ahkarscharte (2,315m, 7,595ft) the highest point on today's direct route, lying between them.

The path winds steeply down to the Oberhüttensattel (1,866m, 6,122ft) a north-south pass between the Forstautal (Vögel Alm) and the Weißpriachtal. Immediately to its north lies the lovely Oberhüttensee with the Oberhütte (privately owned; refreshments) on its western shore near its northern end, about 1/2km off-route and perhaps better ignored in view of the coming ascent of nearly 500m (1,600ft) to the Ahkarscharte.

In good weather it would be a pity not to take in one of the two 'Kalkspitzen', either the Steirische Kalkspitze (2,459m, 8,068ft) to the north, with a quite scrambly path, or the slightly higher, more straightforward Lungauer Kalkspitze (2,471m, 8,107ft) to the south. Despite their names, these two mountains are capped not with limestone, but gneiss! They are both, however, predominantly 'white' mountains. The views are stupendous, with the Dachstein massif majestic to the north. To the east the rock-colourings are richer, and warm reds begin to make themselves felt.

The Ignaz-Mattis Hut by the Unterer Giglachsee looks quite near, but the route to it is roundabout: from the Ahkarscharte go south-east along a ridge to point 2,238m (7,342ft) (map), then east and fairly steeply down to the Znachsattel (2,059m, 6,755ft). Take the north-south pass between the Preuneggtal to the north and the valley of the Znachbach, a tributary of the Weißpriachbach, to the south; then north, past the newish Giglachsee Hut (privately owned, and too near our destination to tempt us today) just west of the Oberer Giglachsee, to the Preuneggsattel (1,952m, 6,404ft); now north-east, well above the two Giglachseen, where beautiful Haflinger horses may be seen, to the Ignaz-Mattis Hut (1,968m, 6,457ft), today's goal.

(This hut can also be reached in about an hour from the Ursprungalm in the Preuneggtal or by a scenically rewarding route up the Giglachbach from Hopfriesen in the Obertal [c 3hrs]. The southern approach from Mariapfarr up the Weißpriachtal is much longer [7-8hrs].)

The area is threatened at the time of writing by a hydro-electric scheme and the other developments which would inevitably follow in its wake: the Alpenverein and other groups concerned with conservation are, of course, opposing the scheme.

SCHLADMINGER TAUERN: WEST-EAST TRAVERSE

The West/East Traverse

Alternative/Escape Route

0 ___ 4 Miles

0 ___ 5 Kilometres

N

To Radstadt

Forstau

Schladming

Aich

Route 782 (cont. as road.)

Seewigtalstuberl

Forellenhof

Bodensee

Hans-Wödl H.

Hüttensee

Filzscharte

Hochstein

Obersee

Neualmscharte Kleine

Wildstelle

Hochwildstelle

Weisse Wand

Obere Gröller Alm

Neualm

782

Riesachfalls

Riesachsee

Preunegstal

Obertal

Untertal

Preintaler H.

702

Untere Klafferscharte

Ursprungalm

Dulsitzsee H.

Greifenberg

Obere Klaffescharte

Vögelalm

Preuneggsattel

Ignaz-Mattis H.

Rotmannlspitze

Krukeckscharte

High Level Path (often dangerous)

Golling H.

Steirische Kalkspitze

Oberhutte H.

Oberhüttensee

Unterer Giglachsee

Trockenbrotscharte

Gollingscharte

Sonntagkarhöhe

Keinprecht H.

Landawirsee Hut

Hochgolling

Seekarscharte

Klammlscharte

702

Lungauer Kalkspitze

Ahkarscharte

Znachsattel

Unterer Landawirsee

Oberer Landawirsee

Seekarhaus H.

To Radstadt

Obertauern

To Mauterndorf

To Weisspriachtal

To Mariapfarr

Day 2

From the Ignaz-Mattis Hut the path descends round the north-east tip (the outflow) of the Unterer Giglachsee, passes a large cattle-shed and then climbs grassy slopes south-east and south through the Vetternkar, whose ruined huts bear witness to the mining activities of earlier centuries. At about 2,200m (7,200ft) the path turns sharply to nor'-nor'-east and climbs more steeply up the strikingly ruddy flank of the Rotmannlspitze (2,453m, 8,048ft)—The Little Red Man's Point—a

Distance: Approx 40km (25 miles).
Ascent Involved: Approx 3700m (12,000ft).
Type of Walk: Unglaciated. Steep ascents and descents. Snow can greatly increase difficulty.
Base: Schladming or Radstadt.
Start: Obertauern.
Best Time of Year: July to September (often snow early in year).
Maps: Alpenvereinskarten 1:50,000 45/2 (formerly No.61) & 45/3: Niedere Tauern II & III. (Also: Freytag-Berndt Wanderkarte 20. 1:100,000; Kompass-Wanderkarte 31. 1:50,000. Radstadt-Schladming.)
Guidebooks: Cecil Davies *Mountain*

Walking in Austria (Cicerone Press). Philip Tallantire: *Felix Austria III Niederen and Hohen Tauern,* William E. Reifsnyder *Hut Hopping in the Austrian Alps.* (Sierra Club Books. San Francisco), Walter Pause: *Berg Heil.* (Walk 87 Klafferkessel und Greifenberg). (English Version: *100 Best Walks in the Alps.)*

The summit ridge of Hochgolling. At 2863 m it is the highest summit in Styria. (Photo: Cecil Davies.)

summit which, though insignificant in itself, offers exceptionally splendid views: to the north across the Enns Valley to the Dachstein; to the west to the two Kalkspitzen; to the south the Engelkarspitze and the Vetternspitze rearing their pointed tops above the Vetternkar; and to the east a mountain panorama characterised and dominated by the great wedge of the Hochgolling. Deep to the north-east, 900m (2,950ft) below, can be seen the peaceful Duisitzsee with its privately owned but hospitable hut. The Rotmannlspitze is indeed magnificent on a fine and sunny morning, but if the weather suddenly breaks the descent that follows can be uncomfortable and potentially dangerous: this is written from personal experience!

The path drops from the summit steeply at first over loose scree and poor rock (alternative routes for a few yards) into a huge boulderfield on the northern slopes of the Sauberg, through whose labyrinth of massive rocks an extraordinarily 'walkable' route has been engineered and waymarked to the Krukeckscharte (2,303m, 7,556ft)—another wonderful viewpoint: the Hochgolling from here is the cover-picture of Peter Goll's German guidebook to the area. Soon the Keinprecht Hut appears below, but a long detour east, with one fixed rope, on a narrow traversing path above dangerous cliffs is required to reach it: a memorial above the cliffs commemorates the death of a young man who attempted a short cut. He was a friend of the Zechmann family, wardens of this hut for over a decade and a half. Grete Zechmann says that the short cut does in fact exist but it isn't recommended.

The Keinprecht Hut (1,871m, 6,138ft) in the 1970s was a tiny affair, with an outside loo and an exterior ladder to the Matratzenlager in the loft. It has since been practically doubled in size without losing either its cosy atmosphere or the friendliness exuded by the Zechmanns, adults and children alike. However, if your time is limited and the weather is good you may continue on the same day to the Landwirsee Hut at 1,986m (6,516ft) (also spelt *Landawirsee* and *Landwiersee*).

Leave the Keinprecht Hut as if about to descend into the Obertal—a rewarding approach to this hut—but soon fork right and pass a small building to traverse the head of the Obertal through lovely alpine meadows. (Notice, but do not follow down the jeep track used by the warden.) After the great parabola of this valley-head traverse, the path swings almost due east and climbs steeply to the Trockenbrotscharte ('Dry Bread Pass') at 2,237m (7,339ft). Guidebooks may tell you that there is a direct path to this from the Neualm, the highest *alm* in the Obertal, where also the high-level path to the Duisitzsee Hut branches off, but Herr Zechmann says that it has long fallen into disuse and would now be impossible to trace. From the Trockenbrots-charte, a waymark indicates that it is possible to ascend Pietrach (2,396m, 7,860ft).

The Landwirsee Hut is below, and there is a direct, uninterrupted view of the Hochgolling and the Gollingscharte. About one third of the way down to the hut a high-level path to the Gollingscharte is signposted on the left as 'only for the experienced' *(Nur für Geübte)*. In some conditions this route (which avoids consider-able loss of height) is positively dangerous. Do not use it against the advice of the hut warden Albert Essl: he runs the hut in an easy-going way but is to be taken seriously on moun-taineering matters.

The hut, originally built in 1911 and enlarged in 1923, was destroyed by an avalan-che and again rebuilt in the late 1970s. It now has a very rough jeep track to it, not, of course, for public use, but providing walkers with a good approach from the nearest car-park in the Göriachtal. This hut is the best base for climbing the Hochgolling (2,863m, 9,393ft), being 300m (980ft) higher than the alternative, the Golling Hut (1,683m, 5521ft). Many people climb the Hochgolling *en route* between huts, leaving rucksacks at the Gollingscharte (2,326m, 7,631ft) 537m (1,760ft) below the summit. But it makes a splendid day's outing, rucksack-free, from the Landwirsee Hut, and if you still have time to spare, the two Landwir-seen (lakes) offer the opportunity for a charming little ramble. You may even encoun-ter a marmot at close quarters, as my wife did.

Day 3

Whether climbing the Hochgolling or not, leave the hut by the jeep track and lose some 200m (600ft) of height before branching left from it up the path to the Gollingscharte, grassy at first, then more scrambly to the left of a small gorge. Note on the left, a little above the gorge, the signpost to the high-level approach. The potentially dangerous section can also be clearly seen above an extremely steep snow-filled gully. Finish up scree and snow—almost always snow—to the bleak, rocky Gollingscharte.

The northern aspect of the Hochgolling from here is both impressive and intimidating, but the fierce, black cliffs are in fact circum-vented. A red-white-red waymark with an arrow, '778 Golling', points the start of the ascent of this, the highest mountain not only in the Schladminger Tauern, but in Styria. This route, the 'Historic Path', was first climbed in the autumn of 1811 by Bavarian surveyors from Salzburg, though several unnamed climbers from Tamswag had reached the summit twenty years before (8 August 1791) by

the west flank of the south ridge.

Begin south-west on a gently rising traverse: there are some stirrups in the rock at the trickiest point, but beware in ice or new snow. (A rope offers little protection on any of this

Dramatic rock scenery like this gorge is a feature of the Hochgolling climb. (Photo: Cecil Davies.)

route.) The traverse leads round a corner on to the wild expanses of steep rock and scree that form the west flank. Follow waymarks up and across this. Presently a sign-post marks the parting of the North-West Ridge Route (left) from the normal route (right). The former is said to be a blocky ridge, narrow in places, with exposed scrambling; Grade II— where a rope is a sensible precaution (first ascent, Hans Wödl, 4 September 1917). As this is better in ascent than descent many climbers make a round trip of it, returning by the ordinary route.

Soon after the signpost there is a choice of ways on the normal route: the upper (left) route includes one or two tricky moves across slabs; the lower presents no problems but involves a small loss of height. The paths meet at a prominent cairn on a small spur. The upper part of the route is steeper, but a former 'bad step' has now been furnished with iron stirrups set in the rock face. The ridge is reached just north of the summit cross, which, as well as the customary book and stamp, has a wooden plaque inscribed:

MÖGEN DIE VÖLKER DER ERDE
DURCH DAS KREUZ GEMAHNT
DEN FRIEDEN FINDEN!
BURSCHENSCHAFTLESSACH
AUGUST 1956

(May the peoples of the earth, admonished by the cross, find peace. Lessach Student Fraternity. August 1956.)

It is an inspiration to Christian and non-Christian alike to be greeted on the mountain-top by such a message, especially when it comes from a *Burschenschaft*—a type of student club normally associated in one's mind with aggressive machismo. Lessach, 7km (4 miles) north of Tamsweg, is geographically the nearest village to the Hochgolling.

The views in every direction are superb, if the cloud that all too often caps this mountain will keep away. Much of the route walked so far can be retraced with the eye. Further away you may see the higher, snow-covered tops and perhaps will be able to identify the Ankogel (3,246m, 10,650ft) 40km (25 miles) to the south-west. To the north-east the Greifenberg, the next summit on the main path, can be seen alongside the jagged Rauhenberg. Perhaps most impressive is the drop of some 1,400m (4,600ft) into the Göriachtal to the south-west. Return to the Gollingscharte the same way; the descent is not much quicker than the ascent as the terrain is so irregular.

Unless you have set aside an extra day for the Hochgolling and are returning to the Landwirsee Hut, continue on R.702 east,

towards the Golling Hut. Do not go down the snow that is usually lying here, but keep well to the right, following the waymarks: it is easy to get too low at first in the boulder-field. Steep, wide zig-zags down scree on the right of the corrie lead to a crossing to the left of the stream and further zig-zags down to the level green floor of the Gollingwinkel, about 600m (1,950ft) below the Gollingscharte and 1,200m (3,950ft) below the summit of the Hochgolling. The north-east precipices of Hochgolling fall sheer to the valley head, making the Gollingwinkel into what at least locally is claimed to be *das grösste Natur-Amphitheatre der welt* 'the greatest natural amphitheatre in the world'. Pleasantly level walking past the side of the former Obere Steinwenderalm brings us to the Golling Hut (1,683m, 5,521ft) which suddenly comes into view a few yards away as we round a slight bend in the valley. (This hut can also be reached from the Untertal, a scenically most attractive route of which only the last 200m (650ft)—by fine waterfalls—of the 600m (1,950ft) ascent, are steep.)

The last three huts to be used on this walk—the Golling Hut, the Preintaler Hut and the Hans-Wödl Hut—are owned not by the Alpenverein but by the Alpine Gesellschaft 'Preintaler', an exclusive Viennese club founded in 1885 and limited to 30 members. (The name is taken from a little known valley in Lower Austria.) Members of the Alpenverein must have a current *Hüttenmarke* on their membership cards to qualify for members' discount at these huts. You will not be overrun by your fellow-countrymen here. Roman Reiter, the efficient warden of the Golling Hut, says that he has about 20 British and 20 American visitors per season. This was the last of the three huts to be built (1904) as there had been a former hut in the area, the Franz Keil Hut, from 1881 to 1891, when it was destroyed by an avalanche. The Golling Hut was enlarged and improved in the mid-sixties.

Day 4

The way from here to the Preintaler Hut is even finer than that over the Gollingscharte. It is scenically the climax of the whole traverse and includes the highest point, the Greifenberg (2,618m, 8,589ft), on the direct hut-to-hut route. On leaving the hut, cross the stream, pass a large boulder, popular with boys who want a scramble and a perch, and follow a rising traverse north-east across and up a slope much overgrown with bushy alder; no difficulty, though a slip, especially in descent, can lead to a nasty tumble.

'Never again!' gasped a woman as she arrived at the Golling Hut. She and her friend had evidently fallen off the path and down the steep, vegetated slope below. The friend was severely scratched and badly shaken. Another member of the party had rendered First Aid.

The path steepens in zig-zags with a fixed rope in one section, turning east, then south, and finally east-south-east up a long, broad, shallow, trough-like corrie to the improbable tarn that lies miraculously on the very saddle between the Greifenberg to the north and the Pöllerhöhe (2,601m, 8,533ft) to the south. (The latter is said to be easily, though pathlessly, reached from here in less than an hour.) This is a magical spot when the morning sun is dispersing the mists, with wonderful views— better pictorially than from the Greifenberg summit, though the dullest aspect of that mountain does block the view to the north. The Dachstein is well framed to the north-west; the Hochgolling peeps over the heights to the south-west; the lake itself is a gem; to the east are the shark's teeth of the Klafferschneide, and deep below to the east and south-east lies the vast corrie that contains the Lungauer Klaffersee and the Zwerfenbergsee at the head of the Lesachtal, a southern approach to the Klafferkessel.

A short half hour of dull plodding and we reach the summit cross of the Greifenberg with its Pisgah prospect of the Klafferkessel (roughly 'The Gaping Cauldron') on whose upper rim we now stand.

The Klafferkessel, one of the natural wonders of the Schladminger Tauern, is even more extraordinary than the Gollingwinkel. It was formed in the ice-age and consists of two huge corries merging into each other, the whole being tipped towards the north as if the vast 'cauldron' were being emptied into the valley. It is nearly 2km (1 mile) across and the Obere Klafferscharte (2,516m, 8,255ft) is over 200m (650ft) higher than the Untere Klafferscharte (2,286m, 7,500ft). Countless lakes and tarns, interspersed with rock and hardy grasses, lie scattered on the bottom of this Gargantuan pot, about 40 being of significant size and some always partially iced. The largest are the Unterer Klaffersee, the Rauhenbergsee and the Oberer Klaffersee. The 'rim' consists of a magnificent cirque of peaks and ridges of which the principal ones are the Rauhenberg (2,585m, 8,481ft), the Greifenberg (2,618m, 8,589ft) and the Waldhorn (2,702m, 8,865ft). In the north, marking like a sentinel the position of the Untere Klafferscharte, stands the massive Greifenstein (2,397m, 7,864ft).

From the summit cross the route drops a little way to the south down a scree track, then turns east on a fine, rocky traverse (fixed rope) down to the Obere Klafferscharte (2,516m, 8,255ft). Here it is joined by a branch of the route to the Preintaler Hut from the Lesachtal. Our own route drops roughly north-east into the Klafferkessel.

The tortuous way through the maze of lakes and hummocks is easy to lose, so follow

The Greifenstein, a dramatic obelisk in the rocky Klafferkessel corrie. (Photo: Cecil Davies.)

Top: **The Huttensee in Seewigtal seen from the Neualmscharte.**

Above: **Golling Hut is owned by an exclusive Viennese club but is open to all comers.**
(Photos: Cecil Davies.)

waymarks closely, especially in mist. This is no place to get lost in. Unless tempted to linger (and in good weather the temptation is great) you will cross the floor of the Klafferkessel in under an hour. Shortly before reaching the Untere Klafferscharte note the memorial plaque to Hans Wödl, and honour the pioneer.

It may take longer than you expect from here to the Preintaler Hut, a good $2^1/2$km ($1^1/2$ miles) away on the map and over 600m (1,950ft) down! The path drops north-east for 1km, turns sharp right to drop down a spur,

crosses the stream, follows the edge of a gorge and finally crosses a spur to drop at last behind the hut and the nearby Waldhorn Alm. In recent years the latter, primarily a cheese-making *alm* and in the 1970s somewhat primitive, has been modestly 'developed' and offers 'Matratzenlager' accommodation—chiefly used by young people, I think. The earliest Preintaler hut here was opened early in the summer of 1891 on a piece of ground '60 square fathoms' in size, bought from the Waldhorn Alm the previous year: it had one room, a single iron stove for heating and cooking, a plank-bed for eight and some straw-sacks in the loft for emergency accommodation. The hut was greatly enlarged in 1924 and several times in the 1950s and 1960s. Finally, in 1976, it was three-quarters demolished and rebuilt according to new plans. Work on it was still continuing in the summer of 1986. It is a most friendly place, obviously owing its atmosphere to its warden, Herr Höflehner: ten years ago, when I was there on my birthday, he presented me with a complimentary glass of wine and biscuits at half past six in the morning!

This hut, too, has a fine direct approach from the north. One can get a bus, or drive a car, as far as the Weiße Wand Guest House (1,058m, 3,470ft) in the Untertal. (Parking is a little beyond the Guest House.) Leaving this valley (which leads, as we know, to the Golling Hut) take a path to the left and go up by the spectacular Riesach Falls—the highest in Styria—to the Obere Gföller Alm: refreshments and fine views of the Riesachsee and the mountains beyond. Continue on the left (north) side of the Riesachsee and picturesquely past the Kotalm up to the hut. Altogether an exceptionally beautiful and interesting path.

Day 5

To start the penultimate leg of our walk, leave the hut past the Waldhornalm and cross the stream. Not far up the hill to the north-east there is a fork. Here we leave the Tauern High-level Path No. 702 which we have followed all the way until now. This forks right and leads next to the Breitlahn Hut (4hrs), the Rudolf-Schober Hut—a long day, at least 7hrs—and thence to the village of St Nikolai im Sölktal. Some people regard that as the 'true' ending to the Schladminger Tauern Traverse. The Breitlahn Hut was only leased (since 1927) by the Graz Section of the Alpenverein. The arrangement was ended in 1986 and this hut is no longer an Alpenverein Hut.

Our route (the usual one) is the left fork, No.

782, known from here to the Hans-Wödl Hut as the Robert-Höfer-Steig, named in honour of its builder. The 782 traverses almost due north, rising or contouring, with a splendid retrospect of the previous day's descent from the Klafferkessel. After about 1½km there is another fork, the 782 continuing up more steeply to the right and the 781 going down, left, to the Neualm (1,857m, 6,092ft). Early in the season, even in June, or after new snow, you should follow the 781 past the Neualm for about 2km, then fork right (sign) for the Kaltenbachschulter and the Filzscharte (2,201m, 7,221ft) from which the path leads north-east down to the Hans-Wödl Hut. This route adds about 3hrs (at least 7hrs from hut to hut) to the walk.

The shorter route, 782, climbs steadily nor'-nor'-east until near the top, when it turns sharply due east to the Neualmscharte (2,347m, 7,700ft), a rocky, narrow and dramatic nick in the ridge whose main pillars are the Hochstein and the Hochwildstelle. Approached thus from the south-west it is not at first the most obvious weakness in the ridge. There is a bronze tablet here now in memory of a certain Günther Malzer (1946–84), placed there by his mountaineering friends. From here a walker can reach the summit of the Kleine Wildstelle (2,577m, 8,455ft) on a waymarked path of scree and grass, in half-an-hour. A further half-hour, involving some Grade I climbing and considerable exposure is needed for the Hochwildstelle (2,747m, 9,012ft) via the Seewigscharte and the north-west ridge.

As one steps across the Neualmscharte the Seewigtal suddenly comes into view with its three jewel-like lakes, the Obersee, the Hüttensee and—just visible—the Bodensee, a tiny cameo when compared with its better-known namesake, but to many eyes, more beautiful. The first few hundred feet of descent, and especially the very first few feet, are across and down very steep and extremely unstable scree. This is the section that must be avoided early in the season and after new snow by taking route 781. Even in good conditions it is uncomfortably insecure under foot and offers no protection. Further down there is a welcome spring (signed *WASSER* on a boulder). After the long descent (nearly 700m, 2,300ft), relieved only by the beauty of the valley and lakes below, it is a relief to walk by the lovely Obersee where day-visitors disport themselves. After this go down steeply again for another 170m (550ft) to the Hüttensee and by this, climbing gently, to the hut near its northern end, which in the opinion of Philip Tallantire is 'the finest hut in the area for situation and scenery.' *(Felix Austria III)*.

It is indeed a pleasant and friendly hut, wardened by identical twin brothers, men of real, old-fashioned courtesy, who were indistinguishable from each other until one grew a beard. The Preintaler Club has certainly chosen its hut-wardens well.

Day 6

Next morning, to conclude the whole expedition, there is a further drop of nearly 400m (1,300ft) to the Bodensee on a finely constructed path near a superb waterfall. Even from this third lakeside you can still see the sharp 'nick' of the Neualmscharte etched against the sky, its characteristic rock tower beside it. Pass by the Forellenhof, a guest-house celebrated for its trout, and walk down the road to the Seewigtalstuberl (large car park).

This is really the end of the walk. The route 782 continues down to Aich in the Enns valley for a good 6km (4 miles) on a newish, raw, hard-top road with quite a lot of tourist traffic. There are no buses, though a minibus comes up from Schladming most mornings for walkers wanting to start their walks from here. If you despair of thumbing a lift and still have some money left, get the waitress in the Stuberl to ring up for a taxi: it's worth it!

Walk 16 NORWAY: A Jotunheimen Traverse by Ingrid High

The Hurrungane seen from the summit of Dyrehaugstindan, an easy climb from Turtagrø. (Photo: Ingrid High.)

East to West through the Home of the Giants

Jotunheimen—the name means 'the home of giants and trolls'—has mountains and glaciers, valleys and lakes, of all sizes. It isn't only a collection of views and spectacular places however, it is wilderness and nature personified. A place where people are reduced to their proper proportions and where one can find peace and solitude for days on end.

Jotunheimen lies in central southern Norway, easily reached from both Oslo and Bergen. In the east it is limited by the road from Fagernes to Vågå (closed in winter); in the north by the main road from Otta to Stryn;

in the west by the Sognefjellsroad (also closed in winter), and in the south by the road from Turtagrø to Tyin. (Author: check I have simplified this correctly).

The many huts and the paths connecting the huts make several routes possible, but the route that I have chosen shows many of the different aspects of Jotunheimen. Starting at the eastern end, at Gjendesheim, which ever since mountain-walking began in Norway has been one of the main starting-places, the route goes to Memurubu hut (over Besseggen ridge); to Gjendebu hut (over Bukkelageret); to Eidsbugarden/Tyinholmen; to Vettismorki/Vetti (via Fleskedalen); to Skogadalsbøen and

146

The first two days of walking cover the length of Lake Gjende. (Photo: Ingrid High.)

ends at Turtagrø. This involves six days of walking. Day-trips can be included from many of the huts, and there are longer alternatives to many of the days. Some days can also be cut out; the boat on lake Gjende can be used, or you can go directly to Skogadalsbøen from Tyinholmen rather than over Vetti. It is also possible to prolong the walk by going back north-east from Skogadalsbøen or Turtagrø across the northern part of Jotunheimen; perhaps including the two highest peaks of Norway.

Before we continue here are some Norwegian words and parts of words which are common and occur in the names mentioned. In general the ending -en/-et/-i is the definite article (the); *heim* means house/home; *bu* means small hut or settlement; *bø* is similar, but is used specifically for a *seter* which means summer-farm; *egg* means ridge; *vatn* means lake (water); *hytte* means hut; *dal* is a valley; *fjell* is a mountain; *bre* a glacier; *hø* a height/hill; *bukk* a male reindeer (or goat); *tind* a peak; *semmel* or *simle* a female reindeer.

The first two days of the traverse are spent along the high ridges on the northern side of Lake Gjende. Then follow two days of more ordinary Jotunheimen valley-walking, passing the other two big lakes, Bygdin and Tyin. (The names of these three big lakes are derived from old words describing their shapes: Gjende— the straight one, Bygdin—the bent one, and Tyin—the one which is split in two.) After Tyin the main east-west watershed is crossed and coming into the Utla-valley you meet the more fertile and wild landscape of the fjord country.

The three first huts, Gjendesheim, Memu-rubu and Gjendebu, were the earliest huts provided for mountain walking. They were first built in the 1870s, when there was a romantic movement among the intellectuals and artists in Oslo, to discover the Norwegian mountains. A local farmer, Jo Gjende, settled in the 1840s at Gjendesheim, and his original hut, built in 1878, has now been restored. It lies opposite Gjendesheim, on the south side of the river, and is accessible by rowing boat. From this low-key beginning Gjendesheim became the major starting place for mountain walking.

Memurubu was originally a *seter*. In 1870 one of the stone huts was taken over by DNT (the organisation responsible for huts and

147

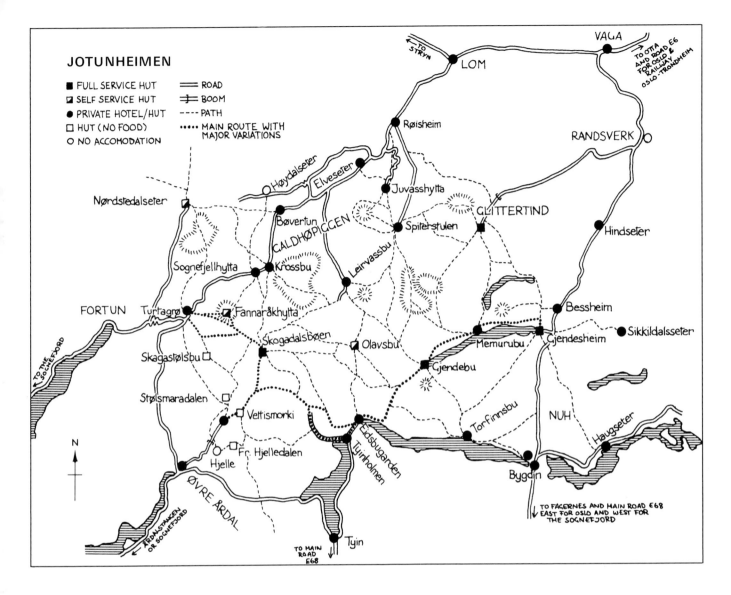

JOTUNHEIMEN

- ■ FULL SERVICE HUT
- ◪ SELF SERVICE HUT
- ● PRIVATE HOTEL/HUT
- □ HUT (NO FOOD)
- ○ NO ACCOMODATION

- ═══ ROAD
- ╪══ BOOM
- - - - PATH
- ••••• MAIN ROUTE WITH MAJOR VARIATIONS

Distance: 80km (50 miles).
Time Required: 6 days.
Type of Walk: Along good tracks, hut to hut.
Start: Gjendesheim.
Finish: Turtagrø.
Best Time of Year: July to mid September.
Maps: At present the 1/50,000 maps are old and inaccurate but half have been replaced. There is a good 1/100,000 map of Jotenheimen. There is no English language guide to this area at present but DNT publish a good Norwegian guide.
Den Norske Turistforening (DNT): This organisation is responsible for huts and paths in Norway. Membership gives up to 40% reduction on beds and meals, but there is no reciprocal rights with other clubs. Address: Stortingsgaten 28, Oslo 1, Norway.
Norwegian Huts are of three types: Full-service (wardened and meals provided), self-service (food available but self-cooking), non-service (cooking facilities only). The last two types may be

padlocked—key on deposit from DNT. In Jotunheimen only Olavsbu and Fanaråken are self-service and the Utla Valley huts non-service. The rest are fully serviced.

All huts have quilts and blankets and no-one is turned away. They are busiest in the last week in July and first two weeks in August.

Allemansretten ensures total freedom of access to land in Norway, including the right to camp for one night anywhere.

paths in Norway) and this stone hut, which is still there, became the first walkers' hut in Jotunheimen.

Gjendebu, built in 1871, was the first purpose-built tourist hut. This hut made the route from Gjendesheim to Eidsbugarden complete.

The remaining stone hut at Gjendebu is today kept as a museum to a girl called

Gjendine Slaalien, who was born in 1871 and lived there until she died in 1971. The composer Edvard Grieg visited Gjendebu for the first time when Gjendine was 17 years old, and impressed with her aptitude for music, returned each year for ten years, writing down many of her songs and also rewriting them as pieces for the piano.

A very readable book about early tourist-life in this area is *Three in Norway, by Two of Them*, first published in 1882, and still available in Norway. This is the story of three Englishmen who travelled from Kristiania (now Oslo), up to Gjendesheim along bad and at times almost non-existent roads. They brought with them a canoe, food, guns and ammunition for hunting. They stayed for the whole summer exploring the area north of lake Gjende. Among their tales is a description of how, after a successful hunt, they baked a delicious reindeer pie in the stone oven they built; this stone oven is still to be seen at Memurubu, where they had their main camp.

Day 1: Gjendesheim to Memurubu via Besseggen

Gjendesheim is now a large tourist centre lying on the main road, but a walk down to the edge of the lake gives you back the feeling of being in the mountains. On the south side of the lake are mountains with ridges, peaks and glaciers in hidden valleys; a wilderness rarely visited these days. On its north side, the lake is walled in by long low hills at the first break of which lies Memurubu. The first two days of walking take you along the tops of those low hills. There is a boat service between the three huts which will take the luggage for you, so it is only necessary to carry a day-sack for these first two days.

From Gjendesheim follow the path going up Veslefjell (the little mountain). A signpost shows the start, and then you follow the red-painted Ts which mark all major paths. Altitude is quickly gained and with it, wide views extending to the end of the lake. This is one place where I don't mind seeing my destination at the start of the day. It looks inviting to be able to spend two full days above that lake which is deep blue in early summer, then green as the surrounding glaciers begin to discharge their mineral-rich melt-waters into it. As the path levels off near the top of Veslefjell (1,743m, 5,718ft) you are on a typical Norwegian stony mountain. Although plant life isn't abundant, that in the area around Gjendesheim is protected by law because of its unusual richness.

As the descent starts, the ridge narrows to the famed Besseggen ridge. It is at least narrow enough to give a view down both sides at the same time: on the right are the deep blue waters of Bessvatn (though it is usually ice-covered until well into July), which lie in sharp contrast to the green Gjende on the left. Besseggen has become the one 'thing' walkers 'do' in the Norwegian mountains, and on a good summer's day there can be plenty of people on it. Many are the tales about the horrors of that (perfectly easy, safe and innocent) path! Besseggen also features in Ibsen's *Peer Gynt*; he had a terrifying ride along the ridge on a reindeer buck. Apparently Ibsen himself never went there but used the vivid descriptions he got from his friends!

From the southern end of Bessvatn the path continues below Besshø which still shuts out the view to the north. A little lake is passed

before the final descent to Memurubu. (An alternative to going over Besseggen is to follow the path along lake Gjende all the way from Gjendesheim to Memurubu (3½ hours).

From Memurubu an extra day can be spent going up the peak of Surtningssui (2,368m, 7,769ft) the seventh highest peak in Norway. It is an ordinary path, taking some 4–5 hours to go up, and 2–3 to descend. The top is said to give one of the best views in Jotunheimen.

Grass, water and rock—a typical combination of terrain. (Photo: Ingrid High.)

Day 2: Memurubu to Gjendebu

The second half of the lake, from Memurubu to Gjendebu is a walk in many ways even nicer than the previous day. After crossing the wild river which is fed by the big glaciers of central Jotunheimen, the path goes steeply up the ridge to the west of the hut. This hill is only 1,400m (4,500ft) so you are below the stone-line the whole day, with grass and flowers along the path. The green lake of Gjende is again company far down on the left, and the mountains on its other side, continue to unfold themselves. In addition, you are not closed in to the north and west, but have long views to the many peaks and glaciers of central Jotunheimen.

At a signpost a path goes off westwards, for a longer way to Gjendebu which avoids the steep descent to the lake-side. Our path, the one going south, soon goes over the edge seemingly heading straight for the lake. It is necessary to follow the T-markings in all their windings, since the terrain otherwise is difficult. This steep place is called Bukkelageret. Along the lake the path goes among small and twisted mountain birches. Luggage which has been sent by boat can be picked up here and the little stone hut where Gjendine lived marks the entrance to Gjendebu.

Day 3: Gjendebu to Eidsbugarden or Tyinholmen

Eidsbugarden and Tyinholmen are not yet part of the dependable network of huts. They both have private hotels and it is necessary to enquire at DNT before setting out, to find out which, if either, is open. Tyinholmen is the most convenient place since getting there will cut the next day to a reasonable day's walking; Eidsbugarden is possibly the nicer place of the two.

From Gjendebu the main path south follows the valley (with the telephone lines). If the weather is good you can alternatively continue the line of the previous two days by going up the hill behind Gjendebu (Gjendestunga, 1,516m, 4,974ft), and then follow the tops until joining the other path at its highest part. Before the top, paths go off westwards for Olavsbu and Skogadalsbøen; ignore these. At the little lake below the hillock called Rundtom (round-about) an alternative path for Eidsbugarden goes off to the right. This is not T-marked. After the descent to lake Bygdin the path follows the lake-side to Eidsbugarden. Bygdin is one of the rare lakes which has a noticeable tidal difference in its water level.

At Eidsbugarden there are a few old houses lying near the hotel as a memory of the early tourist traffic. This was the mountain home of the author Aasmund O. Vinje, who was active in creating the organisation DNT (achieved in 1868). On the edge of the lake, by the large red-painted hotel, there is a statue commemorating him. A short distance along the road is another red-painted house, 'Den Glade

Flowers on the lakeside path to Gjendebu. (Photo: Ingrid High.)

Vandrer' (The Happy Walker), which offers cheap and good accommodation. (A recommended day-trip from Eidsbugarden is to go up the low hill Skinneggen which lies to the south of the lake and enjoy the view.)

In the Tyin/Eidsbugarden area, flocks of reindeer can be seen that are owned by local farmers. Remains of Stone-Age settlements have been found along the shores of Lake Tyin, probably used by early reindeer hunters. In many places in the mountains you will find *dyregraver* (deer graves). These are holes in the ground, deep and with built-up vertical sides that were used to trap reindeer; the main hunting method in earlier days.

At Eidsbugarden we have arrived in Slingsby-country. William C. Slingsby was, since his first tour in 1872, one of the pioneers in mountaineering in Norway. His book, *Norway, the Northern Playground*, first published in 1904, is as readable today as it was then (though, like many mountain classics it is now hard to obtain), and gives much information on both the area and its people. Slingsby stayed at Eidsbugarden during his eventful six-day crossing of Jotunheimen in July 1876. He, his Norwegian mountaineering friend Emmanuel Mohn, and a local farmer (who was an unwilling guide) started at the east end of Lake Bygdin and as they proceeded westwards they made the first ascent of a major peak almost every day: Torfinnstind, Galdebergstind, Uranostind, and after Skogadalsbøen, Gjertvasstind, and then at last, the major feat, Store Skagastølstind, the highest peak of Hurrungane.

Day 4: Eidsbugarden/ Tyinholmen to Vettismorki/ Vetti

This is a long day, but it might be possible to arrange transport by car along the road which leads 6km (4 miles) into Koldedalen. This would mean missing a big lake, as well as some smaller ones, 6km (4 miles) of open landscape with views up the peak of Uranos, its glacier and neighbouring peaks, as well as over two hours of walking.

So, coming either from Koldedalen, or past Kvitevatnet (the white lake) along the path from Tyinholmen/Eidsbugarden, the paths merge near the southern end of Lake Uradalsvatnet. Shortly along the stony lakeside there is a signpost for a path going off up to the left. (The path which continues along the lake is the direct way to Skogadalsbøen.) Our path, marked for Vetti, goes directly up to a little pass with a few small tarns on the main east-west watershed; from now on all rivers drain into the fjords of the west country. This also marks a change in landscape; the bleak and stony landscape of the east changes into that of the fjord country with vegetation, alpine mountains and animals.

After a last look back your attention is caught by the beautifully engineered stone path which was built long ago to take people

In the bottom of the Utla Valley lies the ancient farm of Vetti. There is a tourist hut here as well nowadays, though the road didn't reach Vetti until 1977. (Photo: Ingrid High.)

and animals along the very stony and, without the path, next to impossible hillside. Soon you are out of the stones and in the grass at the head of Fleskedalen (literally pork valley, but implying 'The Valley of Milk and Honey').

This valley, like all side valleys in this area, has a huge heap of stone rubble from the tunnelling operations for a big hydro-power scheme which produces electricity for a large aluminium production plant at Øvre Årdal. But going downhill, you are soon past the eyesore, and the path gently ambles on in a pleasant valley, beside a peaceful stream— could it be more pleasant? At a bend in the river you might see reindeer grazing on the meadows—there is a small protected flock of wild reindeer in this valley.

Where Fleskedalen joins the main valley, Utladalen, there is a little *seter*, also named Fleskedalen. One of the huts is now being rebuilt to take walkers, but it will not have any food. If the day has been long, you might consider staying there.

The *seter* is sheltered from the main valley by a little ridge. Up on this, you can enjoy a stupendous view. Almost a thousand feet below, is a steep-sided and forested valley with an almost hidden wild river in its bottom. On the other side, Midtmaradalen, a U-shaped side valley, goes into Hurrungane, the 'alps' of southern Norway. Snow, ice and steep-sided dark peaks stretch far along it, abundantly feeding the big river which falls down from the valley entrance. Perhaps you might see an eagle fly by below, and it is difficult not to think that there might still be bears down there. Over the last 400 years some 1500 bears have been shot in this valley and its side valleys. It is doubtful whether any are left today, but there are lynx and wolverine, as well as deer, elk and reindeer.

Trees begin to appear along the path, first juniper and birches, then fir trees. Many of the firs and junipers have unfortunately fallen prey to the pollution from the aluminium plant 15km (9 miles) further down the main valley. The fluoride gas causing the damage, which earlier was let out from the plant, is now under control, and hopefully a regrowth is possible.

Less than an hour below Fleskedalen *seter* lies Vettismorki, another *seter* with one of the huts providing DNT sleeping quarters. The hut is small and cosy, newly built, with 4 beds (plus 2 spare mattresses), a gas cooker, crockery and bedding but no food. Most important of all is that it has an efficient woodstove which ensures that any boots dry overnight. With all the vegetation in this valley, the boots seem to get wet whatever the weather. Elk wander around the houses early in the morning.

Here too a little ridge shields the *seter* area from the main valley. The walk over to it goes on soft and deep moss, grass and heather, among the huge fir trees, including fallen giants in all stages of decay. Here you are opposite Stølsmaradalen, another of the big U-valleys leading many miles into the Hurrungane Mountains. Again you have an impressive view of peaks, glaciers and snows. The big river coming out over the lip of this valley cascades widely down the thousand feet of cliffs to the bottom of Utladalen.

(From Vettismorki an extra day is well spent in going down to Vetti, where there is a tourist hut, but more importantly Vettisfossen, Norway's highest free-falling waterfall which thunders 270m (880ft) down to the bottom of the valley. There is a good view of it from a viewing place on the T-marked path from Vettismorki, and from Vetti it is only 20 minutes to walk along the big river to get close to the bottom of the water-fall. In the days when the fir trees at Vettismorki were still cut for industry, the trunks were sent down the waterfall. This was preferably done in winter when the huge ice pillar forming at the bottom cushioned the fall. Vetti's tourist hut provides food and lodging in homely surroundings. From Vetti you can walk to Øvre Årdal where there are bus connections to Årdalstangen from where a boat can take you to Bergen or a bus can take you to Oslo.)

Day 5: Vettismorki to Skogadalsbøen

The path is followed back to Fleskedalen and continued up the ridge above. It leaves the ridge just below 1300m (4265ft) but the continuation up to 1,503-m (4931-ft) high Friken hill is easy. The top gives a good view over to Hurrungane. The main path then gently descends along the side of Friken. Skogadalsbøen hut can be seen far away, and is lost again as the path winds the last kilometres through some forested hillocks. On the other side of Utladalen, Maradalen, the last of the three 'mara' valleys ('mare') opens up its views for a while until you are past that one too.

Does this name 'mare' imply the docile horse or should it be in combination with 'night'? With the impassable mountains and glaciers of Hurrungane, the steep black rock of its many peaks and their inaccessibility, I find it difficult to accept the peaceful interpretation of the name. People have rarely been in these valleys, and it needed a foreign mountaineer (Slingsby) to be the first person to cross the Hurrungane mountains (*hurra* meaning thundering river).

Skogadalsbøen is a full-service, staffed hut, lying high and with good views. The hut itself is ordinary, but with good facilities and food. Above all, the people who work there know the mountains. There was a *seter* here in earlier days when animals and people came along the path from Turtagrø, going over Keisarpasset, this being the easiest way of access.

(There are many day trips possible from Skogadalsbøen. The valley above the hut, Skogadalen ('forest'-valley), is one of the highest places in Norway where trees grow. A river offers many quiet pools for a dip on a hot day, and elk and deer can often be seen. The path leads back to Eidsbugarden. A beautiful but long trip; it is also a possible way to Olavsbu.)

(More ideas for day trips are to walk down the other side of the Utladal to the recently restored farm of Vormeli (warm meadows), which now offers overnight accommodation although you have to supply your own food. Another idea is to climb Friken from here (if you haven't done so already). You go up from its northern end, from the enormous blocks that form the entrance to Uradal.)

Day 6: Skogadalsbøen to Turtagrø

The standard route to Turtagrø is to follow the old *seter* path over the 1,500-m (4,920-ft) Keisarpasset (The Pass of the Emperor). An alternative which is well worth considering, is to go through Styggedalen. Although it is aptly named (Styggedalen meaning 'Bad Valley'), because of the stone-blocks making up part of the path, you pass right below the northern Hurrungane peaks and glaciers. The way follows the ordinary route until below Keisarpasset where it goes left. The path zig-zags past the three lakes; the first and last are passed on the north, the second on its south side. After passing the moraine at the bottom of Styggedalsbreen you follow the hillside to the left, contouring round until you pass a lake where there are *dyregraver*. Eventually the path leads into Skagastølsdalen where the big path for Turtagrø is joined.

If the weather is good, you can spend two days going to Turtagrø by going over Fanaråken and staying in the self service hut on its top for the night (2,068m, 6,785ft). The views include the big glacier of Jostedalsbreen in the west, as well as most of Jotunheimen.)

The hotel at Turtagrø also offers cheap accommodation and once was the centre of mountaineering; it is full of old photographs showing its place in history. From Turtagrø you can go walking, scrambling and climbing in Hurrungane.

Whether happy, or sad, at Turtagrø, 'civili-

sation' has been reached. The road is there to prove it. The walk is ended.

The Way Back

For those who have more time to spare there is plenty more walking possible, for instance by

Skogadalsbøen Hut above the Utla-Valley lies on high ground and has a wide view. (Photo: Ingrid High.)

Norway's highest free-fall waterfall is Vettifossen, 270 m high. The woods above once produced timber for industry and the logs were sent over the fall.
(Photo: Ingrid High.)

going back east through the northern part of Jotunheimen via the huts Leirvassbu, Spiterstulen, Glitterheim and then back to Gjendesheim. These places give access to good peak-days, but the actual walks between the huts are not very special. They are popular since they are easy, so one meets a lot more people in these northern and central parts of Jotunheimen.

Leirvassbu is then the first place to get to. You can go there directly from Skogadalsbøen in one day, along the rather long Gravdalen. This valley has many *dyregraver*. A more interesting alternative would be to first go to Krossbu (5 hours from Skogadalsbøen), which lies on the same road as Turtagrø, then spend the next day in crossing the high glaciers of Smørstabbtindane over to Leirvassbu. Guided tours go daily between the two huts across the glacier, taking (almost) all walkers in big groups (6 hours). Leirvassbu is nicely situated at a lake where several valleys meet. There are many peaks around, inviting to day trippers. The impressive-looking Kyrkja (the church) to the east is one.

From Leirvassbu go on to Spiterstulen (5 hours). From here a path goes up to the top of Galdhøpiggen, at 2,469m (8,100ft) the highest peak in Norway. From Spiterstulen another day (5 hours) is needed to reach Glitterheim. If the weather is good, you can go over the top of Glittertind on the way (add 2-3 hours), else you follow the path below, hoping for better weather for the next day. The height of Glittertind is now recorded at 2,464m (8,084ft) though it is covered by thick snow, the highest point of rock being 2,452m (8,045ft). Depending upon the snow conditions Glittertind is the highest peak in Norway some years, other years only second! There is no hut or shelter on its top, even though some maps indicate there is. The snow covering the top gives poor anchoring facilities.

From Glitterheim you can complete the circle of Jotunheimen by returning to Gjendesheim; a day which leads back into the more open country to the east of the high peaks.

Walk 17 SWITZERLAND: The Grindelwald Cirque by Andrew Harper

A Magnificent Walk Amongst some of Europe's Most Attractive Scenery

Anyone seeking my recommendation for an area that would introduce them to alpine walking would have to wait no more than a few seconds for my reply: *The Grindelwald Area* near Interlaken in Switzerland.

The walking sections can be short or quite long and can be easily tailored to the new-comer to alpine walking. Start and exit points are richly served by a complex system of regular mountain rail, cablecar, chair-lift and post-bus services and access to the area by rail, air or car could not be easier. Wayside camping aside, accommodation is plentiful—especially in the valleys which cater, in the main, for the traditional tourist—but there are excellent facilities at some of the notable high-level vantage points too. Eating establishments that offer variety of both cuisine and price, abound.

The 'Cirque' in the title is a geological description for the upper basin vacated by a receding glacier (long, long ago in this instance) and the walk about to be described goes as far as it is practicable to trace the edge of the rim containing it. The bowl is enormous and features on its southern flank some of the best-known mountains of the Alps—the Eiger, Mönch and Jungfrau—as well as the towering

The Eiger, Mönch and Jungfrau seen from the path between Breitlauenen and Schynige Platte. (Photo: Andrew Harper.)

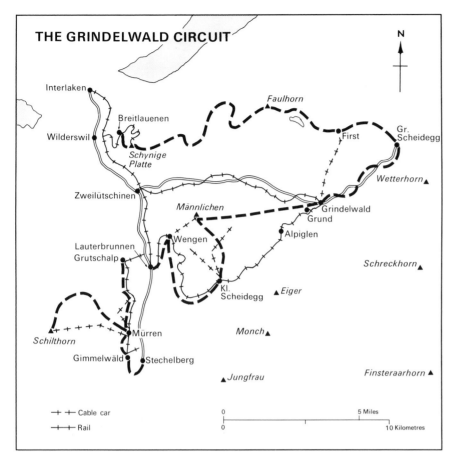

THE GRINDELWALD CIRCUIT

Distance: 70km (44 miles).
Ascent: 4,700m (15,500ft).
Descent: 3,250m (10,500ft).
(These figures allow for the climb to Schilthorn).
Time Required: 4 to 7 days.
Type of Walk: Possibly the easiest kind of mountain walking where the venture can be undertaken without any great apprehension. Bad weather can drastically change the demands made on any walker and the long sections are susceptible to this eventuality. Sign-posting at path commencements and junctions is immaculate. Waymarking is adequate.
Base: Interlaken.
Start: Wilderswil/Schynige Platte.
Best Time of Year: July to September.
Map: Landeskarte 1:50,000 sheet 5004—
Berner Oberland.
Information: Swiss National Tourist Office, 1 New Coventry Street, London, W1. Also the Tourist Offices in Interlaken or Grindelwald.

Wetterhorn at the eastern end of the range. Snow, perpetual snow and ice, share the landscape with the dull grey of rock but these, and the shapes they create, are contrasted by the alpine pastures which are quite often carpeted with thousands of delicate and colourful flowers.

Animal life is not plentiful but it is there to be found just the same. The marmot (a beaver-like mammal) is a charming and playful inhabitant with a danger signal of a high pitched whistle. There are also three types of wild 'deer' to look for, but these are harder to detect as they go about their business more quietly than the marmot and, in any case, are timid creatures that blend in with the landscape to such a degree that sighting them at all can be regarded as an accomplishment. The roaming cows are exceedingly handsome beasts, decorated with a big bell suspended from their necks by an enormous leather collar (these adornments range from the utilitarian to the flamboyant) and in consequence the area echoes to the clinking of these animals at pasture.

Stage 1: To the Faulhorn

The route starts by booking to Breitlauenen

and then boarding the mountain railway train at Wilderswill, on the northern outskirts of Interlaken. Breitlauenen, at 1,542m (5,059ft), is some eight or nine minutes below the upper terminus of the narrow-gauge line which serves the hotel and Alpine garden at Schynige Platte (1,967m, 6,453ft). Alighting at this little halt will allow the thinner Alpine air to be appreciated for the first time. The path wanted is indicated on a post (the whole area is enviably waymarked and indicated): Schynige Platte: 1Std. 30min. It took me three visits to the Alps before I realised that 'Std.' did not stand for 'Standard' but *Stunden* which means 'hours' in German (which is the language spoken throughout the area). Nevertheless, the times given are the standard for walking to the places indicated and are always a very helpful pointer.

Penetrating thin forest, the route eventually emerges to slant alongside a rock wall, allowing intimate sightings down and along the enormous cleft of the Lauterbrunnen valley, showing for the first time the celebrated waterfalls that plunge from its sheer flanks at several places along its length. Passing derelict dairy sheds, the ascending railway line can be discerned over and higher up to the left and after eventually climbing to the same height the path levels to encounter the hotel and restaurant building. The view from the terrace presents the three major peaks of the Oberland, seen beyond the much smaller Männlichen and the dark cone of the Lauberhorn. Facilities exist for acquiring either a bedroom in the hotel or participating in the dormitory-style *matratzenläger*.

The next staging post will be the Faulhorn mountain, where there is a very good restaurant and various categories of sleeping accommodation. The path that leads there starts at the railway station (just below the hotel) with a timing indication of some 4 hours. There is a small chalet offering beverages and snacks at the 3-hour point and, providing it is open, it can be a real godsend.

There is nothing more difficult on the route ahead than that experienced so far—the bulk of the walking being quite carefree and at such a slow rate of ascension that it is barely noticeable. From the very start the view across the void (which houses Grindelwald at its base) towards the enormous Oberland peaks will fascinate—continually changing viewpoints will present them in a hardly-discernable transition and the varying cloud formations will add their ingredient to alter the vista. But not all of the sightseeing pleasures are of mountains: after only some thirty-five minutes the path comes very close to a cliff-edge on the

left and everyone is encouraged to wander to its extreme and gaze down over Interlaken and Lake Brienz. The view also extends right along Lake Thun as far as the conical mountain called Niesen which has the small town of Spiez at its foot. Magic on a clear day.

The path meanders its course, through rocky defiles, along flagstones, curving along terraces and over marshy sheep-inhabited grassland until the deep blue lake can be seen at the far bottom end of the Sägistal. Here it slants up the right-hand side of the valley until, at the far end, it hairpins back on itself into the small Hühnertal where, for the first time, the building on the pointed Faulhorn (2,681m, 8,796ft) can be seen diagonally opposite, its enormous Swiss flag possibly fluttering in the breeze. It will take well over an hour to reach it though. Wild and exposed country, this, with extended views to the north and north-east.

Continuing on the path, quite often through late-lying patches of snow, it takes only some fifteen minutes to reach the small chalet seen on the saddle, where (if open) you can quench your thirst. This little haven goes by the name of Weber-hütte (2,343m, 7,687ft) and is usually hosted by a hospitable family who produce scalding hot drinks without undue delay and a limited selection of snacks. Passing on, the path climbs for a while to reach the shoulder of a flank where, curving to the left, the gentle upward slope permits an easy pace for some thirty minutes during which time the Oberland peaks cannot be seen. The view over to the half-left can be extensive in clear weather. During my last visit a little puff of smoke was discernible at the crest of one of the dark peaks and the explanation of this was, of course, the steam-operated mountain railway from Brienz that climbs to the hotel at Brienzer-Rothorn.

The infamous Eigerwand (North Face of the Eiger) has seen some dramatic Alpine struggles. The view from the Mannlichen to Kl. Scheidegg path. (Photo: Andrew Harper.)

Top: **The Wetterhorn dominates the Alpine village of Grindelwald, once famous for its mountain guides.** (Photo: Walt Unsworth.)

Above: **The Weber-Hutte is a convivial little cafe met on the first day of the walk.** (Photo: Andrew Harper.)

Eventually the ridge is reached and a changed and fine view is to hand. Not only are the three main peaks shown in fresh perspective, but the two spiky summits of the Schreckhorn and the Finsteraarhorn can be seen lurking amongst the glacier icefields that were earlier hidden behind the Eiger. Due to these incredible views, the path is deservedly popular, and hence is well defined and easy to follow.

Coming to the base of the Faulhorn, the weary traveller might foresake the direct approach up the steep slope and take the easier, but longer path that skirts to the right. Whichever you take the panoramic view from the summit viewing platforms will make all the effort worthwhile and with sufficient Swiss francs, a selection made from the restaurant's menu can only increase your pleasure.

Stage 2: Onwards to Grosse Scheidegg

The path from this last venue is carved into the rutted hillside and leaves in a southerly direction, dropping towards the picturesquely situated Lake Bachsee at 2,265m (7,431ft). Until recently this was the route that mules plied to fetch supplies up to the Faulhorn: it now would appear to be more economic for helicopters to 'drop' what is needed, but making the change has removed a quaint link with the past.

Promotional pictures for the area show the distant peaks reflected in the calm waters of Bachsee but luck will be needed to emulate this in your own photographs as the barest breath of a breeze seems to 'etch' the surface. The rate of descent slackens for the rest of the way to a place called First (2,168m, 7,113ft), where there is a good restaurant as well as the upper station to the four-section Sesselbahn or chair-lift system operating from Grindelwald. There is no accommodation available.

The cafeteria terrace makes the most of the promontory position on which it has been constructed and offers splendid views towards the main massif, which can now be seen from closer quarters. On show, too, is the bulky Wetterhorn to the left of all the others.

You will have noticed at least three pathheads labelled for 'Grindelwald' since departing Faulhorn and these wind their way to the resort through meadowland each taking their appropriate time to do so. In the early summer the whole of this area is a carpet of mountain flowers and is best seen by meandering amongst them. However, the recommendation I make is that it is best to continue from First by 'contouring' the hillsides to the east, (taking 1hr 45mins) to reach the hostelry sitting astride

the road pass at Gr. Scheidegg (1,961m, 6,434ft) which can be seen at the foot of the steep northern face of the Wetterhorn. The path is splendid all the way, crossing numerous streams and pastures.

The premises at Gr. Scheidegg boast a splendid restaurant and offer overnight accommodation. A bus service links it directly with Grindelwald.

Stage 3: Down to Grindelwald and Grund

With the Eiger fixed in the eye (showing how narrow its summit ridge is when viewed from this direction) start off on the 2hr 45 min— path which bisects the hairpin twists of the road as both drop gently towards Grindelwald at 1,038m (3,406ft). It is a super experience to stroll down here. Barren landscape gradually gets substituted for toiled land, the few farm buildings offering a colourful foreground for photographs of the massive stone walls to the left.

Drawing towards the Hotel Wetterhorn, with its associated crowds, the view up the gorge harbouring the Obere Grindelwaldgletscher will make you stop and stare awhile. This glacier glints when the late afternoon sun glances from it and looks a picture. Unavoidably plodding along the roadway for a short distance, the remainder of the way into Grindelwald, passes an increasing density of chalet homes which culminate in the whole array of hotels, shops and facilities which form the resort.

Stage 4: The Ascent to Männlichen and then to Kleine Scheidegg

Having done what you will in the place, the traditional route sets out to reach Kl. Scheidegg (situated on the saddle in a general south-west direction) by way of Alpiglen. Although this path trails through woodland initially, it becomes unpleasant where it subsequently shares the wide scars that become ski runs in the winter. What is more, it goes too close to the base of the Eiger and prohibits a balanced aspect of the monolith. Far better then to aim for Männlichen. Both routes commence at Grund (943m, 3,094ft), the lower quarter of Grindelwald, and are signposted adequately. Do not blanch at the extra hour required for the route I suggest, but be assured that it is lovely all the way. You will soon become aware of its attractions and once above the bubblecar mid-way station the pleasure of tramping open hillside will guarantee the removal of any lingering doubt. The sightings of the Eiger north face are superb

throughout the climb and its awesome dominance becomes more distinctive as you begin to look at it 'square on'.

Männlichen at 2,343m (7,687ft) sits on the edge of an enormous cliff and from its viewing platform has commanding views straight down into the Lauterbrunnen Valley. Wengen can easily be recognised at the bottom end of the cableway and it takes as little as eight minutes for a cablecar to bring holidaymakers up from there. Amongst the cluster of buildings at Männlichen there is a newly-constructed and superb self-service restaurant, the choice of foods being quite vast. Do not fail to go to the summit which is some fifteen minutes' climb from the cablecar station: it offers a magnificent panoramic view of the vicinity and you will be able to see most of the places visited earlier on the holiday.

One of the nicest 'balcony' paths in the Alps links Männlichen with K1. Scheidegg. This meanders in the general direction of the north face of the Eiger which imposes its enormity for most of the walk, which takes 1hr 20mins. It is a wide and safe path with occasional bench seats but pay heed to the short stretches that warn of stonefall.

Reaching K1. Scheidegg at 2,061m (6,762ft) will bring you into contact with the hundreds of rail-borne tourists that visit the place daily (although inclement weather can cut their number drastically!), but this also means the provided facilities are up to scratch and use can be made of them. There are numerous restaurants to choose from and the buffet associated with the railway station is excellent too. It is relatively easy to acquire overnight accommodation, but for this do not overlook the first place encountered on the way down from Männlichen.

Stage 5: Wengen, Lauterbrunnen, Mürren

The path to Wengernalp (1,873m, 6,145ft) is signposted and drops away just in front of the railway station and takes about 45 minutes. It shares the general direction of the railway whose presence will be unnoticed until a train trundles past. Over a deep divide, the overpowering scale of the ice-clad ramparts associ-

Above: **The Eiger (left) and Mönch, seen from near Murren. Notice how the signs are in time, not distance, Std is short for** *stunde,* **the German word for hours.**

Facing page: **The crags of the Wetterhorn form a dramatic backcloth to the path between First and Gr. Scheidegg.**
(Photos: Andrew Harper.)

ated with the Jungfrau present an intriguing study. Known for its spectacular avalanches, the *crack* and thunderous roar associated with them would quickly allow you to pinpoint one should it occur. Wengernalp features a modest hotel and it is one of my ambitions to lodge there for a couple of nights to contemplate at leisure its wonderful outlook.

To reach the hotel it is necessary to go through a small pedestrian tunnel under the railway, but the onward path drops to the left just before it. The signpost there will direct you onto a dropping path through the fields. Bearing right to go through some scant trees it then crosses a couple of small meadows, levelling for a while before continuing its drop to reach the resort of Wengen (1,274m, (4,180ft), which is a nice place to saunter through. Lingering awhile under a strident sun can be pleasant enough but you will be seeking the head of the path that drops through the fields towards Lauterbrunnen. As you lose altitude it will be easy to sense the beauty of the deep narrow defile into which you are sinking.

Lauterbrunnen at 800m (2,625ft) has not lost its attraction, despite the intrusion of the railway and the motor car. You could well finish the *Cirque* journey here by taking one of the frequent trains to Interlaken and soon be homeward bound. But for an extra day or so, there is a host of visual rewards to be had by scaling the western flanks. Another highly-respected balcony path is that linking Grüts-chalp at 1,489m (4,885ft) and Mürren at

1,645m (5,397ft). It is possible to join a path departing the centre of Lauterbrunnen's main street but it gains altitude relentlessly through dense woodland and emerges half-way along the path in question. Why not take the funicular railway to lift you effortlessly to Grütschalp leaving you to expend your energy on something more worthy?

The aim is to reach the resort of Mürren and an alternative approach (which does not involve walking along 'the balcony') is to reach Stechelberg (910m, 2,986ft) by walking in a southerly direction along the valley floor (walk the extent of the main street in Lauterbrunnen and, ignoring where road curves down to left, continue straight ahead on a narrow track). It takes 2 hours or so to get to Stechelberg village, which is past the obtrusive lower terminus of the Schilthornbahn cableway system. The path comes to a grey-painted metal bridge and, once over, turns sharp right to gain altitude up a narrow wooded gorge, where you follow directions for 'Gimmelwäld'. With swiftly-flowing water for company, this is a delightful path: steepish at first, but opening out at a junction where you turn right to pass chalets and reach the village. From the bridge it will take approximately 1hr 30mins to reach Gimmelwäld (1,393m, 4,570ft).

From Gimmelwäld to Mürren it is necessary to tread the roadway, but this sure-footed hour will allow continual glances to the enormous mountainscape on your right, where you should be able to pick out the now miniscule Wengernalp hotel and station, whilst a little later on you should be able to recognise the complex of buildings at K1. Scheidegg in the far distance.

Mürren can offer rewarding holidays to visitors throughout the year, peaking with the enviable and awe-inspiring spectacle of its air-balloon festival in mid-summer when the colours of these enormous gas shrouds add another dimension to the venue.

Stage 6: Above Mürren—The Schilthorn

What to do once at Mürren? You could stroll to its southern extremities and explore the lanes beyond which you will discover well-preserved examples of old shepherds' chalets. From their vicinity you will be able to see the continuing Alpine wall that extends west from the Jungfrau, comprising such notables as the Ebnefluh, the Mittaghorn, the Breithorn and the Tschingelhorn—all seen from 'half height' which presents, in my mind at least, the best perspective. It is possible to join the tourists and board the cablecar for the two-stage journey to visit Schilthorn. Here, at

Looking back to Grindelwald from Kl. Scheidegg. In the distance is the Wetterhorn and nearer is the grim Eiger. (Photo: Walt Unsworth.)

almost 3,000m (10,000ft) you will be 'up amongst the peaks' and the view is an absolute gem.

My last suggestion, to complete your appreciation of the area, would be to *walk* up to the Schilthorn (2,960m, 9,711ft) instead of using the cablecar. If you have walked from Lauterbrunnen there would not be time to complete the route that day, but, fortunately, a conveniently-situated mountain *refuge* is located to break the journey. This is called the Schilthornhütte (2,432m, 7,979ft) and the path towards it starts in the middle of Mürren and promises 2¹/₂ hrs of walking. It gets unpleasantly steep only as it cuts past a defile, but the approach to this spot and that which follows is representative of all that is best in mountain path creation. When I was last there I was treated to a playful display by some fawns in a herd of *bergstöcken* who slid, scampered and bounded on the few stretches of remaining snow—what a privilege it was to observe such behaviour!

After a spartan wash at the outside trough and a basic breakfast in the hut, the onward path to Schilthorn rises gently up the right-hand side of the valley floor behind the Birg shoulder which hosts the cableway's intermediate station. It then skirts the base of a snowfield (I have never seen it snow-free) and goes up its left-hand side to gain access to a ridge which leads to the shiny building at the summit. When progressing along this ridge it is possible to see over the intervening valleys in the general direction of Kandersteg with, once again, the splendid vista of distant mountainsides to greet the eye.

Schilthorn's famous panoramic restaurant slowly revolves on its axis. It is understandably expensive to eat there but the cost of a pot of tea is a small price to pay for a life-long memory of the place—although the views from the terraces are entirely free of charge.

I suggest you regain terra firma by descending by cableway: you will probably have earned it!

An introducton to the Alps? Maybe, but I have enjoyed returning to the area on numerous occasions and so, too, have others!

Appendix: BEST OF THE REST
by Walt Unsworth

When I came to compile *Classic Walks of Europe* I found myself faced with a considerable dilemma. I had already compiled *Classic Walks of the World* which included some of the most famous European walks. Obviously these routes would have to be included in the present book, too, yet I did not wish to use valuable space repeating articles which had appeared elsewhere—and in any case, readers who had bought *Classic Walks of the World* would have been justifiably miffed to find themselves buying the same thing again!

Then *The Sunday Times Magazine* commissioned a number of short route descriptions and it seemed to me that some of these would serve

admirably as potted versions of the originals. Here then, for the benefit of those who may not have the book, are brief descriptions of the European routes in *Classic Walks of the World*.

They are arranged in order from the least arduous to the most arduous, though this is arguable. The only one which needs special comment is the Via Delle Bocchette in the Brenta Dolomites. This walk is an extremely exposed *via ferrata,* or climbing path, involving steep ladders up blank walls and ledges protected by cables. It is not in the least strenuous—but it is sensational and should on no account be attempted by anyone afraid of heights.

The Aiguille de la Vanoise. (Photo: Walt Unsworth.)

163

Tour de la Vanoise, France

Distance: 75km (47 miles).
Time: 5 days.
Start: Landry, Isère Valley.
Best Time of Year: July to September.
Maps: IGN CT 235, 236, 237. 1:25,000.
Guidebook: *Walking the French Alps, GR5* by Martin Collins (Cicerone Press).

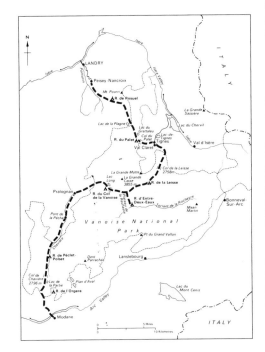

As an introduction to Alpine walking it would be hard to improve on the delectable traverse of the Vanoise National Park, which lies between the valleys of the Isère and Arc in Savoie. The region is well known in winter for its modern ski resorts like Courchevel, but its summer charms are largely ignored—except by the French themselves, who made this their first national park in 1963.

The route starts at Landry in the Isère valley and for the first couple of days travels south towards Tignes and the mountainous heart of the region. A series of high passes served by mountain huts help the traveller on his way. The views are astonishing, ranging as they do over to Italy and the peaks of the Gran Paradiso National Park; once the place where the Italian Royal Family hunted the *bouquetin*, but preserved since 1922.

The peaks of the Grande Motte and the Grande Casse soon begin to dominate the scenery as the walk heads over the easy Col de la Vanoise to the Felix Faure hut: the largest mountain *refuge* in the French Alps. From the hut the way down to the village of Pralognan is sheer delight. Rocky pinnacles rise on either

hand as the path takes to a causeway across the shallow Lac des Vaches. Pralognan itself is an old world village of considerable charm.

South again, the path travels the long vale of the Chavière towards the pass of the same name. The Col de Chavière at 2,796m (9,173ft) has the distinction of being the highest point of any Grande Randonnée in France. It is a suitable climax to the walk: from the col it is down, down, down to the town of Modane and the railway home.

Via Delle Bocchette, Italian Dolomites

Distance: 24km (15 miles).
Time: 3 days.
Start: Madonna di Campiglio.
Best Time of Year: July to August.
Maps: Kompass Wanderkarte 073, Dolomiti di Brenta, 1:30,000.
Guidebook: *Via Ferrata—Scrambles in the Dolomites* by Cecil Davies (Cicerone Press).

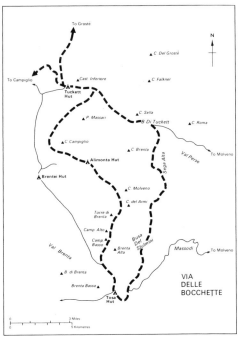

It you are looking for a walk with a difference, then this is the one! Short and sharp, the walk requires little energy but considerable nerve because it teeters across the face of some of the biggest cliffs in the Dolomites. The scenery is always spectacular, the positon seldom less than sensational.

It starts with a cable-car ride up to the Grostè Pass from the village of Campiglio, then a gentle stroll below the pinnacled crest of the Brenta ridge to the Tuckett Hut in time for lunch. At this point the walk gets serious. Our route follows a *via ferrata*, which means 'iron road' and is so called because the walker is given the help of a wire handrail in the tricky bits and even iron ladders. This section of the route is called the Sentiero SOSAT. It gives superb views over the valley to the distant Adamello Alps, which float like white clouds on the horizon.

Soon, however, sterner things come to hand. A deep gully is crossed by means of a long, long, ladder bolted to the rock walls. There is space below your feet—hundreds of feet of it! It is with some relief that the comfortable Alimonta Hut is eventually reached.

The next day sees the highlights of the Via delle Bocchette. The path climbs ladders and then zig-zags through some of the most amazing rock scenery to be found anywhere in the world. The exposure is extreme, but provided a protective cord is used (details in the guide book) it is safe enough. By lunch the Tosa Hut is reached and in the afternoon the route doubles back along the ridge by means of an easier path called the Sentiero Orsi. Here comes the only steep bit of the whole trip—a long pull up to the Bocca di Tuckett and then steeply down to the Tuckett Hut for the night.

All that remains next day is a gentle walk down to Madonna di Campiglio. It is worth glancing back at the pinnacled ridge towering above. It scarcely seems possible that you have just walked through such incredible scenery.

The Pennine Way, England

Distance: 403km (250 miles).
Time: 16 days.
Start: Edale, Derbyshire.
Best Time of Year: May to September.
Maps: OS 1:50,000. Sheets 110, 109, 103, 98, 92, 91, 86, 80, 74.
Guidebook: *The Pennine Way* by Tom Stephenson (HMSO). There are many other good guidebooks to this walk.

This is the first and best known of Britain's long-distance footpaths; it was inaugurated in 1965 after 30 years of negotiation over rights of way. It follows the 'Backbone of England'—in fact it goes beyond the Pennines across Hadrian's Wall and into Scotland. It is a remarkably varied walk and though the hills are not high by world standards, the weather can make the going tough at times.

The Way is usually walked from south to north, beginning at the hamlet of Edale in the Dark Peak and ending at Kirk Yetholm in Scotland. The most convenient accommodation is youth hostels but the guide books give plenty of alternatives.

Several distinct sections can be recognized as the walk progresses, starting in the south with the wild gritstone moors of the Dark Peak, such as Kinder Scout and Bleaklow, where the going can be hard. Black tors edge the skyline and the route passes the sad remnants of Top Withins, the scene of *Wuthering Heights*. Then the underlying rock changes to limestone, dramatically altering the scenery and giving rise to bold features such as Malham Cove and Gordale Scar. There are some fine waterfalls too, like Hardraw Force in Wensleydale.

Tan Hill is the highest pub in England, set in a situation of incredible bleakness. The walk passes this on its way to the Northern Pennines with dramatic landscape like High Cup Nick and the summit of Cross Fell; highest of the Pennine peaks at 893m (2,930ft).

Beyond the Roman Wall the route plunges into dark forests before finishing with a high flourish along the Cheviots. A walk to be proud of.

Corsican High Level Route, Corsica

Distance: 90km (56 miles).
Time: 8 days.
Start: Vizzavona.
Best Time of Year: June to September.
Maps: IGN CT73 1:100,000 and Didier et Richard No.20 Corse Nord 1:50,000.
Guidebook: *Corsican High Route – GR20* by Alan Castle (Cicerone Press).

Of all the Grande Randonées, the Sentier de la Corse, GR20, is generally reckoned to be the toughest. The route is not excessively long but there is some rough ground to travel, involving 6,300m (2,067ft) of ascent and descent. Villages and provisions are scarce and though there are few small mountain *refuges*, most travellers prefer to camp or bivouac. It is, of course, very hot and there is a considerable fire hazard amongst the dense brushwood which covers much of the mountain area—so much so that camping has been restricted in some parts. In addition to all this, some scrambling ability is required at the Cirque de la Solitude, where the paths are protected by fixed chains.

Done in its entirety, the GR20 is 200km (125

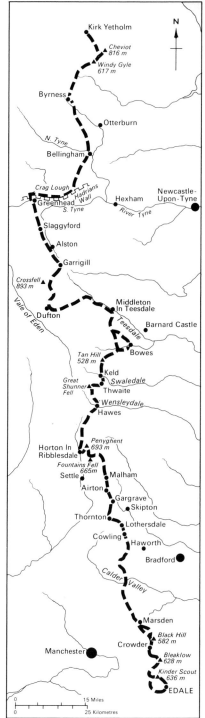

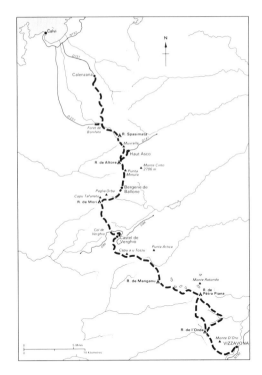

down which the path zig-zags on rocky ledges for more than 200m (650ft). The path crosses the bottom of the cwm in a short distance then climbs up again on the facing rock wall by an easy but very exposed scramble. This is certainly not the place to have vertigo.

One comforting thought is that the rock is good, solid, granite (though stonefall is not unknown in the Cirque it is usually clumsy idiots kicking stones down from above). The granite landscape is never better demonstrated than in the Spasimata Valley: 'sculpted pink rock as if caught in a perpetual dawn,' as my son graphically described it. There are some protected paths here, too, not to mention a dubious looking suspension bridge across the stream.

It is the end of the difficulties and almost the end of the walk; Calenzana is not far away, and beyond it, Calvi and the fleshpots.

miles) long because it stretches diagonally across the island from Conca in the south to Calenzana in the north, which is almost, but not quite, coast to coast. It takes three weeks to walk all this but the southern 'half', from Conca to Vizzavona, is frequently omitted because all the grandeur is in the north. Doing it this way, too, leaves a couple of days for relaxing on the beach afterwards!

Vizzavona is on the main road across the island and on the railway also, with connections to Calvi, Bastia and Ajaccio.

The GR20 never actually crosses the summit of any of the mountains, but a number are quite easy to reach by making small diversions, including one on the very first day, Monte d'Oro (2,389m, 7,838ft), reached by a summit scramble. From the top can be seen the wilderness upon which you are just embarking. It looks extremely savage, and for once appearances don't lie.

A well-filled waterbottle is essential in the days which follow because the daytime heat can be intense. The sun shimmers off the rock and the *maquis*. At the Col de Rinosa the face of the Capitello is reminiscent of the Dru above Chamonix, surrounded by crocodile teeth pinnacles which seem impossible to traverse. Yet this is where the route goes and as is so often the case, with much more ease than seemed possible at first.

Soon the view is dominated by the superb peak of Paglia Orba (2,525m, 8,284ft) and the route comes to a climax in the staggering Cirque de la Solitude; an awesome chasm

Tour du Mont Blanc, The Alps

Distance: 115km (71 miles).
Time: 11 days.
Start: Les Houches, Chamonix.
Best Time of Year: July to September.
Maps: IGN Massif du Mont Blanc (two sheets) 1:25,000.
Guidebook: *Walking Guide to the Tour du Mont Blanc* by Andrew Harper (Cicerone Press).

One of the best—if not *the* best—of the world's classic walks circumnavigates the

Mont Blanc massif, crossing happily without hindrance from France to Italy to Switzerland and back to France in the process. It has all the excitement of the high mountains yet none of the worry of altitude sickness.

It usually begins in the Chamonix valley, though as a circular walk it could begin anywhere on the route. From the hamlet of Les Houches it crosses a wooded spur to the delightful village of Contamines, from where it climbs steadily up an ancient trackway towards the Col du Bonhomme. Roman soldiers passed this way on the conquest of Gaul. In a poor season the Col du Bonhomme and the adjacent Col de la Croix du Bonhomme are likely to be snow covered and off-putting to the inexperienced, but there is no real danger. There is shelter of one sort or another every few miles on this walk.

From the high cols the route plunges down into the lonely Vallée des Glaciers, then climbs yet another high pass—the Col de la Seigne—into Italy. So far the walk has taken you round the western end of the mountains and into the long trench of the Val Veni which runs along the southern edge. Best, however, to quit the valley and climb up to the Chécrouit Alp, which gives one of the grandest mountain panoramas in the world. The whole savage southern face of the Mont Blanc peaks lie revealed; a wilderness of ice and rock.

The path soon leads to the delightful town of Courmayeur and from there along the Italian Val Ferret, below the Grandes Jorasses and other peaks, to cross over into Switzerland by the Col Ferret. The Swiss have also called *their* valley Val Ferret, which is confusing, but the Swiss Val Ferret is far more gentle than the Italian and is like a scene from *Heidi*, with archetypal Swiss chalets and even the occasional alpenhorn.

Soon the path reaches Champex and climbs to the Bovine Alp with superb views down to the vineyards of the Swiss Rhône and across the valley to the distant snows of the Oberland.

At the Col de Balme, the route re-enters France. Mont Blanc floats like a white cloud in the distance; an altogether different mountain from the savage splendour it presents to Italy. Tired legs can gain the advantage of a chair lift from the col down to le Tour in the Chamonix Valley, though the descent is not arduous. The last lap stretches ahead—the walk along the belvedere of the Aiguilles Rouges, with the constant panorama of the Chamonix Aiguilles, the Drus and Mont Blanc across the Vale of Chamonix.

The Traverse of the Pindos (Greece). The Traverse of the Pyrénées

There are two other classic walks which should be mentioned; the traverse of the Pindos mountains in Greece and the traverse of the Pyrénées from the Atlantic to the Mediterranean. These walks are extremely long—the Greek walk takes a month and the Pyrénéan walk takes almost seven weeks—and they are impossible to condense in any meaningful detail. Both are described fully in *Classic Walks of the World*.

The Pindos Traverse was first done by John Hunt's party in 1963. It is actually a traverse from near the ancient town of Delphi to the Albanian border, across the wild Pindos mountains. For those travellers who think of Greece as romantic ruins set by a blue sea, or the cosmopolitan city of Athens, the Pindos will come as a surprise, not to say shock. This is a long, tough walk; not for the fainthearted.

It can actually be divided, like Gaul, into three parts. The first goes from Amfissa, a town 25km (15 miles) west of Delphi, to Karpenisi; the second from there to Metsovon and the final stretch from Metsovon to Mt Gramos on the Albanian border. There is direct access to both Metsovon and Karpenisi by bus from Athens, so the central portion, which is the longest and takes 10–12 days, is readily attainable. It is however, inaccessible except at its starting and finishing points

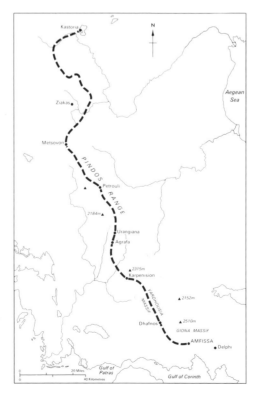

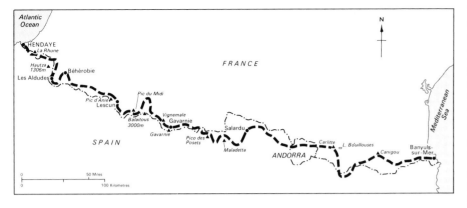

The Traverse of the Pyrénées is also a wilderness experience, but of a different kind. There are actually two major routes along the Pyrénées. One is the GR10; a low level alternative which crosses a few passes but skirts the higher peaks. It is entirely in France. The other is the HRP—Haute Randonnée Pyrénéenne—which tries to follow the watershed, often crossing into Spain, and is a much more serious proposition than the GR10. It is 400km (250 miles) long and there are stretches where neither food nor accommodation is available, so the walker has to backpack. Obviously, it is a walk for those with lots of experience—and lots of time! The trek requires a minimum of 45 days, not counting time out for weather and the like.

A shorter variant, of 24 days, takes in the central portion from Lescun to Andorra. This can be divided into three sections, with rail access to each—Lescun to Gavarnie; Gavarnie to Maladetta; Maladetta to Andorra. Kev Reynolds in his Pyrénéan walk described earlier, shows the sort of country which the Pyrénéan traverse covers.

(Guidebooks: *Walks and Climbs in the Pyrénées* by Kev Reynolds. Cicerone Press, *Pyrénées High Level Route* by Georges Veron, Gastons-West Col).

because it is cut off from civilization by a maze of ravines and ridges.

The final part is the climax of the traverse. It contains the magnificent gorges of the Vikos and Aoos and three of Greece's highest mountains Gamila (2,497m, 8,192ft), Smolikas (2,637m, 8,652ft) and Gramos (2,520m, 8,268ft). Bears and wolves still inhabit this region, though they are rarely seen by walkers. The wild boar is more common, though the most fearsome beasts are said to be the local sheepdogs, which are savage beyond belief.

(Guidebook: *The Mountains of Greece* by Tim Salmon, Cicerone Press).

ADDITIONAL INFORMATION

Maps and Guidebooks

Many of the guides and maps mentioned in this book can be bought from outdoor equipment shops. More comprehensive stocks are held by:

Edward Stanford Ltd, 12-14 Long Acre, Covent Garden, London WC2E 9LP (Tel: 01.836.1321).

McCarta Ltd, 122 Kings Cross Road, London WC1X 9DS (Tel: 01.278.8278).

Cordee Books, 3a De Montfort Street, Leicester LE1 7HD (Tel: 0533.543579).

Many of the European guides are published by Cicerone Press. In case of difficulty they can be ordered direct from Cicerone Press, Police Square, Milnthorpe, Cumbria LA7 7PY (Tel: 04482.2069).

The Walker's Handbook by H.D. Westacott is a useful guide to techniques and areas. Published by Penguin Books Ltd.

Magazines

Magazines often give ideas for new walks and carry reviews of guidebooks and new equipment. The following are the principal ones for European walking: available from newsagents or by subscription. All are published monthly.

Climber and *The Great Outdoors.* Both magazines published by Holmes McDougall Ltd, Ravenseft House, 302 St Vincent Street, Glasgow G2 5NL.

Camper, Haymarket Publishing Ltd, 38/42 Hampton Rd, Teddington, Middlesex TW11 0JE.

Footloose, 26 Commercial Buildings, Dunston, Gateshead NE11 9AA.

High, Springfield House, The Parade, Oadby, Leicester LE2 5BF.